Precision Rifle Marksmanship:
The Fundamentals

**A Marine Sniper's Guide to
Long Range Shooting**

by Frank Galli

Published by

Gun Digest® Books, an imprint of Caribou Media Group, LLC

Gun Digest Media
5600 W. Grande Market Drive, Suite 100
Appleton, WI 54913
www.gundigest.com

To order books or other products call 920.471.4522
or visit us online at www.gundigeststore.com

CAUTION: Technical data presented here, particularly technical data on handloading and on firearms adjustment and alteration, inevitably reflects individual experience with particular equipment and components under specific circumstances the reader cannot duplicate exactly. Such data presentations therefore should be used for guidance only and with caution. Caribou Media accepts no responsibility for results obtained using these data.

ISBN-13: 978-1-951115-10-4

Edited by Chuck Smock
Cover Design by Gene Coo
Interior Design by Jon Stein

Printed in the United States of America

10 9 8 7 6 5 4 3 2 1

Table of Contents

Introduction

Welcome to *Precision Rifle Marksmanship: The Fundamentals*. It's been a long time coming, putting a collection of my thoughts and previous work into a single book. Over the years, the topic of precision rifle shooting, accuracy and ballistics has changed. I like to say from the turn of the 20th century until just before the terrorist attacks on the World Trade Center in New York on 9/11, these topics moved at a snail's pace. For the most part, we just repeated what we were told previously and accepted it as gospel. If we read it or even heard about it, we took it on faith to be correct. It added an air of voodoo to the discussion as if there were secrets ready to be unfolded if you could only crack the code.

Let me start by reporting there is no voodoo. Since 9/11, the precision shooting world has changed how we engaged targets weekly, if not daily. As more money was invested, people started to test the theories previously put forth. At the same time, many respected and accurate methods for successfully engaging a target at a distance have been swept aside or forgotten because of technology. My goal is to mix the two in a way that creates a better marksman, instead of having competent system integrators.

Author Frank Galli in the wilds of Alaska leading a training session. He strives to experience as much variety as possible. Traveling to teach classes gives him a broader understanding of the various effects he sees when shooting a precision rifle.

The author, right, sitting with David Tubb, 11-time NRA World Champion in precision rifle, at the SHOT Show in Las Vegas, Nevada. He thinks Tubb is easily 10 years ahead of the curve when discussing shooting and bullet theory.

By system integrators, I mean shooters who put all their faith in technology or a single method of operation. They are not adaptable, but force you to use a particular product to demonstrate success. Believe me when I say, these are just different tools in the toolbox, and we have more than one method to solve our shooting problems.

Different people have different needs. If I focused this discussion on strictly using my methodology, it would not work for a large portion of shooters out there. I am unique, just like you are, so we all have to fine-tune our techniques to fit our particular styles. That isn't to say we don't have universal truths that go beyond the individual. The fundamentals of marksmanship translate across all disciplines. They are not focused on a specific style of shooting. Yes, we can attempt to write the shooter out of the equation, but is that really why we are here?

It's about best practices and relaying one's experience so you can decide for yourself the perfect path forward. Rather than shrink your wallet or pull a few zeroes from your bank account, I want to arm readers with enough knowledge bombs to clear their paths through the jungle. This is a journey, one that never ends. I started this journey with an air rifle in the backyards of rural Connecticut, continued to the Marine Corps deploying as a Scout Sniper,

The author, left, at a Sniper's Hide Cup competition with Adam R., from Mile High Shooting. The relationships made during shooting events, be it training or competition, can last a lifetime.

Push yourself to the limits. The author is shown here shooting a Seekins Precision SP10M in Hells Canyon, Idaho, in less than ideal weather conditions. Rain, sleet or snow, get out and shoot. The more experience you have, the better.

and it continues today through the Sniper's Hide website and my work as an instructor. It's about passing on your experience to save the next guy the time and effort. But it still takes personal responsibility to get out there and put into practice the topics covered.

It's not enough to read a book or watch a video on the Internet. Nothing beats actual shots downrange or being under the guidance of a competent instructor. Successful employment

of a precision rifle is a thinking man's game. We call it Weaponized Math: using a series of complicated math formulas to align the sights downrange so you can hit the target.

My goal with *Precision Rifle Marksmanship: The Fundamentals* is to give you the tools necessary to purchase a precision rifle system, and, without a lot of drama, set it up correctly, dope it to distance and use it successfully in the field. It doesn't sound like a lot, but you'd

be surprised how many shooters struggle with this. We get vapor lock, information overload, with just enough people telling us how hard it is instead of giving us the right tools upfront.

I wanted to go in a different direction. Some people wanted to hear my personal story. How did I get here? Others wish to see the technical data without having to wade through the voodoo being sold every day on the Internet. Over the years, especially with Sniper'sHide.com and

conversations that take place there every day, we can boil down the B.S. to refine the methodologies into a tasty dish. It's not about "grabbing a case of ammo," but instead having a plan of attack. Having a straight path from beginning to end without being faced with a questionable fork in the road every 100 yards. I am answering the questions upfront.

I call it W.T.F.

Wind, Target, Fundamentals of marksmanship. We look at these three headlines, and only these three first, the rest you can consider decoration for the cake. The wind is the most significant equalizing factor; we have to manage the wind. Why do I put it first? It's something we consider even if we are not shooting a target. When I am driving out to the range, I am looking at the wind. We have wind flags on the highways where I live. So, wind should be our number one consideration.

Target, or what are we shooting at? Until we have a target, we don't need to worry about the other factors; however, once a target appears, we need to know the range to that target. The range tells us what DOPE, or data, we need to input into our sights to get the hit. This is where understanding ballistics comes into play. Without getting too deep, of course, because that alone is a rabbit hole.

Lastly and importantly, the Fundamentals of marksmanship. We used to say at the Rifles Only range when I was instructing there: "There is not a single shooting solution that cannot be solved with the proper application of the fundamentals of marksmanship." It goes back in time to the beginning of rifle shooting. It is knowing how to apply the correct fundamentals as well as where to compromise, trading off and indexing to maximize the outcome in your favor.

In this case, the fundamentals become automatic. We want them to be in our subconscious, so we don't have to think about them unless one is being compromised. How do we make them subconscious? Through repetition. In sports science, some say it takes 3,000 repetitions to build a positive neural pathway, and 10,000 repetitions to fix a bad habit. That is a lot of effort put into a hobby. This is the mindset. It's not just a case of practice that makes perfect, but perfect practice makes perfect.

I write online a lot about putting in the effort. Many new shooters, especially in today's world, are trying to buy a hit. And by purchasing a hit, I don't mean buying an expensive rifle or the best scope they can afford. I mean replacing practice for a product. Thinking, "If I only had this specific tool, shooting would be so much easier." Yes, if you focus on a particular case, within a

Your only limitation is your imagination. Don't be afraid to experiment; to climb on high when looking for a solution.

specific situation, an individual device can make things easier. But it doesn't make you better. You traded becoming a marksman for being an applicator. Marksmanship requires the application of a series of methods; it's not about the use of an individual item.

Take the time to go out and put theory into practice. Go out and shoot, then record the information. When you go out to shoot again, see if the results change. When they do, note the cause. As I stated, it's a thinking man's sport

and needs to be addressed like chess more so than a game of checkers.

I see this book as an extension of my classes. I teach what could only be described as full time. I see a wide variety of students across varied platforms. Even though each student is unique, my goal is to make precision rifle clones. I want each person, operating within his or her means to execute the firing task consistently. Consistency is king when it comes to accuracy and precision. Look at it like this, we call it trigger control, not trigger slap, or trigger tap, or trigger crush. The word control is in the definition.

To expand on the techniques covered in this book, head over to the Sniper'sHide.com website. We have an active forum with thousands of topics every single day. The resources found in the forum are priceless. It is like-minded people crunching numbers and digging more profoundly than ever before. That is why precision rifle shooting is changing so rapidly.

1

Teaching Precision Rifle Excellence

O ne of the objectives in my precision rifle classes is to guide the shooters on their precision rifle journeys. After all, this is a journey, as the sport is continually changing. New equipment changes the game monthly. Different teaching techniques and adapting to the changing demographic landscape have forced us to move in a variety of directions. It's a lot of ground to navigate, which is why it is important to have a guide.

The world is full of good-bad shooters: Guys who have learned to adapt their bad habits along with the right equipment and have found some limited success. Talking with other instructors, we see a lot of people looking to shortcut the system by learning the tips and tricks before the trade. Rather than trying to purchase success, one should evolve, become a more well-rounded marksman through training.

Going hands-on with a student is important to the author when teaching. It's about adjusting the shooter and answering the "why."

Training comes in many forms. There is education you get from a book. There is hands-on instruction. And there is also experience in the way of competition. Any one of these alone is better than nothing, but combining them is divine. A lot of shooters learn by mimicking what they see in images. While the context might be lost, the position looks good enough, so they run with it. Shooting is broken up into disciplines, and those disciplines can have their context for success. We cross-pollinate a lot, however. And understanding the "why" is important.

The why is vital in the age of the Internet. Videos can be edited for success, images can be staged, it all needs a critical eye to weed out the good from the bad. During the breaks in my class,

From setting up the rifle to the shooter, and tweaking the individual's body position, it's critical to understand how each move changes the results downrange.

I play a video that has me shooting my precision rifle. The technique has to be impeccable, the hits on target are impressive, but it's a bit of a lie. It's two videos stitched together, and I explain this in class. You can make anything look impressive if you have some skills. While the video appears seamless, it is actually of two different ranges shot years apart. The color is corrected to

match, and the cuts are done in a way the casual observer has a hard time noticing missing clues. It's easy to get fooled online. Know the "why," and nobody will get over on you.

Step out of your comfort zone. Take a class from a well-established facility or instructor. Go hands-on and then reinforce what you learned in competition. Local or national, it makes no difference. Get out and shoot against others where the rules are written by someone else. We rarely set ourselves up to fail; this fact limits our ability to learn on our own.

Competition is a different animal from training, which should be designed to establish your technique. A match will demonstrate to you how to apply those skills. The beauty

Don't be afraid to manage the shooter based on physical limitations. Moving a shooter to a bench can be the right answer even when the majority of the class is shooting prone.

of the competition circuit is it will be different enough from most training that you will instantly see the need to attend more than one competition to nail down its unique set of skills. In a match, it's all about getting into and out of position efficiently while maintaining your focus to get your hits on target. It's more about your movement, which will then shine a light on the level of your training.

There is a ton of equipment to assist you in a match. Everything from the caliber you choose, to the stock on your rifle, and the bags you carry, will matter. Stay tight and stripped down in the beginning, don't default to these tools. Instead, focus on you and the techniques you employ. Your first three matches should involve employing the bare minimum equipment necessary. It will not be pretty, but get over it; you'll thank me later.

Local, one-day matches are the breeding grounds for success. Many of them are within a two-hour drive and come with no strings attached. Find one and hit it with eyes wide open. Get involved and be curious when attending.

Pay attention to the techniques and movement more so than the gear employed. See how the successful shooters negotiate the obstacles versus what scope is on their rifle. Too many people focus on the equipment and not the training that goes into success. Ask these guys what drills they shoot, not where they bought that tripod. Those things will be evident by the third match. After that third match, you can spend all the money necessary.

Part of my focus is on the gear only because I need to speak on it. If I did not have to chase this aspect of the sport, I would be more worried about my training. I focus a lot of attention to practice and still it is not nearly enough. My other responsibilities reduce my time, so I know it cuts into yours. Have a plan, stick to that plan and put effort into yourself first, the equipment after. The more you experience, the easier your buying decisions become.

Consider me your avatar on this precision rifle journey. Let's step into the abyss of knowledge and try to break down the most relevant points for you to begin your travels.

Precision Rifle Marksmanship: the Fundamentals will take the reader from my beginnings as a Marine Scout Sniper to my present-day job as a marksmanship instructor.

This book focuses on breaking down the fundamentals of marksmanship in easy to understand methodology. We follow a logical order of instruction from shooter to target. There is no voodoo when it comes to precision rifle marksmanship, but there is a technique. Understanding the "why" things happen is a crucial element to learning. We take away the modifiers added over time and bring us back to original intent. The fundamentals of marksmanship are the foundation for all great shooting. See why the Marines are so famous in this area of expertise.

We are simplifying the wind. Through count-

Today, the well-rounded practical marksman will embrace alternate positions. In practical terms, prone is the rare shot, so practice getting off your belly.

ing for both accuracy and precision, *Precision Rifle Marksmanship* is here to deliver first-round success.

The Training Mindset

You see a lot of discussion referencing, "What the pros use" and every one of them focuses on the gear. Well sure, it's easy to point to this element of the sport as most matches record the equipment used by the competitors. I know we do; we have a complete form you fill out when signing up for the Sniper's Hide Cup, which includes equipment. But this only tells a small part of the story. I don't want to focus on the gear, but on your personal growth around the sport of precision rifle shooting.

What do the pros use? Their time wisely. They engage in deliberate practice and many have the talent to back up their performance. This stuff is sports science 101. There are plenty of groups who study the effect of practice versus talent. So, the question you have to ask

less hours of teaching, we have honed our wind skills so every man can grasp, stripping away the mythology. Once you realize there is an answer upfront, you can now put this training into practice day one. Forget the case of ammo to try and figure it out on your own. One shot, one hit is the goal.

The shooter, the weapon system and the external ballistics impact the shot. We are look-

Define your mission. Being successful in a precision rifle match is a goal. The mission matters when it comes to fine-tuning your training.

yourself is, "Can you buy success by studying what the top shooters use when it comes to gear only?" Will a Bushnell scope push you to the next level because a particular team uses it? In a few cases, sure, some of this goes to lessons learned. Picking the right combination of equipment to execute the solution needed to place well in a precision rifle competition is a valid consideration. Some stages favor a piece of gear versus other stages, but how you use it matters too. For me, the key is understanding what goes into successful precision rifle shooting, is how a person puts it all together. You cannot succeed with just your credit card. Just purchasing a book or watching a YouTube video is not enough.

Let's look at competition.

We have precision rifles competitions all over the United States with the groups branching out overseas. Competitions are great way to validate your training. They will help you move

to the next level of your precision rifle journey by forcing you to operate outside your comfort zone.

It takes a certain amount of understanding of the stages you will find at a typical precision rifle match. Many of the matches have similar stages or concepts which allow the shooter to practice these skills effectively and not waste their time engaging in practice that will not yield the desired results. If you can already shoot a three-eighths MOA five-shot group at 100 yards from the prone position, it makes no sense to practice that over and over again. Instead you want to practice on the stages you struggle with. Most likely, this means shooting from alternate positions, so get off your belly. A guiding principle of training needs to be how you execute it.

The best shooters usually have barricades they practice off of more often than shooting in the prone. They are not engaging in endless load

Let the author guide you on your precision rifle journey. He and his fellow instructors travel around the world teaching long range shooting, so learn from their experience.

When you attend a competition, you are no longer subject only to your rules. The match director should be working to push your limits, taking you out of that comfort zone.

development; they have settled on a load that balances speed (muzzle velocity) and accuracy. Their dope has been boiled down, so elevation is never an issue, it is just about the wind. By using your time wisely, you can concentrate on those difficult elements. You learn how to address the obstacles quickly and effectively. It's all about building a stable position while managing your time. With stages that average two min-

utes for multiple shots from multiple positions, you don't have the luxury to waste 30 seconds building a stable position. The top shooters use their time to understand what compromises have to be made. Close shots value speed; the farther shots balance toward accuracy.

We want to break the targets up into high-value and low-value shots. The high-value shots are ones you cannot miss versus the low-value

The relationships made during competition can last a lifetime. Don't be afraid to stretch your legs and travel to other venues in order to grow.

shots, which have the least possibility for success. As match directors, we always build shots into the stage the majority of shooters will not make or reach under the time. Where I see the biggest issue is when shooters attempt to make it to the end of the stage, when I know it was designed not be completed. So instead of taking the shots they can hit under the time, they race to the end missing a majority of shots that

should have and could have been hit. I am guilty of breaking this time-management issue myself. You have to determine what your personal limit is. Is it better to hit all the targets from the first three positions or hit only one target on all four?

I learned a great lesson in this was when I attended the Accuracy International Long Range Classic. On day two, we repeated the day-one stages, allowing us to address the problems

Field matches are the author's favorite style of precision rifle competition. Certain matches have specific styles and tools. Fundamentals work no matter how you are asked to solve the problem.

having learned from our mistakes the first day. It allowed you to take that hindsight we all have and put it to the test. For a new shooter attending a national-level match for the first time, you should take this opportunity as a learning experience before anything else. Instead of going into it nervous and afraid of your placement, use it as a training tool. A way to fine-tune your practice for the next competition. Try taking notes so you can then go home and practice the stages that gave you the most trouble. It requires a certain amount of discipline to record the match from a training standpoint versus any other reasoning. But the dividends it will pay

Sure, you can try to buy a hit by investing in a lot of gear. But it's more about the execution over the specific rifle being employed. Training trumps all.

Be a mentor to a new shooter. Sports grow because of the next generation waiting in the wings. Take a junior member of your community out and spend a day revisiting the fundamentals with him or her.

later cannot be understated.

If you go home and think, "Man, I need a different caliber, scope, or stock," versus "This is what I need to practice," you have missed the point.

We want to practice what gave us trouble, not what made us look good.

So instead of talking to someone about what reticle they have in their scope, ask the next seasoned shooter you meet what their training regimen is. Ask them how they use their time between the matches to practice, so when they arrive, they feel better prepared. Gear can have an effect, but it's not nearly as big as you might think. Don't get wrapped around the axle when it comes to scopes, stocks and reticles. Ask other shooters what the best use of your time is. This will carry you much farther, much sooner. As many have heard before, it's not the arrow, but the Indian behind it. There is a lot of truth to that.

Sports scientists say it can take as many as 10,000 hours of practice to become an expert at a given, complex repetitive task, however they have found this number can be adjusted due to talent. There are plenty of examples of newer shooters to the sport doing very well, very quickly. That is pure talent and copying what rifle and scope they have is not going to infuse

you with more of it. In those cases where talent is not the defining factor, you need deliberate practice. Don't overlook this by chasing the latest and greatest piece of equipment. Save a few bucks, buy more ammo and then hit The Home Depot and build a barricade for yourself. Dry practice is a great training tool. Putting that barricade in your garage and practicing setting up your position quickly and effectively will go a long, long way toward higher placements than any given reticle will.

Finally, if you have other, like-minded shooters in your area, work together in order to push each other in a positive direction. Micro competitions, among friends, or even better, local matches meant to mimic national-match stages can be a super tool for the precision rifle shooter. Push each other to be stronger shooters. Don't overlook your local matches, and if you find the stages don't fit your needs, meet with the match directors and try steering them, (politely) in a different direction. It will not only make your area stronger from a shooter's perspective, but it can help grown the sport, which is the ultimate goal.

The gear comes later. And most of the pieces of equipment that make the bigger differences early on are small things, and not the big expensive stuff.

Perfect Practice Makes Perfect. Not just practice alone. If all you do is shooting from the prone, you'll never excel. Get out of your comfort zone and practice the stuff you are bad at.

2

Early Influences

In the late 1970s and early 1980s, the author's father owned two gas stations in Stratford, Connecticut. The author started working pumping gas when he was 13 years old.

My journey with a precision rifle started in the wilds of southern Connecticut. I include "southern" to give it some legitimacy because nobody thinks about Connecticut when it comes to shooting a rifle. I was born in Bridgeport, a concrete jungle known more for its crime rate and corruption than a city like Chicago. We not only arrested our mayor for criminal behavior, but he was elected again after he returned from seven years in federal prison.

From Bridgeport, we moved to a literal cow town called Shelton about 30 minutes away. This hamlet in the shadows of New York City was where I would hone my shooting skills. At the time, there were fields and dairy farms all over Shelton. Most of my

In Korea, the Army had a Soviet-weapon familiarization program. The author shot a host of Soviet-era rifles.

The author, right, grew up playing military games with his cousins in rural Connecticut. Here he is shown living the dream with a fellow Marine just south of the DMZ in South Korea at Camp Casey. The Army had a short three-week sniper school there which they attended.

friends worked the barns milking cows before and after school. This gave us open access to the farms and pockets of woods in order to set up our military style encampments. We trained endlessly, marching around the neighborhood like an invading army.

Air rifles were my first entry into firearms. I started with a Crossman 760 pump rifle and quickly progressed to its big brother the Crossman 766. We all started with iron sights and were quick learners when it came to mastering shots at extended distanced on small animals

around the farms. My best friend's parents were part of a large set of interconnecting fields owned by their family. Their grandmother lived in the middle with the children's houses on each side. It was easily 10 city blocks long, at least it looked that way. It had rolling hills, open fields and ponds scattered throughout. We rode dirt bikes and spent all hours of the day and night playing outside.

My dad was always a big fan of war movies, shooting and he never shied away from getting out and learning. Our early shooting was typical;

all the classic lines were present. Take a couple of deep breathes, let one halfway out and then hold it while pressing the trigger so you are surprised by the break. Out in the woods it worked like a charm, those 25-foot shots with an air rifle were always on point. We just needed a clean line of sight and a bit of imagination.

From forts, to toy soldiers, we were classic 1970s kids, riding our Big Wheels at Mach 1 down the hills. Playing chase, our version of hide and go seek, just across a wider landscape. It was the perfect environment to stretch our legs and extend our imagination.

Influence-wise there as so many places to draw inspiration. Old war movies from World War II were at the top of the list. We could not watch enough of John Wayne storming the *Sands of Iwo Jima* or Audie Murphy going *To Hell and Back*. They were inspirations for us all. We ate them up faster than a handful of Pez candies.

I remember feeling a sense of pride the first time I mounted a Challenger 4x scope on my 766. It was a huge improvement over my irons. And gave me the ability to place my shots even closer to perfection. I was hooked. Give me a scoped rifle and I would rule the landscape.

One of the first things people mention with me is my size. For the rest of the world I am pretty short: 5-feet, 2-inches tall on a good day, currently weighing about 125 pounds. In my family, I was average. We were all short. What we lacked in size we made up in volume and character. My mom's family is a big Italian Catholic organization, with my grandmother having 14 children. Needless to say, I was surrounded by my cousins. We were a roaming pack of wild dogs back in those days. Military style discipline was pretty much the only answer to maintain law and order. We conducted drills across three cities, from Bridgeport to Stratford, up to Shelton, as we commanded a fierce army

The author was at the head of the platoon during the final formation. His size messed up the height curve, so putting him up front kept the formation looking good.

of Italian Leprechauns.

Still, I was one of only a few to join the military. Most of us were tradesman. Carpenters, electricians, mechanics, so it made sense to follow the various businesses my uncles ran. Not me, I was determined to join the Marines. I had made that decision pretty early on, around 13 years old.

Going to trade school versus a traditional high school, it was easy to meet up with recruiters. They came in what felt like monthly and by my 17th birthday I was ready to join.

Enlisting was not as easy as it might sound. First off, I had to get a ton of waivers. When I was 15, I was crushed by a flatbed truck at my dad's shop. He was having it painted to match his show car, so all the windows were taped up. The rocket scientist he had guiding him into the bay was pushing him right toward the wall. I was outside pumping gas for a customer when I saw the truck was going to hit the wall. I walked

over to the door to tell him to drive right. Turning away, I was grabbed by the bed of the truck and pinned against the wall, injuring the femoral artery in my leg. I was bleeding internally and spent a decent amount of time in the hospital recovering. I needed a signature from all involved in order to enlist. Today, I have a 10-inch scar on my right side where they replaced my broken artery.

My next issue was little tougher to overcome. I was 5-foot-1 at the time and weighed 102 pounds. That is not quite tall enough or heavy enough to join the Marines. Quotas for recruiters being what they are, it was an obstacle to negotiate and they had a plan.

The morning of my MEPS (Military Entrance Processing Station) visit, I was met with a dozen Dunkin Donuts, cinnamon my favorite, and a lot of water. I was the last potential recruit to enter the doctor's office as most of the morning I was camped out at the water fountain drinking as much as I could fit past the donuts.

On paper, I made the cut by a half inch and one pound. Slim to say the least, but the story does not end there when it comes to my height. In fact, the story of my height will never end.

For me, boot camp started exactly like the movies. I arrived at Parris Island in the middle of the night. August in South Carolina was hot and humid with a light drizzle of rain followed by an immediate swarm attack of sand fleas. While I don't recall a lot about the first few hours, the following day I would never forget.

As we received our series orders, I was excited to go to Hotel Company 3rd Battalion. The 3rd has a reputation going back to the 1950s. Every horror story you heard about Marine Corps boot camp from Parris Island involved 3rd Battalion. The swamp marches, drowning, gators on the O Course, all 3rd. See, they are off alone, somewhat out of sight of command. It allowed the Drill Instructors a certain independence that could be considered dangerous in today's world. But if you are going to be a Marine, there is no better place to start. Hard helps. I remember chuckling when I'd hear recruits yelling, "eyeballs" as anyone approached the 3rd Battalion area. It was a warning system dating back to medieval times.

On the first full day as part of Hotel Company, I was lined up with the other wide-eyed recruits. The Drill Instructors were taking up their assignments replaying the "Steers and Queers" scene from *An Officer and a Gentlemen*. In this case, times it by a factor of 10, as there was a lot more recruits and even more Drill Instructors. All of the series were there lined up with each person being singled out for any reason they could find. Me it was obvious: "Who let the grade-schooler through the gates?" I expected to be singled out. It made sense.

The first Drill Instructor to grace my presence immediately started screaming about my height. Swearing at the recruiters for cutting corners and freaking out at my answer to the question, "How tall are you?" "Sir, 5-2," I replied. Sure, I gave myself an extra half inch, just in case. Upon my answer his fake anger turned serious and he said in no uncertain terms I was

out of his Marine Corps before I even started. I know it turned serious because he didn't walk to the next guys to start over, he walked toward the company Gunny Sergeant. He was getting me kicked out. I had no words, as it really hadn't even begun. Before I could process what was happening, he arrived with the Company Gunny, who wasn't playing a Drill Instructor, but took on an even more serious tone.

The question repeated, "Son, how tall are you?" "Sir, Private Galli is 5-2," which was the wrong answer. A few seconds of muted conversation and it was obvious; I was getting kicked out before given any chance to show my mettle. The group turned and started walking away talking to each other while heading toward the officers in attendance.

This is where the world gets surreal. It happened fast, unexpectedly, and can only be described as divine intervention. As the Company Gunny was speaking to a Captain, I was launched backward off the ground. A Drill Instructor, not of my series, yanked me out of line by the collar. Behind us was India Company 3rd Battalion. And being at attention in line I never once turned to look at them, but someone was paying attention.

The Drill Instructor, to this day I have no clue who it was, reached over, picked me off the ground by the collar and pulled me out of line. He went nose to nose with me and in firm muted tones asked me again, "How tall are you?"

I repeated my answer, 5-2. He sternly said, "No, how tall are you?" At this time the Captain, Gunny and Sergeant are walking back toward me. Seeing my time was short, I replied, "Sir, I have no idea what you want, I am 5-2." He looked at me and said, "No, you're 7-foot-6 and the meanest motherf****** on the island." And quickly tossed me back in line without another word said.

Seconds later, which even today feels like five seconds at the most, the Captain squared up in front of me. Flanked on each side by the DIs. The Captain, right on cue, asked me that all-important question.

"How tall are you?"

"Sir, I am 7-foot-6 and the meanest motherf****** on the island," I replied.

A young Private First Class Frank Galli, after graduation from 3rd Battalion.

Without missing a beat, he said, "He can stay." Of course, there were conditions to my acceptance. I had to jump through a few more hoops than the average guy. I was, of course, the House Mouse, which meant I had to clean the Drill Instructors Hooch. In addition to being at their beck and call, I was on double rations so they could stack a few pounds on me. None of this was a big deal, I was used to working hard. The twist was the punishment part of the equation.

If anyone else in my platoon got in trouble, I was in trouble. Don't wait to be told, if someone was ordered to quarterdeck for individual phys-

ical training, I better be there first, ready to go. I left boot camp the same height, but 10 pounds heavier, all muscle tone.

Boot camp was not really a big deal for me. I enjoyed it. In my mind, regardless of all the talk, I knew they were not going to hurt or hit me, and, growing up, my dad had no problem with disciplining us. The day it clicked for me was my last day. We were just a few hours from graduation, getting our dress uniforms ready, preparing the squad bay for our departure. One of the mainstays of the squad bay was the Zit Juice, as they used to call it, a giant jar

The author shown on patrol in Okinawa. He reports the nice part about being in a Surveillance and Target Acquisition (STA) Platoon in the 1980s was the relaxed dress codes. Team members were moving independently and usually dressed for speed and stealth.

of aftershave everyone used. This jug of blue juice was being given to an incoming series and I was designated the delivery boy, or delivery mouse, in my case.

You're still in recruit mode right up until they let you leave. So, the sense of accomplishment never really kicks in until they turn you out

officially. This day was different for me, thanks to my House Mouse role. I carried the Zit Juice over to the new series, requested permission from the other Drill Instructor to deliver my package and accepted the orders to drop the container on the table. After doing so I turned sharply to make my exit. Understand, on this

day I was in my Class A uniform preparing for graduation. I made it halfway past the new recruits standing at attention in front of their racks when I heard the familiar command to freeze.

Immediately, I froze at attention. Then the Senior Drill Instructor commanded the series to place all eyes on me. He let their gaze set in a few seconds before announcing, "He is a Marine, worthy of your respect and honor," adding, "some of you will never know that honor."

Ouch, that stings.

I left there walking a few inches taller that day.

3

The Fundamentals of Marksmanship

Detailed fundamentals are the building blocks of all great shooting. There are plenty of good-bad shooters, as I like to call them, out there. Shooters who have learned to adapt their bad habits into successful shots. Most people focus on results, but the results don't always tell the entire tale.

Properly executed, the fundamentals make the difference between a hit and a miss when it comes to long range precision shooting. There is no voodoo when it comes to engaging targets at long distances. But it does require that you know and focus on the fundamentals of marksmanship down to the millisecond. All shooting is a game of milliseconds and how you control the time between each one matters. Our journey begins here.

Setting up the rifle is the first step in building a solid foundation. When we buy a new car, we adjust the seats and mirrors prior to driving. The rifle needs to be addressed the same way.

Build the trigger mentally from the trigger back, and not the grip forward. The placement of the firing hand needs to support the firing task.

It's important before we begin covering the fundamentals of marksmanship, we take a few minutes to discuss setting up your rifle. This can be the difference between success or fatigue. The closer the rifle is tailored to your body type, the more comfortable you will be behind it. The rifle doesn't care if you are comfortable, it will do the same thing every time based on your actions behind it. In fact, we demonstrate this every class with a tripod. Setting the rifle up on a tripod, pointed at a target downrange, just manipulating the trigger will get us a hit every time. So, if the rifle will do it on command, why can't everyone?

It's a mindset thing. We execute these tasks subconsciously.

Setting up the Rifle to the Shooter

Many shooters are limited by the equipment they can afford. The closer to a bare-bones rifle you get, the fewer adjustments you will find. This is OK. Many a good shooter can do very well with a budget system. But understanding the ways to properly fit the rifle to your body will help you progress in your journey. There is nothing wrong with adding a bit of padding and duct tape to your stock to help with the fit. Looking at the images of Marines and soldiers in combat, you see a lot of tape helping them fit the rifle. They don't have a choice; they are given an issued system and are forced to make it work. Adding a stock pad and using tape are all acceptable methods of fitting the stock to the shooter. Modified is a good thing. Don't shy away from it.

The Proper Length of Pull

Everybody hears a different answer on the proper length of pull, and for different disciplines

Length of pull is used to place the trigger finger in the correct position.

Measure length of pull from the inside of the arm, at the crook of the elbow, with the finger mating to the trigger shoe.

Different styles of shooting create different positions behind the rifle. Alternate positions require a shorter length of pull versus strictly shooting prone.

there might be more than one acceptable answer, however we are covering tactical shooting. If you are strictly a prone shooter, the length of pull can be a bit longer. This is not uncommon. Positional shooters want the measurement to be a bit shorter. So, where we measure from is the real question.

In the past, the mantra was to place the buttstock of the rifle in the crook of the elbow. Then, with our ninja knife hand extended, we measure to the tip of the trigger finger. Today, I recommend a slightly different approach.

Use this same method, but adjust the trigger to a 90-degree angle and measure to the trigger shoe of the rifle. This confirms you can properly

manipulate the trigger without disturbing the lay of the sights.

Picking a Stock for Long Range Shooting

Stocks are a personal choice. Some are expensive, others are less expensive, compromising features for weight and simplicity. Whichever stock you choose, try it to get one that will adjust to the individual shooter.

When talking setup, I like to reference our cars. Look at the rifle the same way you look at your car. We first walk into the dealer, drive the vehicle of choice. Then we settle in with the

The author focuses on rifle setup, as it's the adjustment for the shooter behind the rifle. The more adjustability in the stock, the more comfortable the shooter will be in the long run.

representative to pick our features and get one in the right color. It's almost the same when we look at a rifle. The main difference is, when the dealer finally hands us the keys, and we sit in it for the first time, we adjust things. Seats and mirrors, these two elements are our sights and stocks.

After a short amount of time, our driving becomes subconscious, just like shooting. We can cruise down the highway talking on the phone, adjusting the radio while talking to our passenger. Very little effort is spent focusing on the lines. However, if you look, we are making micro corrections with our hands on the steering wheel. To press the point even further, if we change one thing, move the seat for different driver, or adjust a mirror, immediately we notice

it. Shooting a rifle needs to be like that. This level of familiarity.

Setting up the Cheek Weld

Before we set up the cheek weld, we have to mount the scope. The scope should be mounted in the rings ahead of time and can be attached to the rifle, but it should not be tightened in place just yet. In the section on sight picture, we will cover setting up the scope properly, but first let's explain where we need to position it on the rail.

We will assume the rifle has some form of Picatinny rail on the action. These Picatinny rails will help you set the eye relief, which will determine how we set up the stock. When setting the scope in the rail, it is best not to put it in the last slot at the back. Give room, both in front and behind the rings, so you can move the scope either forward or backward. It should also be noted that you bring the system to you. Don't try to wrap yourself around the rifle. Sure, we can get away with it in the short. But, over time, the mismanagement of the set-up will show.

Choosing a stock with an adjustable cheek piece will further assist the shooter in setting up the rifle. This will, again, aid in comfort when it comes time to shoot. Additionally, it will help you get a consistent cheek weld from shot to shot.

We do this by addressing the rifle in the prone position. The shooter should be straight behind it, not at an angle to the stock, with spine in line with the bore. Rest the head naturally on the stock, obtaining a good solid cheek weld. Looking through the scope there should be instant edge-to-edge clarity. Shadowing will tell you which direction to move the scope or cheek piece on the stock. If you are looking through a donut with shadowing all around, move the scope forward or backward in the rail. If you have shadowing at the top or bottom of the sight picture move the cheek piece up or down and repeat the process until the picture is clear.

Straight Back Behind the Rifle

We have all seen images of service rifle shooters using a sling in the prone position shooting offset at an angle. They point the foot and raise

Manipulation of the trigger without disturbing the lay of the sights sounds easy, but some shooters can put a lot of movement into their shots because the rifle is not properly set up for them.

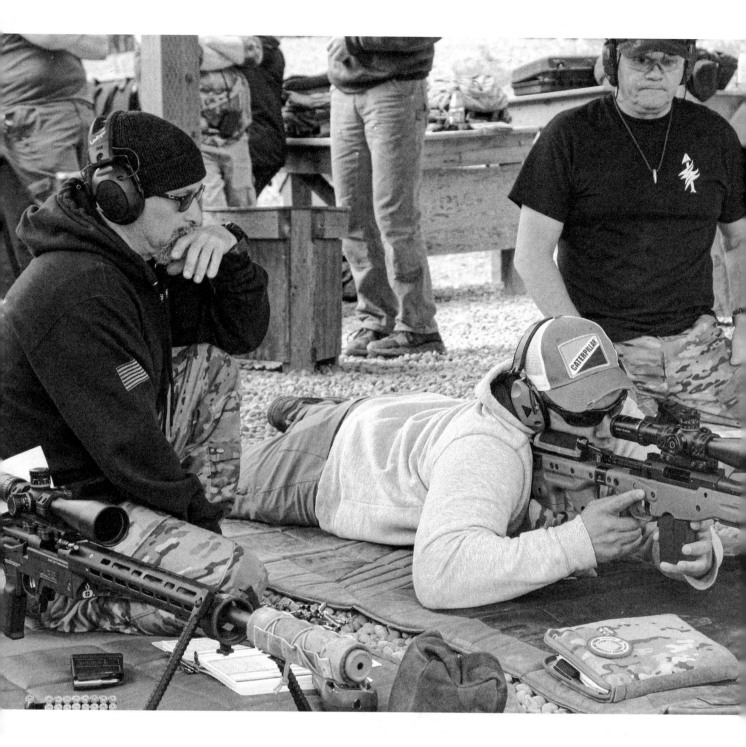

their knee to establish a good prone position. This works great for a sling shooter. But for the tactical shooter using a bipod, especially with a heavy caliber, the proper position is straight back behind the rifle. Recoil will exploit any angle between the body and stock. So, while the little green Army man position might look good from a historical perspective, it's not a position we should be using in modern times.

The reason a sling shooter gets off to the side of the rifle is to place the support arm directly under the stock, so the forearm is straight, and in line, underneath it.

Being straight behind the rifle is going to pay off down the road. It's going to allow the recoil to move down your body and exit your legs equally. If you are properly squared up (your shoulders straight across, regardless of being in the standing or prone position) the rifle will recoil and return to target. The movement will be

Demonstrating the different variations is important, as not every shooter is built the same. Set up the rifle to the individual, not some arbitrary idea of why, simply because someone else did it that way.

On the firing line, the author focuses on each shooter's position throughout day one. He is building clones.

The position needs to be consistent and repeatable behind the optic. We are aligning our head and body behind the rifle. It needs to be automatic.

minimal, allowing the shooter to maintain sight picture throughout the firing process. When we ask shooters to demonstrate a supported standing position, they will always blade to the target; there are many things wrong with this position. When shooting from the standing position, practice being square and creating a tripod between your body and the support. You'll see the benefits right away.

Use this straight behind the rifle method to set up the stock and cheek piece. This is also the way to set the eye relief on the scope. Get into position before mounting your scope. Get a good natural feel for the rifle in your shoulder pocket, making sure your bipod is correctly adjusted for your body. After your cheek weld is established, put the scope on the Pic rail and bring the sight picture to you. By mounting the scope this way, you get a good natural position

with a comfortable sight picture. Remember, we don't want to have to work for edge-to-edge clarity. We want that good sight picture when we address the rifle. This is the proper way to set up the scope and fit the rifle to the shooter.

Set up the rifle in the position you feel most likely to use most often. Put your shooting discipline into context when adjusting the rifle system. If your local range only lets you shoot off a bench, set up the rifle for the bench. If you are shooting multiple positions, set up the rifle so you can address each position with a minimum amount of compromise.

Breaking Down the Fundamentals of Marksmanship

OK, now we're going from the analogy about our car to a discussion of golf. And trust me, I am not a golfer by any stretch of the imagination. In any sport we engage in, soccer to football, golf to shooting, they all have a specific set of fundamentals. We want to break down those fundamentals, wiping away the flourishes that have been added over time. We are looking at original intent here, with a twist. Most of the original intent was written with iron sights in mind, as well as being shot unsupported or with a sling. Today we have bipods and front rests, so we need to consider those tools in the context of our fundamentals.

Natural Point of Aim

Stepping up to the tee, we have to address the golf ball with our body and align the club. This adjustment of our body position to launch the ball at our desired target is similar to natural point of aim.

Natural point of aim is a very simple concept, but is often misunderstood. In order to establish a good firing position, we want our muscles to be relaxed. When the body mentally perceives recoil, it will subconsciously relax for a microsecond. This relaxation of the muscles can move the rifle to the point where it is naturally aligned. So, if the shooter is forcing the position, even a little, the body will subconsciously steer the rifle off target during firing. This is why we want to establish our natural point of aim.

The way to check for our natural point of aim is to align the sights on the target. While in position, go through a couple of breathing cycles with your eyes closed. Upon opening your eyes, see if the sights moved off the target. If the sights have moved, realign the rifle and your body as one unit on the target. Small movements will go a long way here. The movement should come from the shooter's core and not

Demonstrating the proper prone position to each student helps establish a quick baseline. Once demonstrated, it's the instructor's job to tweak the shooter's position to fit his or her body type.

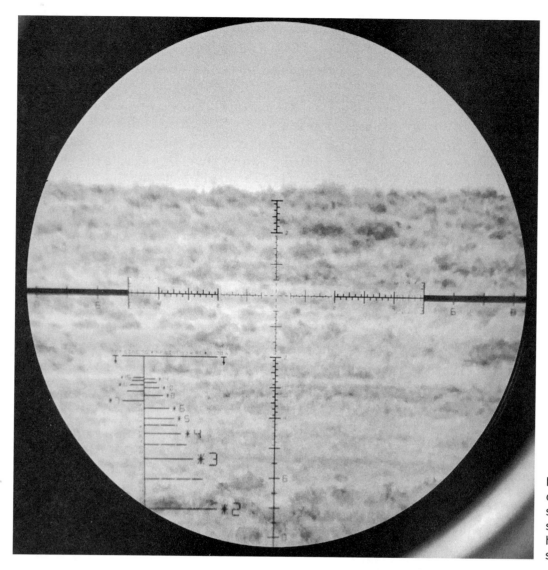

Edge-to-edge clarity, with no shading, is key. Be sure you are not hunting for a clear sight picture.

the shoulders and/or arms.

Taking a couple of deep breaths relaxes the body just enough for the brain to change our position, should it find that position uncomfortable. When we opened our eyes, if the sights are off target, we have to fix this alignment. We call this the gross adjustment for natural point of aim.

By practicing getting into position straight behind the rifle repeatedly, one can help shortcut this process by being square not only to the target, but behind the rifle. Indexing with the legs and the knees, the shooter wants to point his or her body to the rifle, which is pointed at the target. This will help align the shooter quickly and effectively in the field.

The fine-tune adjustment for natural point of

aim is the dry fire. This will show the shooter if his position is perfect. Given time and opportunity, always dry fire before going live. If the reticle moves, that is a clue to adjust your position ever so slightly.

Sight Picture, or Aiming

Those shooting iron sights will first consider sight alignment and then sight picture. Because we are using a scoped rifle, we don't necessarily need to discuss sight alignment in the same way. By setting up the rifle correctly in the beginning, we have, it is hoped, determined a good cheek weld. This is very good first step when it comes to sight picture. However, as a tactical shooter, we might find a situation where our cheek weld

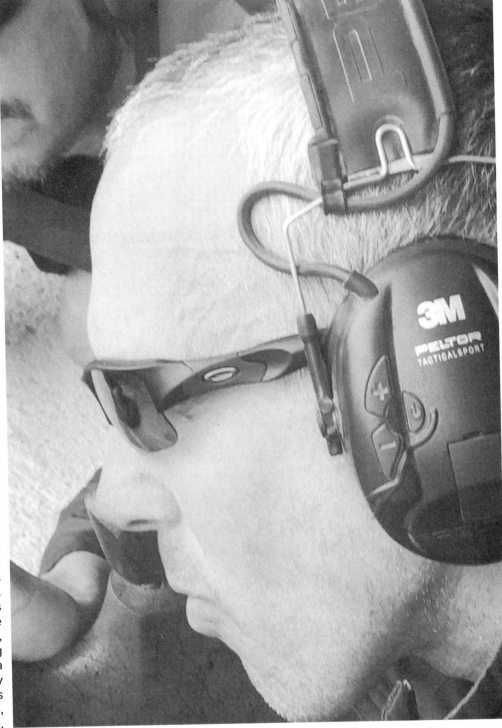

Instructors see when students are holding their breath when shooting. The negatives far outweigh the perceived benefits of not breathing. The author teaches students to breathe through the shot, with it breaking at the bottom of a natural respiratory pause. If the sights are not lined up, keep breathing.

is slightly compromised. The way to fix any potential aiming issues from this is to use the parallax adjustment on the scope. The parallax adjustment, if set correctly, will essentially turn the day optic into a red-dot-type scope by putting the reticle, the target and the shooter's eye on the same focal plane. As with a red-dot sight, most understand the dot does not have to be in the center of the optic for the shooter to hit the target. The red-dot sight is a parallax-free system; by using the parallax adjustment on the day optic, it will basically do the same thing.

Proper sight picture is important. Correct sight picture means you have edge-to-edge clarity with no shadowing of any kind. If you find shadowing, even a small amount, it is recommended that you move the scope or move the cheek piece to line up the shooter's eye directly behind the optic. Eliminating any angle is key. Your head should be square with the ocular lens of the scope so that your head quickly and naturally aligns to the proper sight picture. Any shadowing seen in the sight picture is a result of the eye looking at the inside of the scope tube. Building up the cheek rest or moving the scope to the eye will help eliminate this. Proper sight picture is key because that is going to tell us where the bullet is going to go.

How Do We Check for Parallax?

Back in the old days, most day optics had the parallax set at the factory. There was no adjustment on the scope. They usually set them around 150 yards to suit the average hunter. With most optics under 10x, parallax is not a big issue. It gets worse with magnification, so it is not uncommon to find an optic less than 10x with no parallax adjustment. We are referencing modern higher-powered optics with a parallax adjustment.

To check for parallax, line up the reticle on a target and move your head ever so slightly, side to side, or up and down. Don't move your head enough to cause shadowing to appear around the edges. Use very small motions, to see if the reticle appears to "float" on the target. A way to demonstrate this is to take a pencil tip and hold it out between you and some object a distance away. When you move your head, the target will move away from the pencil tip, this is parallax. But, if you move the pencil tip on top of the target object so it is touching, then move your head, the pencil stays in place. We want to re-create this through the scope by adjusting the movement out. Just remember, in some optics, focus is not parallax and being parallax-free might put you out of perfect focus.

Much of sight picture is established when setting up the rifle. We don't want to hunt for the proper sight picture, something I notice a lot of new shooter do. We want to fall in behind the stock and have our head naturally aligned to the optic.

The scope should be set up in position, placed on maximum power, if using a variable-power optic, and then fine-tuned in place. At this point, lowering the magnification for different positions will open up the eye relief, thus creating a more forgiving eye box. This minor compromise is necessary as different positions will move the head ever so slightly behind the scope.

Breathing

We do not want to focus on our breathing. Let's start off by saying we need to breathe. Period. Holding your breath is the last thing you want to do when shooting. When we are hammering a nail or driving our cars, we don't think about our breathing. Correct? Instead, we continue to breathe normally. The same thing applies when shooting a rifle. What we need to know about breathing while shooting is where to break the shot, which is at the bottom of our natural respiratory pause.

Let me repeat that: Break the shot at the bottom of our natural respiratory pause.

For years, people were taught to take a deep breath, let it halfway out and hold it. This is incorrect, and in many ways counter to achieving accurate fire. Why? Because we have no way of knowing what "halfway" is under typical circumstances, and we have no concept of how long we are actually holding our breath. The longer we continue with this practice, the longer we will hold our breath, and the first thing affected is our eyes. Your vision becomes impaired, your body begins to strain and you're no longer in a relaxed state.

We all have a natural respiratory pause, even if we are running with 80 pounds on our backs; there is a bottom of the breathing cycle. That is where we break the shot. If your shot is not lined up right immediately, continue to breathe until it is. The best part about this is, under stress, we can exaggerate the process to help us breathe through a physical event.

We do not have to tell our body to breathe

heavily when exerting ourselves. It just does it naturally. In order to clear out of this condition, we need to breathe more and not less. So, holding your breath in the case of shooting is a very bad thing and does not make the shooter steady. We just turn on a few pieces inside our brain that give us the appearance of being steady. We have image stabilization behind our eyes.

Breathing is my personal Achilles' heel. I find myself reverting to bad habits all the time and, in my case, holding my breath is that bad habit. Oxygen deprivation is not the issue here, carbon dioxide is. We have hypersensitive carbon dioxide sensors in our brains that immediately throw up warning signs when they detect elevated levels. We can hold our breath for at least a minute before a pulse-ox will measure it, however the brain is reacting inside and will compromise us on the firing line.

Trigger Control

Trigger control is defined as the manipulation of the trigger without disturbing the rifle or the lay of the sights on the target. Most errors when shooting can be attributed to improper manipulation of the trigger. In fact, we are such creatures of habit, we can improperly actuate the trigger over and over yet still manage to group well. This is the most influential point, because we are turning on the machine. Pressing the trigger to the rear starts the process. In most people's minds it is also the end, which causes them to inadvertently affect the shot placement. We literally beat the bullet out of the bore by

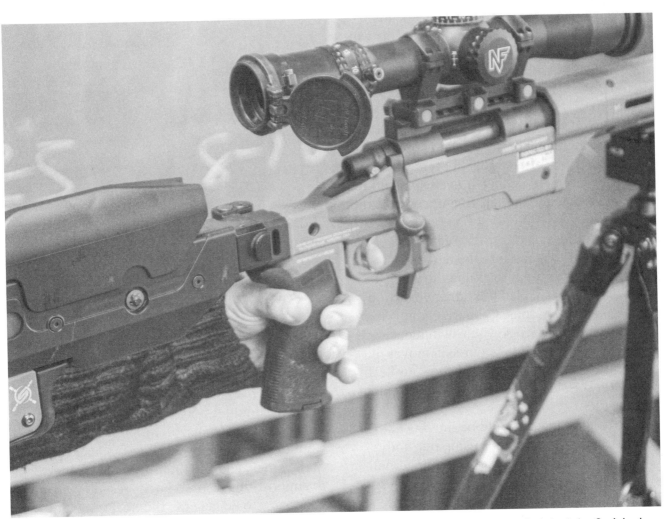

Look at the trigger finger when placed on the shoe. Is your finger starting and stopping at 3 o'clock (or 9 o'clock for a right-handed shooter) when manipulating the trigger?

moving the rifle and altering the sights off the target. In some cases, the shooters are so relieved at having fired the shot that they immediately disengage from the rifle. This is a bad idea.

The purpose of the firing hand is to manipulate the trigger and hold the rifle into the shoulder pocket. We aren't gripping it like a handgun, rather holding it straight back to the rear. This requires very little pressure, so we don't want to have a death grip on it. The shooter should establish a firing position on the stock that starts from the trigger back and not from the stock forward. This is more a mental process than a literal one, as we don't want people putting their fingers on a live-weapon trigger first. The initial practice should have the shooter visualize the trigger finger before the grip. You can do this during dry practice, which is highly recommended.

We want to place the trigger shoe squarely on the pad of the finger, creating a 90-degree angle with the finger and second joint. This will vary slightly from shooter to shooter based on their hands, and type of stock, but the goal should be to get the fingernail to point to 9 o'clock for a right-handed shooter, 3 o'clock for a left-handed shooter. This right-angle position should be there before the trigger is pressed and remain there afterward. Shooters who find their trigger fingers curling or even flying off the shoe, need to work on their trigger control and follow-through.

When addressing the stock, regardless of the type, we want to make sure the movement of the trigger finger is not touching the stock. In the old days, they called this "dragging wood" for the obvious reasons. If the trigger finger is resting against the stock, you will influence the rifle, which is not good. As our skin moves, it compresses the muscles and pushes our flesh out under the skin creating a lateral movement on the stock.

The trigger finger should be moving like a hinge, straight to the rear using our body mechanics to our advantage. If the fingernail starts at 9 o'clock and ends at 9 o'clock, you can rest assured you are manipulating the trigger straight back to the rear. In many cases, you'll find the finger is moving much less than

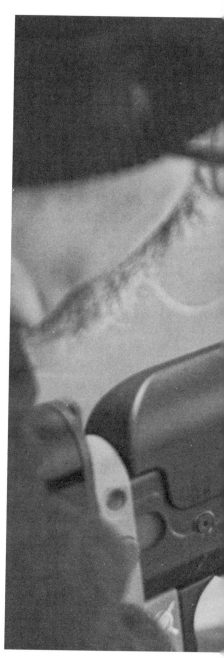

Press, break and freeze. That is the mantra.

it moves if you are incorrectly pressing the trigger shoe.

The three fingers below the trigger finger should be pressing the stock straight back into the shoulder pocket. The pressure should not be so great to discolor them visually. We want to develop a front-to-back management of the stock, and the thumb should be there to support this front-to-back pressure. It's not necessary to engage the thumb. Depending on the stock type, many will lay the thumb on the strong side or use it as a reference point on the

stock, putting it in an out of the way place. We call this floating the thumb, and it is a perfectly acceptable position as we don't need our thumb for the task of shooting.

Correcting a shooter's trigger control is our main priority when teaching classes. One of the most common errors in trigger control is variety. We see shooters manipulating the trigger in a different way every single press. No consistency is what we observe.

Do not underestimate dry practice. It takes roughly 3,000 repetitions to create a new positive neural pathway and about 9,000 repetitions to fix a bad habit. The worst part about fixing bad habits is those 9,000 new repetitions have to all be exact. When dry firing, you can watch your finger.

It's OK to dry fire your centerfire rifle. There should be no damage to the system. If you feel uncomfortable doing so, invest in a snap cap to absorb the impact of the firing pin. But it is generally safe to dry fire a centerfire rifle.

Dry practice needs to be carried out as if it is a live shot. Sloppy dry practice will instill sloppy fundamentals. Invest in perfect practice.

Don't just sit there snapping the trigger, engage the rifle like your life depends on it. The more you dry practice, the better shooter you will become. For indoor dry practice, consider purchasing an Indoor Optical Training Aid (IOTA) lens device; this allows you to focus your scope indoors at 11 feet.

Given time and opportunity before a shot, always dry fire. Set up your position so, without breaking that position, you can easily reach over and insert a live magazine or load a live round so the actual shot mimics the dry fire. We see shooters all the time dry fire perfectly and then change their hand position or cadence of fire by simply going live.

Follow-Through

Follow-through is the forgotten fundamental of marksmanship.

In everything we do, we need follow-through. I wrote earlier about other sports like football. Watch any Sunday game during a kickoff. When the ball sails past the receiver into the end zone,

On the firing line, we execute the fundamentals to the highest degree of accuracy possible. We want to be consistent behind the rifle.

head or, worse, let go of the club. If he saw me do that, he would reprimand me like a puppy who just peed on the floor.

The final act of firing the rifle is follow-through. As I wrote earlier, pressing the trigger starts the machine and begins the bullet's journey down the barrel. As with everything, this takes time. We have to allow the system the time to complete the cycle, so we have to follow through with our trigger press. This will assure shooters they are not disturbing the rifle and the sights before the bullet leaves the barrel. It's a very simple concept. But many people, when focusing on precision, like to "tap" the trigger, allowing the finger to fly off the trigger shoe. At the same time, we don't want to squeeze the finger and "crush" it to the rear because this also moves the rifle.

Follow-through is simply holding the trigger to the rear until the recoil pulse has ended. We don't want to be in such a hurry that we are rushing for the bolt to reload before the bullet has left the bore. It is possible to disturb the system and cause the round to deviate off target.

When the rifle is firing, picture it as a large tuning fork. If we are allowing the trigger mechanism to move during the vibration period, when the bullet is still in the barrel, we can adversely affect the vibrations, thus changing the harmonics of the system from shot to shot. This is especially true with a larger caliber semi-automatic platform. Our goal is consistency. Not following through is anything but consistent and it will cause deviations downrange. With the finger giving the same consistent pressure it took to break the shot, the shooter wants to maintain that 90-degree position of the fingernail and hold the trigger shoe to the rear.

Lastly, we want to continue to watch the reticle on the target. Before breaking the shot, a shooter can lose focus, thinking about all the fundamentals, one then another, then another. The last thing we want to mentally think about, and focus on, is the reticle on the target. We need to watch this throughout the entire firing process. Here is where you want to put the bullet. So, it is here you need to focus. Observe the sights during the firing sequence. We al-

the kicking team will run beyond the receivers until they reach the end zone themselves. This is a basic example of follow-through.

Recently, I was browsing Twitter when I saw famous golfer Phil Mickelson shooting a 6.5 Creedmoor rifle. He was tapping the trigger with zero follow-through behind it. I sent a reply Tweet to him reminding him of this observation. Imagine if I took a golf class with Phil and after addressing the ball and adjusting my club to line up the shot, I swung and immediately upon making contact with the ball I stopped the club ready know what to do. We can press our finger without looking, we can break at our natural respiratory pause without thinking, and we can hold the trigger to the rear thanks to repetitive practice. So, the focus needs to be on the sights. If they are beginning to drift off target, we have to stop the process and reset. You'll see it move, so if something is not correct, the sights will show you. Don't fire. Reset your position.

I like to mentally follow the bullet to the target before moving at all. That means a delay in running the bolt. I have mentioned this before: Distance should give you time and opportunity to put all the fundamentals into play. If I am trying to spot my impact on target, if I start moving the sight picture will be compromised and I might miss the result. If I hit the target, I want to know without the aid of a spotter, and if I miss, I really need to know where so I can correct it. This flies in the face of old-school doctrine that once advised: The gun is broke, or empty, so run the bolt as quickly as possible. Most of the time of flight we are dealing with is relatively short, so don't sweat the few seconds we are asking to freeze in place.

Some people might blink, lose focus, subconsciously look inward, etc. There are a host of things we will think about as part of the firing task, but not in the correct order. So, build the position and, when you are ready to shoot, focus on the sights and where they are in relationship to the target. Unsupported sling shooters will talk about calling their shots. Where were the sights when the shot broke? In supported shooting, especially on a bipod with a scope, the shooter should see the bullet impact the target and know "where" the sights were the entire time. Follow the bullet to the target by watching the sights. Through a scope, this is entirely possible if your position is correct and you follow through with your shot.

Follow-through is my personal pet peeve when it comes to the fundamentals of marksmanship. I harp on it more than any others. With our current state of affairs in terms of rifle systems, we can get away with many bad habits. We have exacting triggers; they break crisp

Does your instructor shoot in front of the students? The author and his instructors tag-team the rifle in each class, demonstrating the fundamentals.

and clean with minor contact. So much so, we see shooters employing triggers adjusted in single-digit ounces. Anything from 8-, to 4-, even 2-ounce triggers are hitting the street. This is an attempt at a mechanical fix to fundamental issue.

Sure, you can buy a fix for just about anything these days. Add weight to the rifle: In fact, some stocks today come with heavy steel weight systems. Decease the caliber and in-

crease the speed in which the bullet leaves the bore. The faster the bullet exits the less influence the shooter has on the shot. Employ a ported muzzle brake to keep the recoil inline so you can get back on target quicker. All this helps, but what happens when you can't make these physical changes to the rifle system. Lighter bullets will have less recoil, less recoil means less movement behind the rifle by the shooter. All this is a factor.

Recognizing Time

With trigger control and follow-through working together, we have to recognize time. Every rifle system has a lock time. That is usually applied to the firing pin movement. The time from the trigger break to the primer being hit. However, our lock time does not just apply to the firing pin movement. We have to consider the time it takes for the brain to relay the will to press the trigger to the hand. Different shooters have different reaction times. That can mean a shooter with a slower reaction time using a bigger lead on a moving target. Then we have to look at the time it takes for bullets to the leave the barrel. We know about barrel harmonics, but did you know you can look up the harmonic nodes using a time stamp?

The trigger is the start button and the stop. We are turning the machine on, not off.

I see it a lot with shooters who hold their breath. They immediately disengage from the rifle because they are sitting there holding their breath prior to the shot. They hold their breath for a number of reasons, but mainly because they feel it makes the shot steady. It's a huge relief when the rifle fires because they are quickly running out of air.

Your precision rifle is a machine, we are turning on the machine in order to send the bullet downrange to the target. I would submit to you, the shot is not over until the bullet has hit the target, or we have confirmed a miss. Stay engaged with the rifle and sights until we are sure we need a follow-up shot, or we are sure the target has been successfully engaged.

Calling Your Shot

We have gone through the fundamentals of marksmanship, so you can understand what it takes to successfully engage a target using a rifle. All this information is great as a theoretical exercise. But how do we know we are doing it right in our practical application? The best way is with a competent instructor to watch you shoot and correct any errors in your form. The next best way to know you are doing it right is "Calling your Shot." Because telling you how to do something is not enough. We need to put it in practice and look at the end result, as it appears through the scope.

Calling your shot, again, comes from the competition world. It is very important to sling shooters. However, because we tend to do things slightly different, we have to modify the way it was done in the past. Unsupported sling shooting means the body will react to recoil to higher degree than shooting from a supported

Fundamentals translate regardless of the position. What changes is the amount of practice we put into the task.

position, such as off a bipod. Because we focus on being straight behind the rifle, and managing the recoil, we will have far less movement of the system. This is easy to see by watching a video of a successful tactical shooter. Video makes it clear just how little the rifle will actually move, allowing the shooter to remain on target. This will help shooters fine-tune their training and take target analysis beyond the target to their sight picture.

The most common expression when talking about calling your shot is:

"Where were the sights when the shot broke?"

It is expressed this way because the instructor was talking about unsupported sling shooting. The shooter will move with recoil and rock off target then roll back on, reacquiring the sight picture. In the 21st century, we do things slightly different, so we have to adjust this thinking to account for supported shooting. How we speak to ourselves matters. In this case, asking the question in the past tense is wrong.

The tactical shooter needs to ask, "Where are the sights when the shot broke?" It's a small but important distinction that will begin to condition our mind toward the positive. It will force the shooter to focus on the sight picture during the critical moment when the shot is fired. Shooting is a game of milliseconds and if you divert your attention from the target, you risk drifting off target. In so many cases, shooters will not even notice this. They will establish their sight picture, consider the crosshairs on target and then begin to think about something else. It's during these moments where we miss the movement caused by a poor trigger press, or a subconscious shift in our body. We need to carefully watch the reticle so we can answer: Where are our sights during the firing sequence? This is the modern, more effective way to call your shots. If the sights remain on target and we deviate from impacting at our expected location, we then need to examine the firing sequence, so we identify the issue. "Was it a case of letting a fundamental go; poor natural point of aim; a failed trigger press; or lack of follow-through? Or do we need to adjust our zero? Calling our shots will help identify any number of issues. It can even help in recognizing faulty equipment such as scope that fails to hold zero.

If we have practiced and trained our body to execute the fundamentals correctly, during live fire the benefits will be immediately apparent. This also extends to positional shooting, from any position. Making this a part of the firing sequence will train you to be more effective.

Recoil Management

In classes, I talk a lot about the fundamentals of marksmanship and how they are the building blocks to all great shooting. When we break them down into a logical order, they address the core elements of a shot. From our body position to our sights, the fundamentals guide us toward a better result: hitting the target.

When addressing the rifle, we look at natural point of aim: rifle pointed to the target with the body pointed to the rifle. Sight picture has become modified when using a scope from sight picture and sight alignment to aiming. Granted, we still have sight alignment, our eye relief, and sight picture is about edge-to-edge clarity behind the ocular. However, these actions are not part of the shot sequence because the scope should be set up ahead of time. When using a rifle scope, it's more about aiming, unlike iron sights.

Bipod design matters when it comes to recoil management.

Once our body position is established, it's about the firing sequence. In the past, we would tell the shooter to control his or her breathing giving it that slight pause before breaking the shot. Today, we look at the natural respiratory pause, breaking at the bottom of our exhale while avoiding the urge to hold our breath. Think about this. Movement, going from Point A to Point B quickly, increases our heart rate and breathing. The worst thing you can do under these elevated conditions is to hold your

breath. So, we breathe through and merely break the trigger at the bottom of our natural respiratory cycle. Trust me, you have no concept of time under these conditions so don't attempt to hold your breath.

While ignoring our breathing, we want to begin to take up the trigger without moving the sights off target. Trigger control or the manipulation of the trigger without disturbing the lay of the sights, might sound easy, but it's our most significant point of error. We combine trigger control with follow-through, the act of physically and mentally holding the shot on target. In our mind's eye, we want to follow the bullet to the target until the recoil pulse has subsided. We do that by physically staying engaged with the sights on the targets. One hundred percent of your focus should be on the target/reticle relationship during this sequence. Once the recoil pulse has ended and we have observed the results of our shot downrange, we can then run the bolt for the next round.

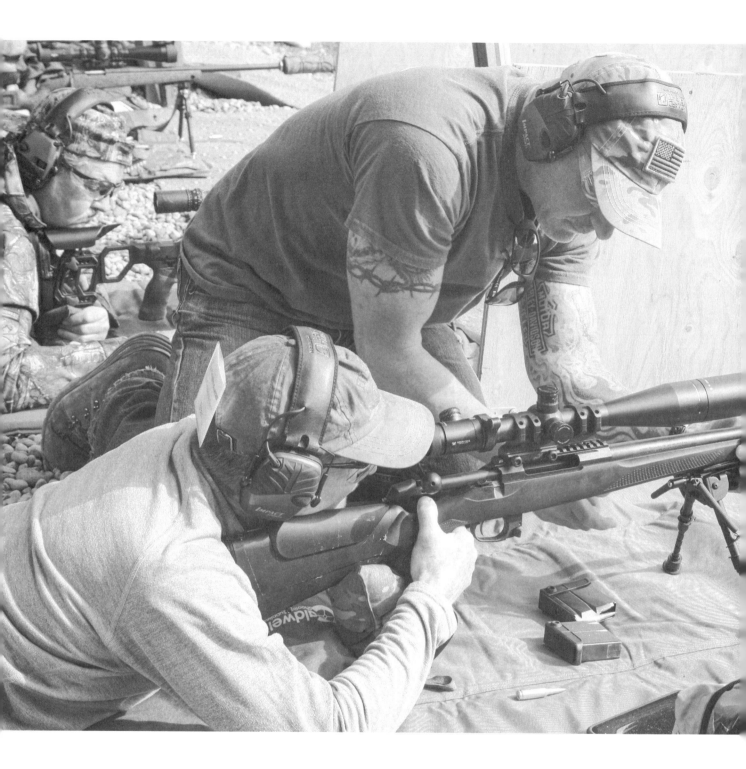

These are the fundamentals of marksmanship as needed to engage targets at a distance successfully.

But there is more. Today we shoot slightly different than the originators of the fundamentals. They were sling or unsupported shooters. While various front rests existed, the technique did not change much when using one.

For the modern shooter, a solid front rest is the most common way to engage targets. We use bipods, which means we have to modify our body position in a way to allow the shooter the ability to see the results of the shot. No longer do we rely on the spotter to do the heavy lifting. Back in my Sniper School days, the spotter was the Senior Marine who guided the trigger monkey on target and established the variables for the engagement. All the shooter does is follow

During this short period, new shooters tend to move causing deviations in the position of the barrel. More influence at the back of the rifle, increases movement at the front. If we are consistent, as in we shoot a group, it's our job to adjust the sights to center the group around our aiming point. This recoil management is why your zero is different than your buddy's; each person is addressing the rifle in a slightly different way; hence the recoil management changes.

Today, the military addresses recoil management as part of the firing task, the same as follow-through. However, recoil management starts during the beginning phases of the shot sequence. We want to load the bipod or stack our weight behind the rifle, eliminating angles during natural point of aim. Then, when the shot breaks, we ride the rifle through recoil, maintaining our sight picture and our reticle's relationship with the target. This is the part of recoil management that works with follow-through.

Loading the bipod is often misunderstood. People think it's about pushing the rifle forward with the shoulders. This is incorrect. You are loading the bipod from the core, our hips. It's not about pressure, but more about dead weight giving the rifle a slab of meat to recoil against. It's also bipod-dependent, as you are merely taking the slack out of the system.

A Harris bipod, one of the most common on the market, has very little to no perceived movement in the legs. We load a Harris using one technique, where an Atlas Bipod has slack in the legs and movement. That requires are a different technique. The Harris is more of a rise with a knuckle under with the rubber feet. We do not push any bipod forward, but rather bring the rifle back into our shoulder pocket and move our core up. It's a pinching method of holding the stock between the bipod and body.

The Atlas comes back into our shoulder pocket, then operating as one unit, we remove the slack from the legs using our core weight to hold it. This way, when the rifle recoils, it just flexes on the slack of the legs. About a quarter inch of movement. Once the recoil pulse has ended, the rifle will return to the original starting point.

This works in alternate positions, too, when

Part of setting up the rifle to the shooter is balancing the proper height on the bipod legs, so recoil will come back in a straight line.

directions and press the trigger without disturbing the lay of the sights. Today, we have learned that recoil management is an essential element related to the fundamentals.

Recoil management tells the bullet where the barrel is when leaving the bore. It controls your zero. Depending on how you are positioned behind the rifle, once it fires, there is time between the primer strike and the exiting of the bullet.

we are not even using a bipod. Take a barricade drill as an example. How do you position your body and stack your weight behind the rifle? We want our shoulders square and in front of our hips and the rifle held into the shoulder pocket. Picture the prone body position and translate that same upper chest and head location to other positions.

Recoil management is every bit of a fundamental as the fundamentals themselves. We can spot our own shots; we stay engaged with our targets; and can quickly follow up and fix a miss without assistance. Seeing is essential. The more we can see, the more we can locate, close with and engage. It's about being our own spotter, and not taking our most senior member out of the fight. Two guns are always better than one.

Sniper's Hide website (www.snipershide. com) has a robust online training section in the forum. I have more than 45 minutes of video breaking down recoil management under a variety of conditions. From prone to shooting off a bench, the way you position yourself behind the rifle matters. I have found that you can see as much as a 20fps difference in muzzle velocity by just mismanaging the recoil management. Yes, you read that correctly, your muzzle velocity can and will change based on your position and how you manage the rifle. It's a critical element and needs to be understood.

Some ranges only let you shoot off a bench, but many of the competitions we participate in are either prone or a variety of alternate positions. When putting new shooters on a bench, we turn them around and square them up. The benches that force you to sit sideways and bladed are a no-go for us right from the start. Turn that bench around and sit squarely. Being up tall and bladed will push you off balance and bleed velocity off compared to the prone position.

It's important to understand the type of shooting you are engaged in, the discipline. Each discipline has its little variations. I would not preach recoil management to the benchrest crowd, but that is not my discipline of choice.

The best advice I can give the new shooter reading this is to relax behind the rifle. You need to be a slab of dead meat and not to push or

Different rifles have different recoil pulses, so match the system to the technique employed.

to hold tension in your shoulders. We used to read about guys trying to practice recoil management based on the written word. Many will complain about the bipods rolling or creeping forward. That tells me you are using your shoulders and not your core weight. It's about sliding that belt line forward about a half inch. Next, make sure you are not unloading the bipod by

reversing the order. Guys will move forward first and pull back into the shoulder pocket second. This unloads the bipod.

Fixing That Bipod Hop

Bipods don't hop. There is no "UP" component. That comes from the stock bouncing off the shooter. The bullet goes one way, the recoil goes the other way and, like electricity, that recoil will follow the path of least resistance. If you feel you are straight and square behind the rifle and the system is still jumping to the side, consider that your 6 o'clock hold might not be right for you. Instead, the stock might need to be closer to 7 o'clock on your body versus that

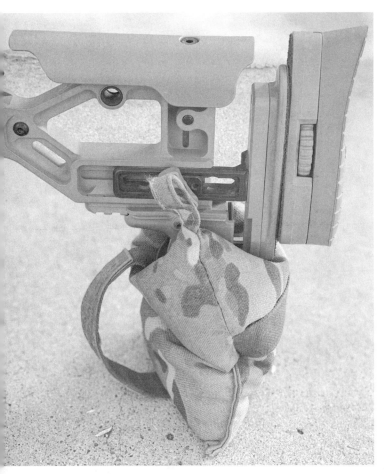

Balance the rear bag under the toe of the stock. Be sure to support both the rifle and the rear bag.

I have mentioned it several times: Recoil management is not just part of the prone position. It's an element of your body position, regardless. Get aggressive, place your shoulders over and in front of your hips and secure the rifle in the shoulder pocket. Think of a lean, more so than a push.

Rear Bags

You want to be using a rear bag. This means a rear bag and not a rear rest. If you are using a front rest instead of a bipod, you can pair it to a rear rest, but for most of us who include movement into our shooting, it's a rear bag.

The rear bag is there is to support the back of the rifle. If we look at the movement we induce into the system, it's all at the back of the rifle. This means it will magnify as it travels forward toward the end of the barrel.

How you manage the rear bag will determine the direction the recoil pulse travels.

6 o'clock hold. A Harris bipod is generally the worst offender when it comes to the rifle jumping to the side. Be sure to come one notch up on the legs to remove the spring from the system and check square. It's a more difficult method to start with it because a Harris is so ridged.

Trigger control and follow-through also contribute to the movement of the system. If you are tapping the trigger, or not following through, you are adding motion to a process where no movement is required.

Recoil management is an integral part of driving the rifle correctly. The fundamentals of marksmanship are the foundations for all great shooting. We combine the two as part of one action, execution of the firing task. The rifle will recoil in a straight line; the scope will be zeroed to the rifle and not to the shooter's bad body position. It's all about consistency, doing the same thing the same way for every shot.

The author slides his hand inside the strap, then using his pincher fingers, he supports the rear of the rifle and not just the bag.

I like to pair my rear bag up so it levels the rifle to my firing position when in place. Then I look at my hands as a choreographed movement between the rear of the stock and firing hand. To start off, the firing hand brings the rifle into the shoulder pocket. That holds the rifle firmly in place allowing you to relax the shoulder. There is no tension there as the hand holds the butt-stock. When it comes time to run the bolt, the firing hand will let go of the stock to manipulate the bolt, and the support hand needs to hold the stock in place while the bolt is being run.

It's a tradeoff. The firing hand runs the bolt, the support hand holds the rifle.

The hold accomplishes a few things. It prevents the rifle from fishtailing in the shoulder pocket. It keeps us on target, so we don't have to re-acquire it. And it minimizes all movement when behind the rifle.

Some negatives we see with improper rear bag use is:

- Sympathetically squeezing at the same time, when we fire the rifle
- Holding just the bag and not the rifle
- Not using either the bag or supporting the rear of the stock
- Using the wrong size bag for the shooter's body position

We have heard of students not using them, and I have seen it a few times in class. Trust me, your performance will increase three-fold with the correct use of a rear bag.

Going back to the days of the sock filled with sand, remember: Something to support the back of the rifle is better than nothing. Pinch the stock between the thumb and index finger while adjusting and supporting the rear bag with the three lower, gripper fingers.

It's a key piece of equipment and should be paired to the bipod for maximum effectiveness.

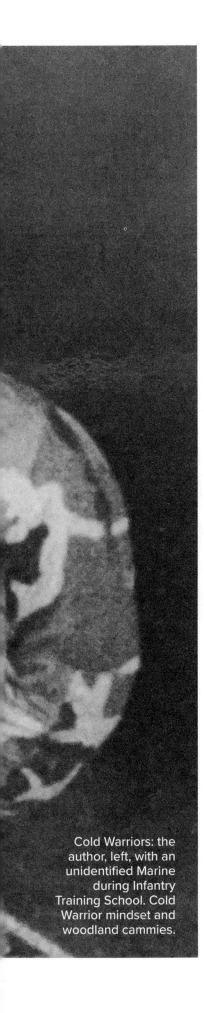

Cold Warriors: the author, left, with an unidentified Marine during Infantry Training School. Cold Warrior mindset and woodland cammies.

4

Infantry School to Amphibious Reconnaissance School

From boot camp, I went to Infantry Training School (ITS) at Camp Geiger, in North Carolina. Camp Geiger is an offshoot of nearby Camp Lejeune. I had a ton of fun at ITS, it was the ultimate example of playing Army as an adult. This part of the Marine Corps is exactly what I envisioned growing up in Connecticut.

During my time at Infantry Training School, I got in tight with our Captain in charge. During these early years in the Marine Corps, I would often get letters from federal prison. I had an uncle serving time for Mafia-related activities and, for me, he was just being federally educated. Some people go to college, other people go to federal prison. I was called out in boot camp for it, and when I arrived at Geiger they wanted to know more.

This was a typical 1980's-style uniform in the field. Training was focused on the Soviet threat.

Our Captain was fascinated with mob stories. During overnight exercises he would visit with me for hours talking about my experiences. It was all very Sopranos growing up. It's funny what some people consider to be normal. I thought it was normal. Northeast Italians were supposed to be connected. That is the perception.

He suggested I attempt the recon indoctrination given during Infantry School. He felt for my size (5-foot-2, 112 pounds), a role in a recon unit would be a good fit. Recon in the USMC is not an easy thing. The schooling alone is pretty extensive.

At the time the recon indoctrination test was:

1st Class PFT, 20 pullups, 200 situps, and then a three-mile run in less than 20 minutes.

Immediately after that, you had to do the full obstacle course twice in less than five minutes. After the obstacles, you immediately went to the pool for the advanced swim qualification. I know the USMC has changed the swim qualification requirements, so I don't quite recall all the differences in the four levels. The advanced qual featured the underwater swim, in which you have to break the surface to simulate there being a layer of oil or fire on the surface. This was the biggest difference I personally remember. How much time you had to tread water might also be a factor.

When all this was concluded, we headed over to Onslow Beach where the Recon Battalion was located. On the beach, you had to complete a five-mile ruck run with 50 pounds of sand and no frame. We used a standard Alice Pack, and the Marines conducting the test all got a good laugh putting me on the pack scale. At this point, I weighed a whole 112 pounds.

Running five miles on a beach with no frame was certainly going to test my ability to adapt, overcome and excel. The reality was, I did not finish the ruck run in time. We had 58 minutes to complete it, and that was just not going to happen. There are two things to understand at this point, the day before this Indoc test I had received a flu shot from the USMC. I was sick as a dog at this point in the test. I managed to pass everything else up until the ruck run. During the run it was hard to maintain my breathing as I had a line of snot pouring out my nose down to my knees. One of the tricks I used to keep in the game as long as I did was to pull the main compartment straps over my head to get the bulk of the weight on top of my shoulders. From there, it was just not quit. When the time officially expired, I was still on the course moving forward. The Recon team rolled up in a Willys Jeep, versus a Hummer, and ordered me in the vehicle. The Indoc was over they wanted to go home; it was Saturday afternoon. I never really

The patrol phase of Amphibious Recon School. The rifles were fake because of the amount of water the author and his fellow students traversed.

The author always liked carrying the PRC 77 back in those days. It was a bit of character building, and they could do so much more damage with a radio.

looked them in the eye and just said "F*** You" and kept walking forward. Not to be deterred, they repeated the order, and I repeated my response, this went back and forth for about five minutes before they left me alone and waited at the finish line.

I was the last guy to arrive and, upon dropping my pack, rolled right in with everyone else, like I just passed the test. Truth was, I was 15 minutes late to the party. To this day I believe there was a little bit of divine intervention from my ITS Captain, as I was given orders to Am-

Sure, they lived in tents. Most would call it squalor, but the author and his fellow Marines loved it.

phibious Recon School in Virginia.

I found recon school to be the hardest of all my certified training schools attended in the USMC. I had a tough time with the open-water swims when hauling all my gear. Pulling 80 pounds through the water when you weigh 112 pounds is not easy. During the patrol phase, I had no issues at all and did quite well. It wasn't until we flew to Key West, Florida, for the water phase that I struggled.

The thing with me was testing. I tested above average, and I excelled at anything books related. It was the daily two-mile swims in waters around Key West that kicked my butt.

I did not graduate ARS, but I completed it. I made it to the last day and was prevented from going to a Recon unit due to an issue with another student. In our class, we had one officer, a Lieutenant from 2nd Recon Battalion. I remember his name, but not how to spell it, so let's call him

Lt. Cocteau. He started a bunch of drama with me the day of the final exercise, where I had no recourse. It was basically him against me, and being I was a Private First Class at the time, there was no way I was winning this one. In hindsight, I want to say it was coordinated to keep me from Recon, because I did struggle. The water phase kicked my butt, and I get it. You have a specialized unit with guy who is 5-feet, 2-inches tall, weighing 112 pounds, not everyone is going to be a fan. Looking back over the years, he did me a colossal favor, so there is no reason to be bitter about it. They originally explained that all the students were equal, however it was funny how fast rank became a factor. He had a similar run-in with a group of Force Recon Marines in the class that was overlooked as they had a unit and command behind them, while I was more freelance at the time. I was just a Marine in transition, versus one attached to actual unit.

The tried and true M60 machine gun. Later, when the author spent some time in a National Guard unit, he was forced to qualify this weapon for them because nobody knew how to take it apart.

My punishment was to be returned to a line unit.

After ARS, I was back at Camp Lejeune and assigned to Bravo Company 1st Battalion, 2nd Marines. Camp Lejeune in 1986 was still trying to determine if we wanted to be old school or move toward the future. There was a weird dynamic to it. Court Street was still in full swing, but in the process of being closed off. Court Street was where the bars and hookers were along with a few choice tattoo parlors. If you were stationed at Camp Lejeune, you knew all about Court Street, and I use the name as a point of reference.

My first two weeks in a line unit turned out to be quite memorable. I was a semi fresh-faced PFC and my best friend was my roommate Craig Gardpiey from the West Coast. We had a third roommate, a gang-member type from East Los Angles. We'll call him Cheech for this part of the story. Cheech liked to go out and drink to excess, and he did not hold his liquor very well. On one particular evening, Craig and I were in our racks like good little Marine PFCs with beds made to boot-camp standards. I have no idea what time it happened, but I know it was after midnight when I was startled awake by Cheech.

He was sitting on my rack with his face super close to mine telling me to wake up. He had a Raven .25-caliber handgun pressed against my head babbling in a mix of languages. "Galli, you're a good dude, but you need to get death in your body," he was telling me. I looked over at Craig who was also awake, his eyes as big as flying saucers. He was explaining to me the rules of life while tapping me on the head with his pistol. Getting death in my body was requirement according to him. At this point, I let him talk and said nothing, which was the smart move as he got bored rather quickly and staggered to the door. We lived on the first floor, so after opening the door you are staring at the courtyard.

With the rack being made to boot-camp standards, you are essentially locked in place. There is no way you are getting out of bed quickly, so not moving was the plan of the day until this unfolded. Cheech, standing in the open doorway began to yell in multiple languages at the world,

a mix of Spanish and English. He received a reply from another Marine walking through the courtyard, a big F*** You. Cheech proceeded to shoot him, as he did others out in town that night. Nothing critical, just enough to wake up the entire barracks.

Cheech was wrapped up quickly after that, spending the remainder of his Marine Corps time in the Brig.

Shortly after this, I took a critical step in my USMC history by being volunteered to attend the International Naval Review in New York City. Ronald Reagan was about to reopen the Statue of Liberty for the Fourth of July celebration in NYC. With half of them having just returned from Okinawa prior to my arrival, many of the senior Marines were home on leave. They needed a few guys to float up aboard the USS Austin so the Marines could take part in the festivities.

They called it a Tiger Cruise, a mini float where civilians are present. We sailed from North Carolina to Brooklyn, New York, were the ship was docked. During the float up, I was introduced to one of the most influential Marines of my early career: Doug Henderson. Doug was a Corporal from STA Platoon. STA stands for Surveillance and Target Acquisition, and it was the part of a Marine Unit where the snipers are located. While on ship, I explained my position to Doug, and said I wanted to go to Sniper School. I told him about Amphibious Recon School and what transpired there, so there were no questions.

While in NYC, our position within the International Naval Review changed. We were supposed to work during the day hosting a Dog and Pony Show. Dog and Pony Shows are where you stand there and talk about military jobs to visitors on the ship. Whatever it was supposed to be, that was not the reality on the ground. They basically cut us loose after morning formation to wander the streets of New York and be nice to people. That turned into a full-time drunk fest. With me having family close by, it was very entertaining. I escorted a lot of new visitors to NYC to the better bars to hang out, including the guys from STA Platoon.

Establishing my good nature with Doug, I

Traveling to New York City for the Fourth of July was dream duty for the author, even if only for a few short days. It took him one step closer to Sniper School.

asked to go to the next Sniper School class upon return to Camp Lejeune. Doug agreed to get me a slot and not much was said after that, at least by the members of STA. PFC Galli was telling everyone who would listen I was going to Sniper School during the next class and the laughter could be heard to this day.

No way was a PFC going to Sniper School, and the Battalion would have only two slots. Sniper School at the time was often used as a re-enlistment tool. The requirements were pretty clear and, frankly speaking, I was missing a few elements. I needed three expert rifle qualifications and I didn't even have one. I only qualified in boot camp, and while I shot expert most of the time, on qual day I choked and missed expert by one point. Still, I was confident I was going to Sniper School, after all Corporal Henderson told me so.

Between the Fourth of July and October, the

A trip to Bridgeport, California, and the Mountain Warfare Training Center, got the author in shape for the start of Scout Sniper School.

timing for the next Sniper School class, I attended Mountain Warfare training as part of Bravo Company. We traveled to Bridgeport, California, and took the final summer course of the season, which, of course, turned into a winter wonderland by the end of the trip. I liked camp life at Bridgeport, but hated force-marching up mountains. The idea I was going to Sniper School became a bit of a running joke to the senior members of my platoon, especially to my Platoon Commander.

We returned to Camp Lejeune just after October and, sure enough, Doug Henderson kept his words; orders for PFC Galli to attend Sniper School arrived. Saying my unit was pissed would be an understatement. During Sniper School I received my Lance Corporal rank. Getting rank in the Marines is usually a big deal.

Big Battalion formations, attention to orders, a big focus on all those receiving awards. Hazing was still allowed, so not only did you get your metal chevrons driven into your collar, you got punched by all those in your Platoon with equal or higher rank. Not for me. I was called into the First Sergeant's office, he threw my chevrons at me, and told me to get out. I smiled and said, "Bye, I am going back to Stone's Bay now." They were not happy, but I was.

Amphibious Recon School and the lessons learned there really helped me in Sniper School. There is more than just education when it comes to these schools. There is political, there is gaming the system, there is knowing where the lines are formed. I took that failure to heart and learned from my previous mistake. The nice part, no officers to get in the way.

5

Before You Go to the Range

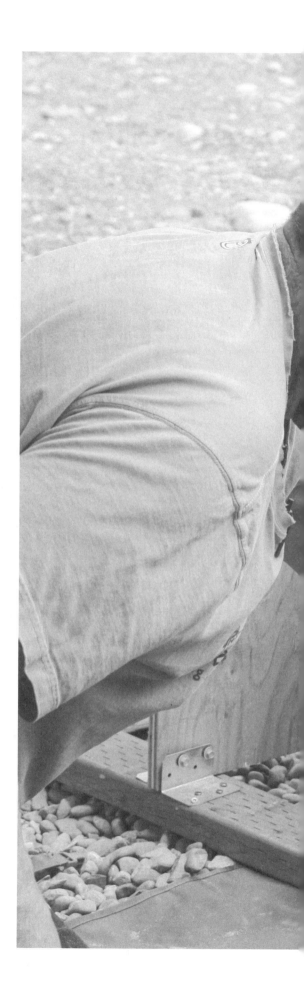

The author spends an extra amount of time setting up the rifle to the shooter. Don't overlook this important element to success.

When you purchase a new precision rifle, there are a few things you need to do prior to shooting it. The first thing is properly setting it up for the shooter. Rifles need to be looked at the same way we look at our cars. The stock is the seats, the scope is the mirrors, and how you are address the bolt is the same as looking at our steering wheel.

Rifle setup can change over time, usually a short amount of time, but it's not always a static prospect with a new shooter. We settle into our rifle systems, so expect a minor amount of change to happen within the first 500 rounds.

Prior to setting up the rifle, I recommend a minor cleaning of the action and the bore. Think of it as getting to know your rifle. Take a single wet patch of a cleaning fluid of your choice and punch the bore. Then send a few dry patches to wipe it clean. We want to make sure there is no fluid or debris in there prior to shooting. I also like to check and wipe down the action, maybe put a tiny bit of white grease on your lugs. It's at this point I want to test the comfort of the stock, sans scope.

There is a ton of debate in terms of triggers. I happen to be a fan of two-stage triggers. I want to marry my finger to the trigger shoe without fear of it firing unexpectedly. Today we see guys pushing the trigger weight limits to the Nth degree. I was highly critical of 8-ounce triggers for tactical rifle competitions, but those have given away to 2- and 4-ounce variants. Super unsafe in my opinion, especially for a field rifle. If you want to participate in benchrest or F Class using a trigger set that low, OK I get it, but a tactical rifle that will be employed in the field is dangerous.

My thoughts for tactical triggers hover around 16 ounces and above to about three pounds. If you travel back in time, the mindset was the trigger break should surprise the shooter. This is completely false. The shooter should know exactly when it breaks. Trigger Control: See, it's right in the name. On the military side, consider a command-fire drill. This is something like what you'd imagine in the Captain Phillips engagement, when Somali pirates hijacked the MV Maersk Alabama ship in April 2009. After Captain Philips was taken hostage, the SEALs took out the pirates using a command-fire drill in which all shots are executed as one. You cannot do this without understanding your trigger break.

Set the trigger prior to setting up the scope as you might have to pull the barreled action out of the stock. Find that point where you can still control the movement without disturbing the lay of the sights.

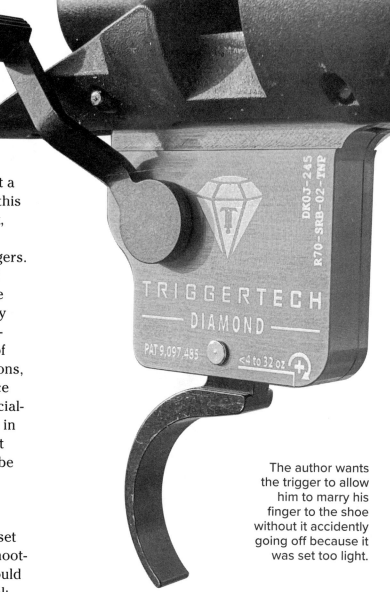

The author wants the trigger to allow him to marry his finger to the shoe without it accidently going off because it was set too light.

My favorite part of modern triggers is the ability to move the shoe forward and backward, depending on the size of the shooter's hand. This is that extra layer of control you can achieve by a tiny amount of movement. These triggers shoes move maybe a half inch, but that is enough to align the trigger fingernail to 90 degrees. I get intimate with my rifles before setting up the scope, as I want to feel it without being distracted by the glass. We love our scopes; they are like the icing on the cake and shooter will focus on the optics before setting up the rifle properly.

Once I have it set up for me, I have considered my use and what positions I will be shooting the rifle. For example, if my local range only lets me shoot from a bench, I am going to set it up for that position. If am going to be shooting prone, which is preferred, I set it up for that position.

It's at this point I mount the scope.

Prior to attaching the scope to the rifle, I set it up in the rings. I personally use a Badger Dead Level device to mount the scope in the rings. The key to properly mounting the scope is aligning the reticle to the fall of gravity. There are two methods I would recommend for accomplishing this task.

1.First, set the scope up so the reticle follows a plumb line: A weighted string hung in a way I can align the reticle to match. The bullet only cares about gravity, so using a plumb is the best way to knock this out without spending any money.

2.The second method is using the bottom of the scope. The majority of scopes out there have a flat machined into the body under the scope saddle. This can be used to align the bottom of the scope to the top of the picatinny rail. When you pair up these two sections, the reticle should be leveled.

Inside a room, using a dead level with the flat of the scope matched to flat of the rail is super easy. Use a set of business cards, feeler gauges

The author likes a two-stage trigger, when available. The two-stage trigger allows him to marry his finger to the shoe so he can control the trigger break, which should not be a surprise.

The author's scope is mounted and leveled first and applied to rifle after. He sets up the scope using a Badger Ordnance Dead Level tool.

or a machines square. You don't need expensive scope-leveling tools and, honestly speaking, they are not correct, thus a complete waste of money. Buying a scope-mounting package with four sets of levels might seem worthwhile, but believe me, they are wrong in their application.

A critical component to all this is, of course, the bipod. We often see a lot of new shooters glance over their bipod choices. They go for the basic model they can find, never understanding just how much control the bipod affords.

Bipods have changed since the Harris was introduced. These models are the lowest common denominator where the design has not changed since the beginning. Today we now look at a bipod in a whole new light.

Straight and square are not wording I would use with Harris bipods. These stamped metal devices are often out of square and balance the

rifle on the top of the pyramid. It's a bad way to do business, however it's how everyone has done it for 40 years. We generally look at pictures on the Internet and repeat what we see, especially if we see it enough. There is no "why," just a "because." "Because Bob did it that way" is not an answer.

The bipod sets the tone; it manages the shooter's comfort level behind the rifle. It's funny when I see big, 6-foot-plus guys trying to shoot prone with their Harris 6- to 9-inch model set at the lowest level. You set up the bipod based on the shooter's body type. Taller for bigger guys, shorter for smaller people. You want the shoulders level and straight. So, if you have to roll your head over or dip a shoulder to address the stock, the bipod is too low.

Prone is the lowest position. We often hear students talk about getting as low as possible

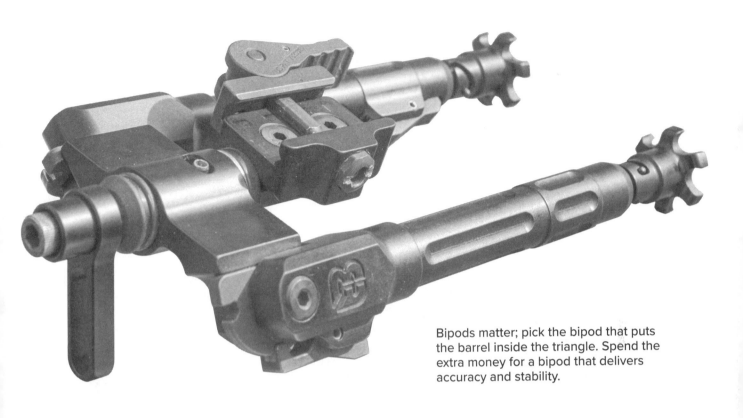

Bipods matter; pick the bipod that puts the barrel inside the triangle. Spend the extra money for a bipod that delivers accuracy and stability.

The bullet only cares about gravity, so level the reticle of the scope to gravity. Do not obsess over it. Simply match the flat of the bottom of the scope to the flat of the rail. You don't need four levels to properly set up the scope.

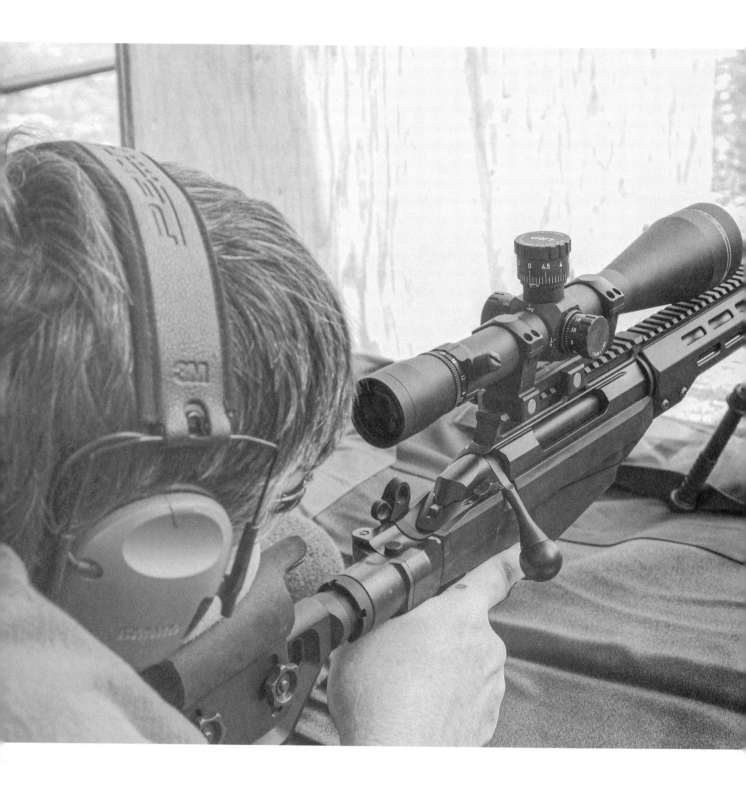

to be more accurate, more stable. Well this goes back to the game of Telephone. You know the game of Telephone, when several people take turns whispering a phrase from one to another, seeing how the phrase changes from the first to the last person. The idea that you need to get as low as possible comes out of this, but incorrectly tries to apply this theory to a single position

versus the correct examples comparing the common positions like kneeling or standing.

First, we have the standing positions. We walk up, level the rifle to our eye and fire. The only thing holding up the rifle is our two hands, and they are not supported. We have our feet on the ground and the size and weight of the rifle, will dictate our success. If we want to get more

The wider the stance, the better the stability. You want the bipod to support the front of the rifle without compromising accuracy.

Adjustability costs money. The more adjustment in the rifle, the more expensive it will be. The Sniper's Hide Edition Rifle from Ashbury Precision was designed to put effort into the stock so it will actually fit the shooter correctly.

stable, or increase our accuracy, we need to get lower, so we transition to the kneeling position.

The kneel is lower than standing and helps us support the firing task. We drop down to one knee widening out our base, making us more stable. We then can hold up the support arm using our knee. With our forearm straight and correctly aligned under the rifle, holding it up

becomes easier than the standing position. It's lower than standing and more stable. If we want to increase stability, we can then move from the kneeling position to the sitting position.

The sitting position puts our butt on the ground, increasing stability. With our legs, we can hold up the rifle by supporting both arms. Our firing elbow is balanced on one leg and support elbow is balanced on the other. We want the forearms under the rifle as straight as we can get so the rifle has bone support.

These positions are what you read about when they write about the elements of a good shooting positions. Bone support, muscle relaxation, aligned with our natural point of aim, we then properly align and hold the rifle on target.

Finally, if you want to get more stable than sitting, we go prone. We are lying on the ground, so we have maximum support. Our arms should be up on our elbows, and not lying on our forearms. This is a key element for the prone position and the best way to explain it is using children. If you watch small children on the floor, reading, watching TV, or playing on a computer, they typically sit up on their elbows.

Shooting courses vary, so set up the rifle in a way you can manage more than one position correctly.

Prone is the lowest position. Once in the prone position, set the bipod for the shooter's body type.

We don't have to tell our kids to do this, they just naturally balance high on their elbows. It's normal, so why fight the natural position our kids demonstrate every day?

There is no position lower than prone, except dead. Sure, we can write about a Hawkins position as used by the military. The Hawkins position is used to reduce your profile on a small crest. You lay on the rifle stock, balance the front of the rifle with a fist, and make like a lump of grass. It can also be used to shoot under things instead of a roll-over supine position. Hawkins was used a lot in the USMC, especially in the early days of the sniper program because it made you a smaller target.

After all that, it's all about the bipod. Invest in a good solid, and square bipod because it matters. The bipod also controls rifle cant, or tilt. Canting a rifle is bad. It throws the shot low and sideways increasing the wind hold. If you

are shooting a target with others, especially if you have a left-to-right wind and you need more windage than the other guys, you might be canting the rifle. I write a lot online about setting up the rifle to your natural hold. Why I cover this so much is because canting is subconscious, even with a level, most people don't realize they are doing it.

If we look at bipod designs, the ability to lock out the side-to-side motion is key. Right-handed shooters will push the rifle to the right with their heads. Then, when running the bolt, they will pull the rifle to the right. With these two actions, the body will fall into the position and

We want to eliminate angles. Lining up straight behind the rifle is step one. We also want to look at our head behind the rifle. The bipod controls the angle of the head on the stock. Raise the bipod to align the head correctly.

and the mind is looking at our hand. Forget follow-through as that is the forgotten and the shooter is probably going to tap the trigger. Once the first shot is fired, they ignore level and now they are focusing on their groups. All the while, they are slowly pushing and pulling the rifle to the right. A lefty will do the same, just backward. We notice this downrange when we observe the groups. There will be multiple shots touching, but separated as the shooting is firing.

Shot One: Centered and straight

Shot Two: Slightly canted right, could be less than a degree

Shot Three: Another canted shot, maybe as much as two degrees

Shot Four: Centered and straight after correcting the observed cant

Shot Five: Slightly canted again like shot two

We are not very good multi-taskers; we miss a lot of information right in front of us because the brain is preoccupied with the results instead of the process.

A bipod with the ability to lock down the sideways movement is key. You can forgo the level, just align the rifle on target, observe the top of the scope to make sure it is straight and before even addressing the rifle, tighten the bipod to minimize the want to push it over.

A level is a training tool, and not a shooting aid. If every time you address the rifle, looking at the level saves you from firing canted, you have a rifle setup issue. It's the definition of insanity if you think it about. Every time the shooter has to look at the level to fix a canting problem, his body is telling him something important. Listen to your body. Adjust the system so the natural hold is correctly addressing the rifle without the need for a level. We have the charts and math to show why. The problem is, are shooters listening, or trying to buy a hit with a piece of gear?

I put a lot more weight on the right bipod versus trying to save a few dollars. We are shooting a precision rifle. Skimping on the bipod is a bad way to do business. We have $5,000 rifles with $2,500 scopes and guys want to spend $89 on the bipod because it's an afterthought. It needs to be looked at with the same weight as a scope.

relax. This means most shooters will miss even a two-degree cant induced into the system.

Think about this mindset. The shooter sets up on target, focuses the reticle to the point of aim, then begins his mental checklist. We think about breathing, and our brain looks at our chest. We consider our trigger control

It controls not just setup, but the firing task by supporting the rifle in the shooter's shoulder pocket.

Bipod placement and design have a factor on precision. The farther out the bipod is mounted on the stock, getting it closer to the end of the barrel, the more precise the shots will be. Why is this? Physics. It directly relates to the movement of the rifle at the shooter as translated with the release of the bullet.

Where the barrel is upon release of the bullet affects our zeros. Why do shooters zero where they do? Recoil management. What is the key component to recoil management? The bipod along with the shooter's body position. When the rifle recoils, the barrel moves, we then zero the scope to the align it to the barrel at the point of release. Crazy as it sounds, this is why

You can see the triangle of the bipod along with the triangle of the shooter's position behind the rifle. Camera angles might skew this look, but understand we want to strive to be straight.

The rifle needs to set up straight, so recoil will go in a straight line through the body and out the legs.

one person has a particular zero versus another shooter who, when shooting the same rifle, will not be zeroed in the same location.

Having a wider stance on the legs and putting the barrel inside the triangle, all this increases precision downrange.

At this point in the process we can now finish mounting the scope. We want to bring the scope to the shooter. We don't want to hunt for a proper sight picture. The goal is edge to edge clarity in the optic. We don't want any shadowing, which tells us we are looking off center insider the scope tube.

We set the scope up on the rifle with its magnification set to maximum power. The scope's eye relief, the distance between the ocular lens and the shooter's eye, is measured on maximum

In class, the author and his fellow instructors work on tweaking the shooter through the course. Moving the scope, raising the bipod, all help fit the rifle to the shooter.

magnification. The higher the power, the shorter the eye relief. When moving positions, we can reduce the power and open up the eye box making the optic more forgiving to off-center positioning. Most scopes have 2.5 to 3.5 inches of eye relief. This distance between the shooter's

eye and optic will change with magnification. You often read scope reviews where the writer will talk about the eye box. How forgiving the eye box is can be a real concern for the tactical shooter because positions are not fixed.

At maximum power with parallax set to infin-

The higher position behind the rifle allows us to run the bolt without moving our entire body.

ity, we can then adjust the reticle focus on the scope. This is another pre-shooting, pre-range task that must be established when setting up the rifle. Think about the eye doctor, as it's a similar trial-and-error situation. The eye doctor sits you down and begins to test prescriptions, "better or worse?" he asks you. Same with the reticle focus. We don't want to stare at or watch the reticle when focusing it. Instead turn away, make a small adjustment and then ask yourself, "better or worse?"

If your reticle ever blurs, splits or changes in front of you, that is your body rebelling and telling you the scope is properly adjusted for you. We want a sharp crisp reticle, as letting the brain control your focus will knock it out of whack.

In the end, I want to address the rifle like my car. I can see all around the car with the mirrors, and the seat and steering wheel are in comfortable positions. I am not searching when running the gun. I am moving in a smooth, natural way so not to cause body discomfort.

As instructors we cannot see what the individual student sees. This part of the process is dependent on the shooter's understanding of the concepts put forth. Just because a gunsmith delivers a rifle with a scope attached in a certain way, does not mean we can ignore rifle setup. When the car dealer hands you the keys to your new car, you don't just drive off the lot as is. You adjust it to fit you. Same concept.

So now you have the rifle set up for you, the scope set up for you, and when you address the rifle, you should not be searching for any of the sights or controls.

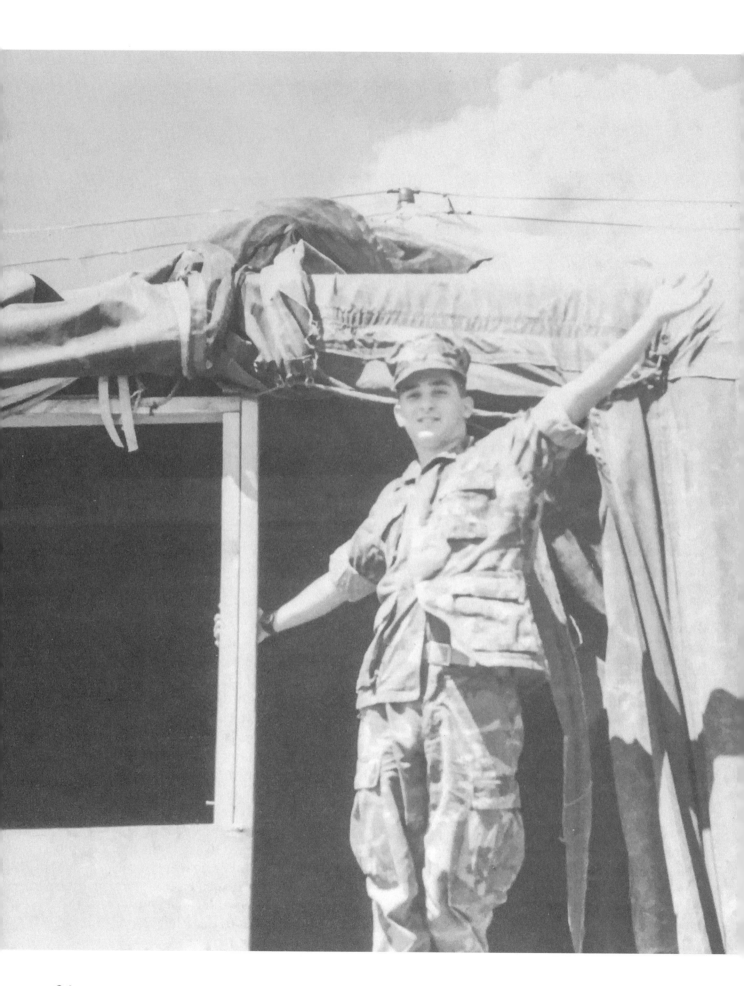

6

Sniper School

I attended Sniper School in October of 1986. I entered the course as a PFC, which was pretty rare. In fact, I was the lowest ranking member of the class. My partner from 1st Battalion, 2nd Marines was a Corporal from Charlie Company.

Entering Sniper School was less intimidating than you might imagine. I would suspect my time at ARS helped prepare me for the course. You can see why they don't want junior Marines attending and how the failure rate was so high.

For your basic infantry Marine skills, it was sprint to the finish line. Immediately upon arrival to Sniper School you are tested with a short land navigation course. They expected you to understand and be proficient in these skills. It makes perfect sense, "We don't have time to re-train you, so bring your A-Game."

Bridgeport, California, not to be confused with the author's hometown of Bridgeport, Connecticut, was his home sweet home for 30 days prior to Sniper School.

The school was located on Stone's Bay, just off Main Side Camp Lejeune. I drove my Datsun 240Z out past the training areas, which allowed me to kick the Z in the ass. I was caught by the MPs one trip doing 96 mph through the training area and lost my on-base privileges. Lucky for me, it did not apply to Stone's Bay, or I would have been walking.

Sniper School can be broken down into the skills taught. Field skills, like land navigation, were emphasized, but not to the degree found at Amphib Recon School. Instead, we first focused on concealments, a static form of stalking. You had 10 concealment exercises where you had to hide from the instructors. This was the precursor to stalking. With USMC Scout Sniper School, if you fail any one of these tasks twice, you failed out of the course. So, basically, you have to score 8 out of 10 for each given task. The written test, I believe, was given twice, sort of a practice quiz then a final exam.

One of the tasks which failed a lot of students were the observation exercises, which were fun, but nerve-racking in a lot of ways. The instructors could load the dice on these types of courses. The areas used not only for observations but

Creating a ghillie was one of the first tasks to accomplish. You wanted the colors to match your current surroundings.

also for stalking had different levels of difficulty. You could wind up on a hard course or an easier one. The objects hidden could be easily identified or very difficult.

Hiding a magazine spring or taping an antenna in the tree line is not an easy find. The worst was using the old World War II colored barracks as a backdrop. One day, the instructors decided to place a clear plastic map protractor into the wood siding of the building. Days like this increased the pucker factor.

In terms of pure fear of failure, nothing is harder than stalking. We used a lot of power-line breaks as stalking lanes. As the power lines cut through the woods, we set up on either side in order to stalk toward the instructors. They allowed you one meter, or the length of an M40AI rifle, from the cut grass toward the woods. You were allowed to travel along the edges, but you could not flank them by going into the woods.

You ended up low crawling for 90 percent of the stalk. The instructors dedicated to you were located on the opposite side of the stalk lane. They had a great angle on the students and took a lot of pride in busting you. We had one instructor who loved to yell, "I see you dickhead," which we took as a term of endearment. As you got closer to the instructors, you were keeping one eye on the walkers hoping none of them traveled in your direction.

One particular area, we called it the Pool Table, was especially difficult to navigate. Not only did it have a minimum amount of vegetation to hide in, there was one section of swamp which included cattails. The issue with the cattails is they wave at the instructors when you brushed up against them. You always carried hand clippers when stalking. With cattails you cut the bottom ever so carefully and then lower the flag down. All this is done in hyper slow motion.

In the end, it's all about route selection and masking. How many natural objects can you put between yourself and the observers? I am sure my size helped me hide. Being small can have an advantage.

Most of Sniper School was uneventful; there were no real close calls for me until the end. We had really crappy weather when it came time

The author drove to Sniper School in his custom Datsun 240Z. During one such trip, he was clocked doing 96 mph in the Lejeune training areas. His base-driving privileges were suspended for a month.

to qualify with our M40A1. My graduation date was mid-December, and we had a lot of sleet and freezing rain. Through the course, my shooting skills were never a question, but none of us can control the weather. I had to use every option in order to pass the final shooting test.

It's amazing looking back at the equipment used to qualify when you consider what we shoot today. The M40A1 rifle with Unertl 10X USMC Sniper Scope was more than capable as an 800-meter rifle, but the ammunition used was definitely subpar. The 173-grain Special Ball is pure surplus garbage. In today's world, if we asked you to compete in any form of precision rifle competition and we handed you special ball, the odds of completion would be slim.

After a day of practicing in the weather, I managed to qualify and thus sealed my fate graduating USMC Scout Sniper School.

During our time in Sniper School, Gunny Hathcock released his book, *Marine Sniper: 93 Confirmed Kills*. We all had dog-eared copies of it in anticipation of the Gunny attending our graduation. For each graduating class, a group of

The Marine Corps' Combined Arms Exercise, or CAX, takes place in California at Twentynine Palms. After graduating Sniper School, the author, having gone through several schools to drop artillery and bombs, spent most of his time there dropping ordnance.

The author at CAX in his chocolate-chip "cammies." He reports being a sniper at a live-fire range was very entertaining.

instructors would travel to Virginia Beach, pick up the Gunny and then we would spend a night and the day with him.

The first night Gunny arrived at Camp Lejeune, we hung out in town at a local dive bar. In his own, soft-spoken way he relived a bunch of the stories in the book. The next day, we had our graduation ceremony. I recall him chuckling about my size and wishing he had me in Vietnam to gain an advantage. "Gee, I bet you can really hide." You bet Gunny, they'll never find me. Gunny Hathcock signed my copy of *Marine*

Sniper, 93 Confirmed Kills, as well as my Sniper School diploma. Under my name is the signature of Gunny Hathcock and today that piece of paper sits in plexiglass.

Sniper School was my ultimate goal and just graduating was a huge win for me. When I first enlisted in the Marines, the guys at my dad's shop had bets going on how fast I'd be home, forget about the sniper part. This puts a big exclamation point on the discussion. In Sniper School, I had received my Lance Corporal ranking, so I no longer felt like a boot.

7

On the Range with a New Rifle

Before I move on, I want to state that you want a 100-yard zero with all rifles with tactical, raised, or what we call target turrets. A 100-yard zero is the best option out there, even for hunting rifles. I will expand after a few other topics.

Bore-Sighting

Prior to firing our first rounds, we want to bore-sight the rifle on a target at distance. Sure, there are a host of ways to skin this cat, I get it, everyone has their own idea of zeroing. It can definitely depend on the type of rifle you are shooting whether you can "look" down the barrel in order to line up the sights. Some rifles make this process easier than others.

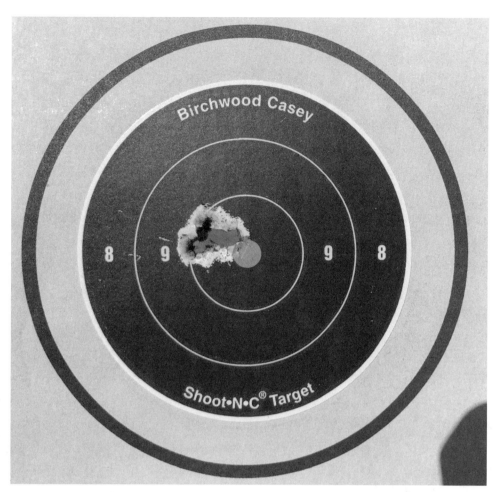

Where on the target do we zero our rifles? The author likes to be centered up elevation-wise, but just one-tenth or one-quarter inch left of center, for a variety of reasons. Number one: He is a right-handed shooter.

You can certainly shoot the rifle inside 100 yards, like at 25 yards, but you should familiarize yourself with the mechanical offset associated to your system. The mechanical offset is the height of the scope over the bore. We look through the scope and the bore is two inches or so below this, so we have to account for the mechanical offset. At 25 yards, you will have a significant amount of dope dialed on the scope to make up the difference. That means your 25-yard initial zero has to be as high as your scope is mounted.

AR15 shooters understand their mechanical offset because they shoot inside 100 yards all the time. If you want to hit a target inside a

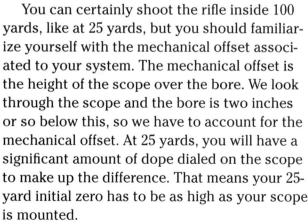

The author does not zero his semi-auto precision rifles any differently than his bolt-action rifles.

Prior to zeroing your rifle, you want to be correctly set up and the rifle adjusted to the shooter. Once the rifle is set up, you can then zero the shooter.

room, you have to aim over it to account for the sight-above-bore offset.

Back in the day, everyone wanted their scopes as low as possible. This was to help with hunting, using a point-blank-range zero. The lower your hunting optic is mounted, the easier it is hold over and hit an animal at a particular range. That range was usually pretty close.

Today we have monolithic rails, we have

adjustable cheek pieces and we have software to translate the offset. You need to know about mechanical offsets in order to hit targets inside 100 yards, but from a 100-yard zero everything is up. What I mean is, you will always add elevation to shoot these targets and you will not have to hold under.

I like to have a smallish, round brightly colored target at 100 yards I can point the barrel at it and see it from the action. Then I can glance up and align the reticle to the center of this target. Doing this gives me a good solid bore-sight. This is dependent on being able to remove the bolt and look through the action, at times this means moving the cheek piece out of the way. For this action, the rifle on a bench with a front and rear rest is easiest to manage. It's one of the few times I would recommend a Lead Sled to hold the rifle in place.

With the rifle bore-sighted on target, it's time to address the 100-yard zero.

Our first reaction is to chase the zero. By chasing the zero, I mean we forgo the groups for adjusting individual shots. At a bare minimum, we want to move the center of the group to the center of the target. It's all about point of aim matching up to our point of impact. It's during the zeroing process I am focusing on my fundamentals of marksmanship. I mimic Tom Cruise during this stage when he spoke about No Mind in *The Last Samurai*. No mind: We want to be completely blank behind the rifle and let our body act.

When the rifle is brand new, we want to knock out a few groups in order to settle in and get comfortable with the recoil pattern. It's not about barrel break-in as much as it is about us getting our positive repetitions in. Years ago, I tried to mandate only five-shot groups on my Sniper's Hide website. That proved to be a futile request to my members. So rather than harp on the benefit of a five-shot group, I will allow three-shot groups. It's been said, three shots test the equipment, five shots test the shooter. I want to push myself to the next level. So, shooting a nice five-shot group and then moving that group to center of the target is important to me.

I can race to complete this process, but I usually take my time. I want to look at the

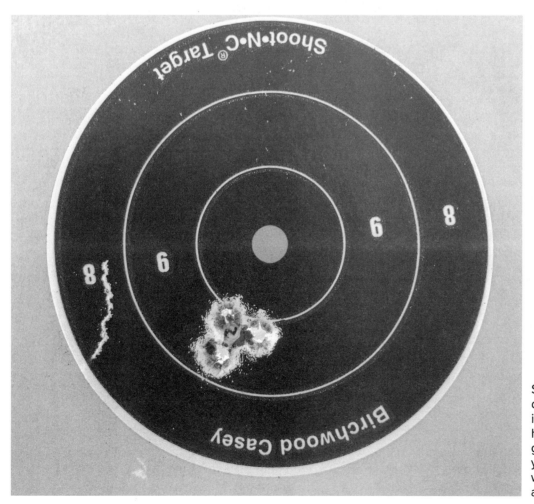

Shoot a group; don't chase the impacts. Once you have an actual group on paper, you can measure with the reticle and adjust.

Testing your optics tracking is vital. Optics are mechanical devices prone to trouble. A tall-target test will make sure your scope is in the proper working order.

group size, the recoil pulse, the view through my scope. As I noted earlier, I want to become intimate with the rifle, and zeroing is the most delicate of processes.

I shoot my group, then measure the distance from center, or my point of aim, using the reticle. The reticle is a calibrated ruler three inches in front of my nose. The reticle, especially in modern optics when the system of adjustment using the turrets matches the system used by the reticle, is completely straight forward. What you see is what you get. If the reticle reads, 1.2 Mils left and .7 Mils high, the adjustment is easy, exactly what you see. I don't need to walk downrange; I don't need to use a grid. I can stick

a single dot on a plain white piece of paper and simply measure the group distance from center.

I do have a thought on cheating the 100-yard zero. When absent of any other reasoning, I always zero just slightly left of center. One click, regardless of the scope used, to the left helps me in a variety of ways.

1. It gives me the edge as a fine aiming point should I need to fine-tune the 100-yard shot.
2. I counteract any right-hand drifts some might talk about.
3. It keeps my ultra-fine, quarter-inch aiming point intact. It's the same concept as the benchrest target, when you aim low and hit high.

We use a 100-yard zero because it's consistent. It has a very short time of flight, so as the conditions change, the zero is not affected like if we zeroed at farther distances.

Imagine zeroing your rifle in Florida at a distance beyond 100 yards, then having the shooter travel to Colorado where the air is thinner. You can easily see a change in that zero, which will only grow the farther you shoot.

When we use to consider 400 to 800 yards to be long range, these offsets were not really noticed. Especially when people took this concept into the terms of hunting. Hunters back in the day were trying to get as close as possible. You will not see the issues inside 400 yards by any stretch of the imagination. But, today, with

A tall-target test for your optic can include a grid target, and, for the author, a four-foot level, to test the reticle movement.

An Accuracy International AW Rifle with the backup iron sights. A well-rounded marksman understands how to use both sights and a scope.

people shooting beyond a mile and taking game beyond 500 yards, we absolutely see it.

We have epic debates with all sorts of reasoning when it comes to zeroing a rifle. Every week the members of the Sniper's Hide forum are discussing the pros and cons of zeroing at distance. One of the most common misconceptions is zeroing at distance adds more to your elevation. It doesn't work that way. If you can zero at 100 yards, and you don't, you gain nothing. The only time this is necessary is when guys are shooting extended ranges where they have so much cant in their base, they cannot dial down to 100 yards. Place a 60MOA base on a rifle and your 100-yard zero goes out the door. This is a specialty thing and should not be looked at as the rule, but the exception to the rule.

We put in our repetitions and we fine-tune our zero, so it is point of aim. Now we have to reset our turrets on the scope. Nothing drives me crazier than people coming to class with a zero scattered on the turrets. Ask the student: "Why are the turrets on 3.1 Mils with your windage at .8 right?"

Your turrets are designed to be reset so they read, zero-zero.

Reset your scope turrets to zero windage and zero on the elevation. You need a reference point, and this gives you one. You would not believe how many students in class arrive with a scope in a condition other than zero.

Reloading is one method to get the maximum effectiveness out of a rifle system. Shooters move from factory ammunition to reloading as a part of their personal development.

Muzzle velocity is not just for reloading or ballistics computers. Having a baseline number will help you diagnose barrel issues or know when it's time to replace the barrel.

This gives us a valid starting point and positive return location. We can dial anything on the scope and always come back to zero. Reset your turrets, and if you do not have a zero stop, take a picture of the location as referenced by the markings a manufacturer will include on the scope.

There was a time, that as soon as I was done zeroing, I would set up a chronograph to measure my muzzle velocity.

We need to know our muzzle velocity in order to determine the range we can shoot. We use the bullet's ballistic coefficient to describe drag. The ballistic coefficient translates the bullet's shape, area and mass into a number we can use. Combine that information with the air density and muzzle velocity and we can then predict a range.

I have changed my thinking, mainly because of software, so I don't necessarily chronograph

anymore. I use drop, but chronographing a rifle is an important component to data collection.

If you are a reloader, you absolutely need a chronograph. And today our choices in chronographs are excellent. The issue in the past was the sunlight and using the sky screens. Variations in sunlight caused problems with consistency, as well as the spacing between the screens limited the accuracy of the systems. With devices like the LabRadar and the Magne-toSpeed, we have first-class options.

I will admit more information is better, so if you can chronograph and get a solid set of data, absolutely, I am all for it. Also consider firing at least 200 rounds before the barrel may or may not settle into a specific speed.

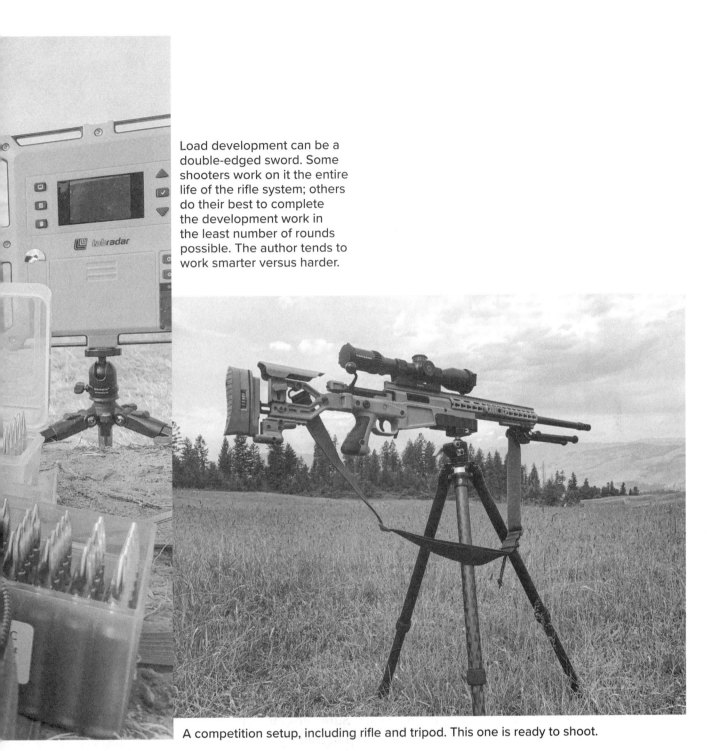

Load development can be a double-edged sword. Some shooters work on it the entire life of the rifle system; others do their best to complete the development work in the least number of rounds possible. The author tends to work smarter versus harder.

A competition setup, including rifle and tripod. This one is ready to shoot.

Different calibers have different routines, so I hesitate to make a general claim here. The best reason to use a chronograph today is to figure out when your barrel needs to be replaced. Variations in your muzzle velocity is a pretty good sign your barrel is going south. Changes in standard deviation can be noted using a chronograph.

It's at this point, before doping the rifle at distance, I engage in collecting muzzle velocity numbers. You need a starting point with software, so if you have access to it, chronograph data is necessary to get the ball rolling. Personally, I have enough experience I can swag a value that will be within 50fps, and software will do the rest.

8

First Deployment with the Marines & Weaponized Math with Marc Taylor

Back when I deployed to the Mediterranean Sea aboard the USS Guadalcanal as member of Bravo 1/2, we had a situation erupt in the Arabian Gulf. Sure, we can call it the Persian Gulf, but that gives ownership to Iran. This was during the Iran/Iraq War and for the United States we were supporting Iraq in that fight.

We were the first Special Operations Capable (SOC) Marine unit. We called the SOC designation Spread Over Continents because they divided our float up in a weird sort of way. We had ships in the Mediterranean, our ship had just sailed to Mombasa, Kenya, and we had ships docked in Haifa, Israel. Aboard the Guadalcanal, we were deployed to the Arabian Gulf only to exit it quite quickly. We traveled through the

Strait of Hormuz and then right back out to a tiny island in the Indian Ocean called Diego Garcia.

On Diego Garcia, we were slated to pick up a bunch of mine-sweeping helicopters as the Guadalcanal was a landing platform. From a distance, it looked like a mini aircraft carrier. We were on a short company run around the island when we returned to the ship. At the top of the gangway was the boat's Captain who explained to us that we had to get off. They ran out of room and were dropping us off at the naval base so they could return to the gulf with the mine sweepers.

The Iranian navy was mining the shipping lanes and attacking Kuwaiti oil tankers as they traversed the gulf region. The United States was about to jump into the war with an active role escorting the foreign tankers. We spent the next two weeks in a warehouse on Diego Garcia sleeping on cots. Because I was split off from our main unit, and the fact a new front was emerging with the Iran, a change was about to happen.

Even though I had recently graduated Sniper School, Bravo Company was unwilling to let me go to a Surveillance and Target Acquisition (STA) Platoon. We are always short men for deployments and giving up a Marine was a tough sell. The creation of a new unit was going to allow me to be billeted as a Sniper with the STA Platoon guys.

The members of 1st Battalion, 2nd Marines stuck in Diego Garcia were flown back to Camp Lejeune via a C5 cargo plane. Twenty-seven hours in a plane sitting backward is no fun, but we made it work. The idea was to create a MAGTF, Marine Air Ground Task Force, with the members of 1/2. This put me in a position to finally get picked up by the Sniper teams present.

At the time, the Sergeant in charge of STA Platoon was Marc Taylor, an instructor-school honor grad with a lot of experience under his belt. He brought me over to the Sniper teams placing me under Ken Hagemann.

Taylor was hardcore and had a reputation for demanding a lot out of his Marines. It's what you want if you want to hone your skills. Initially, I

The author's ship, the USS Trenton, supported and was protected by the wooden mine sweepers. Iran was placing mines in the shipping lanes during the Iran/Iraq War.

Team leader Ken Hagemann, Platoon Sgt. Marc Taylor and the author pose in front of a 25mm chain gun that had been placed on the ship for swarm-attack protection.

was placed with Jeff Thompson, but he did not travel with us on our return to the gulf. Regardless, I have a great Jeff Thompson story:

Jeff Thompson and I caused a bit of a stir during the train-up phase of the MAGTF. We were flown via C5 back to North Carolina. While the rest of 1/2 was still in the Mediterranean, we were housed in transient barracks next to the Marine Corps Band. Living out of sea bags, we were not allowed to go off base. We were considered deployed and still received sea pay. Every time a senior officer or non-commissioned officer saw us, they complained about our attire endlessly. Salty, faded utilities completely out of spec, but we were deployed so there was nothing they could do about it. You can tell the guys who were deployed, the salty cammies were faded due to the Navy laundry practices. After a float, you were supposed to toss the utilities for new ones.

During the train-up, we were out by Stone's Bay, an area we knew well. At the time, SOTG, or Special Operations Training Group, was creating a small compound and there sat a Willys Jeep. Jeff and I had the bright idea to steal it, so we made our way toward the compound. With me in the driver seat, Jeff pushed the Jeep so I could pop the clutch and start it. Fired up, we turned the corner to leave the compound in our new whip, only be stopped by the rightful owners. With no place to go, we were caught, and the MPs were called to haul us into jail.

When we reached main side and were placed in custody, the MPs there began to question us:

Who are you?

I don't know, who are you? (We didn't have ID cards or dog tags. If they were smarter, they would have checked us for a "meat tag" which was a tattoo snipers had to replace the dog tag.)

Who are you with?

(Oh cool, a question we can answer.) We are with 1st Battalion, 2nd Marines.

But 1/2 is in the Med right now.

I know. We were just there.

We ended up spending eight hours in jail because we refused to answer the questions in a meaningful way. You see, it was raining, and we didn't want to go back into the field. So, sitting in jail seemed like a better idea at the time.

Once the rain stopped, we informed the MPs who to contact. Our XO, a Major Kelley, was there to wipe the police blotter. Since we were not supposed to be in the United States, and because we were part of a new unit, they could not have us getting in trouble. Score one for the sniper guys.

The Major was super cool about it, gave us a nice little pep talk, emphasizing that snipers are not supposed to get caught stealing stuff, but good on us for trying. He rewarded us with a can soda, and trust me, a can of soda was a reward at the time, then back to the field we went.

This building of the MAGTF took about 30 days before moving the unit to the USS Trenton in order to sail back to the gulf for an additional seven months.

I was now a billeted sniper in a position to use my new skills, MAGTF 2-88 was off and sailing.

Taylor had a huge impact on my sniper upbringing. He was a studious taskmaster in the best ways possible. Taylor is a no-compro-

The author was part of the first Marine unit to field the .50 Caliber Sniper Rifle. Here is the Iver Johnson 50 they used. Originally this was designed by Daisy; yes, the BB-gun company.

Soviet-weapons familiarization was part of the author's training at Camp Casey on the DMZ in Korea.

mise Marine and allowing me to be part of the team was a big leap of faith on his part. I was no slouch when it came to the basics, so his initial observations on my performance were strong. But STA 1/2 was built on a buddy system. We did not do things just because, nor did they take the traditional routes. After all, Doug Henderson was able to sign me up for Sniper School, pretty much sight unseen. There was no Indoc with STA 1/2, it was all gut feelings.

Weaponized Math with Marc Taylor

Fast forward 20-plus years and Marc Taylor and I are still working together. Marc moved to Alaska and runs Wiggy's Alaska, a cold weather gear and sleeping bag company. Marc has also written books on hunting in Alaska, so he is tied in with the shooting community there.

Today, Marc and I teach precision rifle classes together. He is the driving force behind the Alaska Precision Rifle Course. In the last five years, we have taught more than 400 students in that one state alone.

With such a diverse field of shooters, we wanted a computer-free solution to doping a rifle. Alaskan shooters are not fans of electronics. Battery-powered devices don't work well in the cold weather. In any given class, we could have a student shooting a .30-378 alongside a student shooting a 6.5 Creedmoor, with another block of shooters using a 270WIN. We don't want students with their head in their phones to start with, so how do we dope all these rifles sans a software-bullet library?

The answer came from the mind of Marc Taylor. Enter: Weaponized Math.

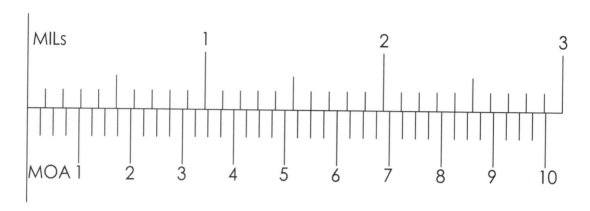

Mils – MOA Conversions

Mils	MOA	Mils	MOA	Mils	MOA	Mils	MOA	Mils	MOA	Mils	MOA	Mils	MOA
0.0	0.0	3.0	10.3	6.0	20.6	9.0	30.9	12.0	41.3	15.0	51.6	18.0	61.9
0.1	0.3	3.1	10.7	6.1	21.0	9.1	31.3	12.1	41.6	15.1	51.9	18.1	62.2
0.2	0.7	3.2	11.0	6.2	21.3	9.2	31.6	12.2	41.9	15.2	52.3	18.2	62.6
0.3	1.0	3.3	11.3	6.3	21.7	9.3	32.0	12.3	42.3	15.3	52.6	18.3	62.9
0.4	1.4	3.4	11.7	6.4	22.0	9.4	32.3	12.4	42.6	15.4	52.9	18.4	63.3
0.5	1.7	3.5	12.0	6.5	22.3	9.5	32.7	12.5	43.0	15.5	53.3	18.5	63.6
0.6	2.1	3.6	12.4	6.6	22.7	9.6	33.0	12.6	43.3	15.6	53.6	18.6	63.9
0.7	2.4	3.7	12.7	6.7	23.0	9.7	33.3	12.7	43.7	15.7	54.0	18.7	64.3
0.8	2.8	3.8	13.1	6.8	23.4	9.8	33.7	12.8	44.0	15.8	54.3	18.8	64.6
0.9	3.1	3.9	13.4	6.9	23.7	9.9	34.0	12.9	44.3	15.9	54.7	18.9	65.0
1.0	3.4	4.0	13.8	7.0	24.1	10.0	34.4	13.0	44.7	16.0	55.0	19.0	65.3
1.1	3.8	4.1	14.1	7.1	24.4	10.1	34.7	13.1	45.0	16.1	55.3	19.1	65.7
1.2	4.1	4.2	14.4	7.2	24.8	10.2	35.1	13.2	45.4	16.2	55.7	19.2	66.0
1.3	4.5	4.3	14.8	7.3	25.1	10.3	35.4	13.3	45.7	16.3	56.0	19.3	66.3
1.4	4.8	4.4	15.1	7.4	25.4	10.4	35.8	13.4	46.1	16.4	56.4	19.4	66.7
1.5	5.2	4.5	15.5	7.5	25.8	10.5	36.1	13.5	46.4	16.5	56.7	19.5	67.0
1.6	5.5	4.6	15.8	7.6	26.1	10.6	36.4	13.6	46.8	16.6	57.1	19.6	67.4
1.7	5.8	4.7	16.2	7.7	26.5	10.7	36.8	13.7	47.1	16.7	57.4	19.7	67.7
1.8	6.2	4.8	16.5	7.8	26.8	10.8	37.1	13.8	47.4	16.8	57.8	19.8	68.1
1.9	6.5	4.9	16.8	7.9	27.2	10.9	37.5	13.9	47.8	16.9	58.1	19.9	68.4
2.0	6.9	5.0	17.2	8.0	27.5	11.0	37.8	14.0	48.1	17.0	58.4	20.0	68.8
2.1	7.2	5.1	17.5	8.1	27.8	11.1	38.2	14.1	48.5	17.1	58.8	20.1	69.1
2.2	7.6	5.2	17.9	8.2	28.2	11.2	38.5	14.2	48.8	17.2	59.1	20.2	69.4
2.3	7.9	5.3	18.2	8.3	28.5	11.3	38.8	14.3	49.2	17.3	59.5	20.3	69.8
2.4	8.3	5.4	18.6	8.4	28.9	11.4	39.2	14.4	49.5	17.4	59.8	20.4	70.1
2.5	8.6	5.5	18.9	8.5	29.2	11.5	39.5	14.5	49.8	17.5	60.2	20.5	70.5
2.6	8.9	5.6	19.3	8.6	29.6	11.6	39.9	14.6	50.2	17.6	60.5	20.6	70.8
2.7	9.3	5.7	19.6	8.7	29.9	11.7	40.2	14.7	50.5	17.7	60.8	20.7	71.2
2.8	9.6	5.8	19.9	8.8	30.3	11.8	40.6	14.8	50.9	17.8	61.2	20.8	71.5
2.9	10.0	5.9	20.3	8.9	30.6	11.9	40.9	14.9	51.2	17.9	61.5	20.9	71.8

Mils – Weaponized Math - Try Dope

True dope	1.75 x 300yd		1.45 x 400yd		1.4 x 500yd		1.3 x 600yds		1.25 x 800yds		1.24 x 800yds		1.22 x 900yds
Yards													
300	400	400	500	500	600	600	700	700	800	800	900	900	1000
start	1.75		1.45		1.4		1.3		1.25		1.24		1.22
TRUE	Try	TRUE	Try	TRUE	Try	TRUE	Try	TRUE	Try	TRUE	Try	TRUE	Try
						2.4	3.1	3.4	4.3	4.6	5.7	6.0	7.3
						2.5	3.2	3.5	4.4	4.7	5.8	6.1	7.4
						2.6	3.3	3.6	4.5	4.8	5.9	6.2	7.5
						2.7	3.4	3.7	4.6	4.9	6.0	6.3	7.6
		0.9	1.4	1.7	2.4	2.8	3.6	3.8	4.8	5.0	6.2	6.4	7.8
		1.1	1.5	1.8	2.6	2.9	3.7	3.9	4.9	5.1	6.3	6.5	7.9
0.4	0.7	1.2	1.7	1.9	2.7	3.0	3.8	4.0	5.0	5.2	6.4	6.6	8.0
0.5	0.9	1.3	1.8	2.0	2.9	3.1	4.0	4.1	5.1	5.3	6.5	6.7	8.1
0.6	1.1	1.4	2.0	2.1	3.0	3.2	4.1	4.2	5.3	5.4	6.7	6.8	8.2
0.7	1.2	1.5	2.1	2.2	3.1	3.3	4.2	4.3	5.4	5.5	6.8	6.9	8.4
0.8	1.4	1.6	2.2	2.3	3.3	3.4	4.4	4.4	5.5	5.6	6.9	7.0	8.5
0.9	1.6	1.7	2.4	2.4	3.4	3.5	4.5	4.5	5.6	5.7	7.0	7.1	8.6
1.0	1.8	1.8	2.5	2.5	3.6	3.6	4.6	4.6	5.8	5.8	7.2	7.2	8.7
1.1	1.9	1.9	2.7	2.6	3.7	3.7	4.7	4.7	5.9	5.9	7.3	7.3	8.9
1.2	2.1	2.0	2.8	2.7	3.8	3.8	4.9	4.8	6.0	6.1	7.5	7.5	9.1
1.3	2.3	2.1	3.0	2.8	4.0	3.9	5.0	4.9	6.1	6.3	7.8	7.7	9.3
1.4	2.5	2.2	3.1	2.9	4.1	4.0	5.1	5.0	6.3	6.5	8.0	7.9	9.6
1.5	2.6	2.3	3.3	3.0	4.3	4.1	5.3	5.1	6.4	6.7	8.3	8.1	9.8
1.6	2.8	2.4	3.4	3.1	4.4	4.2	5.4	5.2	6.5	6.9	8.5	8.3	10.1
1.7	3.0	2.5	3.6	3.2	4.5	4.3	5.5	5.3	6.6	7.1	8.8	8.5	10.3
1.8	3.2	2.6	3.7	3.3	4.7	4.4	5.7	5.4	6.8	7.3	9.0	8.7	10.6
1.9	3.3	2.7	3.8	3.4	4.8	4.5	5.8	5.5	6.9	7.5	9.3	8.9	10.8
2.0	3.5	2.8	4.0	3.5	5.0	4.6	5.9	5.6	7.0	7.7	9.5	9.1	11.1
		2.9	4.1	3.6	5.1	4.7	6.0	5.7	7.1	7.9	9.8	9.3	11.3
		3.0	4.3	3.7	5.2	4.8	6.2	5.8	7.3	8.1	10.0	9.5	11.5
		3.1	4.4	3.8	5.4	4.9	6.3	5.9	7.4	8.3	10.3	9.7	11.8
		3.2	4.6	3.9	5.5	5.0	6.4	6.0	7.5	8.5	10.5	9.9	12.0
		3.3	4.7	4.0	5.7	5.1	6.6	6.1	7.6	8.7	10.8	10.1	12.3
		3.4	4.9	4.1	5.8	5.2	6.7	6.2	7.8	8.9	11.0	10.3	12.5
		3.5	5.0	4.2	5.9	5.3	6.8	6.3	7.9	9.1	11.3	10.5	12.8
		3.6	5.1	4.3	6.1	5.4	7.0	6.4	8.0	9.3	11.5	10.7	13.0
				4.4	6.2	5.5	7.1	6.5	8.1	9.5	11.7	10.9	13.2
				4.5	6.4	5.6	7.2	6.6	8.3	9.7	12.0	11.1	13.5
				4.6	6.5	5.7	7.3	6.7	8.4	9.9	12.2	11.3	13.7
				4.7	6.6	5.8	7.5	6.8	8.5	10.1	12.5	11.5	14.0
				4.8	6.8	5.9	7.6	6.9	8.6	10.3	12.7	11.7	14.2
				4.9	6.9	6.0	7.7	7.0	8.8	10.5	13.0	11.9	14.5
				5.0	7.1	6.1	7.9	7.1	8.9	10.7	13.2	12.1	14.7
				5.1	7.2	6.2	8.0	7.2	9.0	10.9	13.5	12.3	15.0
						6.3	8.1	7.3	9.1	11.1	13.7	12.5	15.2
						6.4	8.3	7.4	9.3	11.3	14.0	12.7	15.4
						6.5	8.4	7.5	9.4	11.5	14.2	12.9	15.7
						6.6	8.5	7.6	9.5	11.7	14.5	13.1	15.9
								7.7	9.6	11.9	14.7	13.3	16.2
								7.8	9.8	12.1	15.0	13.5	16.4
								7.9	9.9	12.3	15.2	13.7	16.7
								8.0	10.0	12.5	15.5	13.9	16.9
								8.1	10.1	12.7	15.7	14.1	17.2
												14.3	17.4
												14.5	17.6
												14.7	17.9
												14.9	18.1
												15.1	18.4

Marc Taylor, who teaches precision rifle classes with the author, developed his Weaponized Math system based off percentage of drop versus muzzle velocity or ballistic coefficient.

Weaponized math is a way to dope a new shooter without using software. It works regardless of caliber, though small changes to the numbers can be made to adjust it to the individual, so you can true it when faced with varying conditions. But it gets you started. We like to call it: try dope.

Try dope is what our grandparents did back in the day using manufacturer inches of drop data. Before the advent of computers, we used to dope our rifles initially using inches of drop. You converted the manufacturer supplied drop to minutes of angle (MOA) with a simple long-hand math formula. Then you went to your local range with its standard 6x6 NRA Target and dialed in the dope necessary to hit the X Ring. Once you doped the rifle, your try dope was thrown away.

Today we have computers, and everyone wants to hit a 1-inch dot on the first shot from 800 yards away. Not really practical, but it's the mindset.

How do we start off doping the rifle when we are missing some key elements? Well, using this simple weaponized math formula. Is it perfect, no, but it should put you within .3 Mils or 1 MOA of the center of the target at the given ranges.

Marc looked at the percentages of drop, and, using a simple multiplier, we were able to run down the firing line giving all the students data.

Here is Marc's thoughts on the use of weaponized math and its inception.

Students generally bring one of only six or eight ballistic profiles to a course: slow .308 Win., fast .308 Win., slow 6.5, fast 6.5, the occasional 7 SAUM or WSM, or the lightning bolt of a long-action .30 cal. In our Alaska Course, this might include .270, .243, .338 Win. Mag. and even .30-.378. There is about an even split between hunters and tactical shooters in Alaska, so we have to be ready for nearly anything. Alaska shooters are also not overly dependent on data acquired from smart phones because they don't work when cold. Hard data is more preferred, especially among the hunters. Regardless of cartridge, they all have a very common characteristic: The percentage of drop utilized between each 100-yard increment. We teach on a 1,000-yard range, so most everyone except the

"shortys" and "gassers" with 168 SMKs are still supersonic and will be predictable and repeatable at 1,000 yards.

At our Alaska Precision Rifle Course, we had a real struggle that was costing us valuable time. A dip in terrain at the 900-yard line required us to get our 900-yard target high in the air in order for the student to see it clearly for a shot. The problem that presented to the instructor is that our call, being generic, did not close the danger space tightly enough to assure a near-center plate hit on the first or second shot. And the dip in terrain made a splash, which appeared to miss low, but was actually a miss high that impacts seventy or so yards beyond but was viewed under the target. And a miss low fell into dead space where we could see no impact.

We had to skip the 900 and go to the 1,000, then back into the 900. But I'm better than that. After all, I have a high school education from central Mississippi, the finest the nation has to offer.

We, as instructors, simply had to get better at our predictable calls.

So, I started thinking about the percentage of drop difference between 800 center-plate data and the 1,000 center-plate data. I "figured" that the bullet dropped 45 percent between the 800 and 900, and 55 percent between the 900 and 1,000 of the total drop of 100 percent. I just actually pulled that number out of the air. So, I went back, way back, to simple-man Mississippi math, and worked out a formula to get that magic 900-yard data call, regardless of ballistic profile or rifle.

It went like this: 1,000-yard data MINUS 800-yard data EQUALS a number. That number represents the drop between 800 and 1,000, in Mils or MOA. Take that number and multiply it by .45 and it would give me the 45-percent drop between 800 and 900 that I was looking for. And it did. Almost every time.

Student influence on bullet travel is still in it, so it did not work out perfectly every time, but boy, was it a time and ammo saver!

Take my 6.5, for instance. At my home range: 8.7 at 1,000 minus 5.8 at 800 equals 2.9 Mils of drop in that 200-yard gap. If I take that 2.9 and multiply it by .45, it gives me 1.3 Mils. Add that

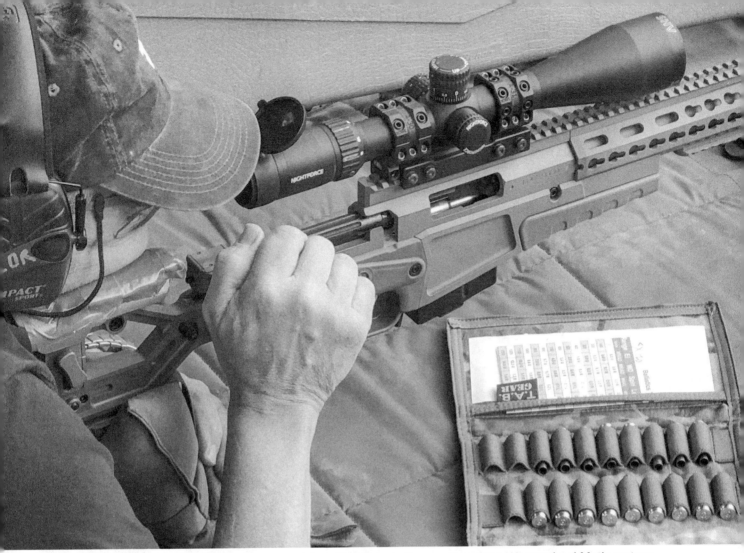

Marc Taylor, behind his AX Rifle during a precision rifle class, is the creator of the Weaponized Math system.

to my 800-yard data of 5.8 and it gives me… guess what…? What my TRASOL spits out for my 900-yard data!

8.7 - 5.8 = 2.9

2.9 x .45 = 1.3

5.8 + 1.3 = 7.1 Mils

7.1 Mils to a waterline hit

Before you ask, I ran these numbers at 1,500 D.A., 4,500 D.A., and 7,500 D.A. The error was very slight, measured in only one or two tenths of Mils. Less than an MOA. A ballistics solver prediction is much more precise, but requires a lot more input.

This was great. Problem solved at 900 from now on, and it saved student ammo and instructor aggravation. I could now concentrate on the student's wind call knowing the data I gave him was elevation-correct, minus his input and windage. And it works in MOA or Mil, of course. I had created voodoo.

Played out the data looks like this:

300-yard drop data X factor 1.75 = 400-yard data
400-yard drop data X factor 1.45 = 500-yard data
500-yard drop data X factor 1.40 = 600-yard data
600-yard drop data X factor 1.30 = 700-yard data
700-yard drop data X factor 1.25 = 800-yard data
800-yard drop data X factor 1.24 = 900-yard data
900-yard drop data X factor 1.22 = 1,000-yard data

Combine this weaponized math with a hard-copy chart and we have a winning combination to get shooters on target without software and without any real ballistic background. It's nowhere near as sensitive to inputs as software is, and it doesn't need batteries.

Since publishing the weaponized math, students have tested and embraced the data in a variety of ways. We know it works because the Internet has been relatively quiet on the subject.

9

Doping and Cleaning the Precision Rifle

By using the weaponized math system, you can easily dope your rifle to distance. We need to gather as much information as possible, so that means shooting targets at distances and recording the results.

From a 100-yard zero, we now need to engage a target at 200 yards. It's pretty easy, as most rifles will use 2 MOA or .5 Mils to hit the target. This barely changes. You might find a .50 MOA of variation or .2 Mils, but you will be super close. Where things begin to change is at 300 yards.

Shooting at 300 yards needs 1 Mil of adjustment, or roughly 5 MOA. This will vary a bit more than 200 yards, but it will get you super close. We want to fine-tune each yard line, so the point of aim matches the point of impact.

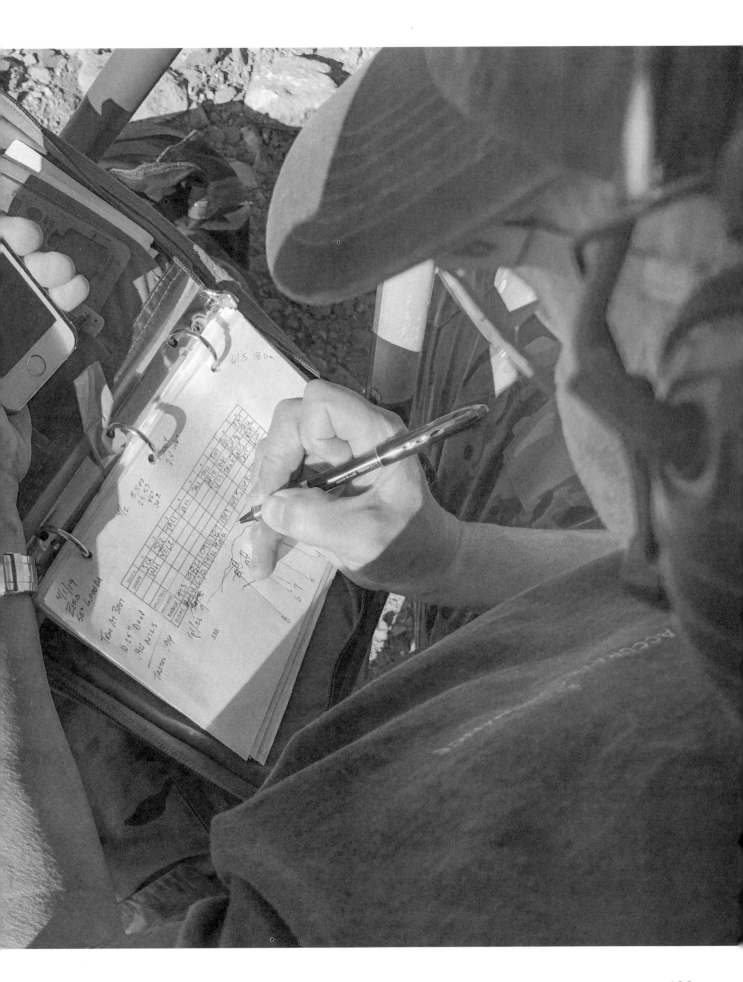

Computers and smartphone apps are all too commonplace today. The author recommends their use, but warns against putting too much focus on them. Old School data collection is still the best answer when combined with modern techniques.

Best practice for doping the rifle would be to shoot each yard line on paper, with the center of the group aligning to the center of our point of aim. However, we often use steel and that can induce a bit of error.

Steel is big, the vertical spread on piece of steel can easily amount to 4 MOA of variation. It's dependent on target size and distance, but the reality is, steel is often taller than necessary. So, we want to use a "watermark" on the target to create a fixed point of aim. The watermark is a simple painted line used to put the reticle on. From there, you adjust the point of impact up or down, so the group is centered around that line.

To take this idea one step forward, I created a Truing Target with Austin Angus of AA Targets. Again, we see a ton of software in our classes.

We want to support all the software out there. In order to do this, we have to "True" the computers to the rifle system. We cannot match a rifle system to the software, we have to match the software to the rifle. To gather accurate data the truing bar was built.

Working by range or distance, we want the truing bar to be .2 Mils wide at every given yard line. If a milliradian is .36 inches at 100 yards, .2 Mils would be .72 inches, then matched to the individual ranges. At 200 yards the truing bar is 1.44 inches wide. So, basically, we just multiply .72 by the first number in the yard line. At 800 yards our truing bar is 5.75 inches.

Hit the center of the truing bar, and you know the data is solid.

When you have your 300-yard data secured,

the use of our weaponized math will make the rest pretty simple. Focus on the fundamentals and shoot good groups.

Better Record Keeping Means Better Results

Be sure to write down everything and don't simply default to your computers.

The question constantly comes up about lining your dope to your software. The problem is people go out to the range with software in hand and then can't quite understand why it is not matching up or they have troubling "truing" it after the fact. Not all. Some find it pretty easy, but Internet forums are full of people commenting about the ballistic software errors.

There are several reasons why software might not line up properly, but part of the problem is using the software first and not doping the rifle prior to exploring the ballistic solvers. When using software prior to shooting, I call anything the computer spits out as "Try Dope," because you are just trying to hit the target, not much more. It's not 1 MOA accurate. Remember, manufacturers' drop data was designed to get you on an NRA 6x6 target board. It is up to the shooter to fine-tune that drop to hit the center. We never questioned it; we just knew we needed to put in the effort.

My personal argument has always centered around the human factor. That regardless of what Doppler says, what the computer model says, the human factor has a much bigger say as to where the shot actually hits. I have heard several times that what they saw in a fixture was

Better record keeping means better results. Make sure, regardless of how you manage your data, you keep a hard copy of your information as a backup.

not what happened when they put a shooter behind the rifle. It comes down to recoil management. This is why one shooter will hit using Solution A, and the next shooter needs Solution B or C. How they manage the recoil and exactly where that barrel is upon release of the bullet matters. It's why your zero and your friend's zero are inches apart. No software out there considers you; it only considers an empty, near perfect world.

The next problem is the promotion of "drifts." We have a lot of new data that points to a series of drifts that can affect the placement of the shot. The promotion of these is a relatively new phenomenon. When I went to Sniper School back in 1986, we didn't worry about Spin Drift, (*wasn't even mentioned*), we didn't worry about Coriolis, Cross Wind Jump, or any of the other examples we see today. Baron Roland von Eötvös, who the heck is that guy? In all, we have about four drift factors that are discussed and some people start employing a correction

We have great modern tools for the precision rifle shooter. The human factor is still your biggest variable when it comes to actual shooting.

Don't just rely on your phone or computer. The author manually records the data to hard copy as a backup to his computers.

for them as close as 400 yards. Am I saying they don't exist? No. But am I saying they are being blown out of proportion? I think much of it is used to take the blame away from the shooter.

Here is why:

We gather our dope by walking our shots out, actually shooting each yard-line distance, and in recording the data we include everything. Drifts, too. There is really no such thing as a no-wind day. If you experience one, consider yourself lucky, but practically speaking, windless doesn't

exist. Under normal circumstances, we zero and dope our rifles with everything already included. Then when we go to our "Data on Previous Engagement" we're taking into account these factors. If, today, I am shooting to 1,000 yards and used 7.4 Mils to hit center along with .75 Mils of wind for a 5-mph breeze, that assumes all the drifts and drop data. If conditions change because of the location or atmosphere, a computer will help account for it rather than the old, outdated rules of thumb, but still, hitting the

The Sniper's Hide Training Fundamental Checklist. The author and his fellow instructors look at what the shooter is doing.

target usually happens. We see this every week in tactical rifle matches around the country. Guys travel from their home location to ranges 500 miles away and hit targets. Why do they hit? They practiced and recorded their dope. Talking to several high-scoring PRS Shooters, they strive to nail down their data, so elevation is a given and the only question becomes wind. In known-distance courses, they consider this information their zero data. They essentially re-zero the rifle for each yard line.

Now wind is the biggest drift factor we have and actually will offset some of the other drifts. It depends on the direction, and speed, but it will cancel out or increase several of the other factors. It's important to understand the wind. No dispute, you need to know what is going on here as it can control so much of how we hit

the target. That includes elevation changes. To expand: It's not unheard of to have a terrain feature in or around a specific yard line that causes an elevation issue, so even if everything with the computer lines up, your 700-yard dope is off because the wind changed the flight path to hit that one target. It often has people scratching their heads. One shooter is everything BUT "X" range perfect? Odds are, it's the wind.

Still, if we recorded our data, we know what the wind was doing. So, if we doped the rifle in a 5-mph wind, going to an 8-mph wind is not like starting from zero. While they might say an 8-mph wind will move the impact .1 Mils up or down, it's really only 3 mph wind we are dealing with. We already accounted for 5 mph. Why add 8 mph on top of the 5?

If you're modeling the shot on a computer, I

can see the importance of all this. But it's not the same as shooting it. Not to mention we miss out of adding our own spin to the bullet. Poor fundamentals will NOT line you up with the model. If you are adding .2 Mils of trigger hook to your shot and you want to call it Spin Drift, well OK, I suppose you can, but are we really talking about the same thing. Why did I not use any, and you are using .2 Mils for the same target? Why is my wind call 1.5 Mils to hit the target and you are using 2 Mils to hit the same target? Happens every week. Maybe it's rifle cant?

The point is, while all these effects exist, they are not equally distributed among the shooters. We all release the shot in our own way. So, before you go adding all the drifts to your ballistic solver, try doping your rifle first without any software. Develop YOUR dope to distance and record everything, then True the software to what you shot, rather than worrying about what the computer said before your first round went downrange. It doesn't take very long to dope our rifles out to 1,000 yards. Now I can go back and line the computer up at my leisure. I think you will find the variations are much smaller than you realize. Solid Dope is hard to argue with as we all know the bullet has the last word.

There is no disputing what is being said, there is disputing how much it actually affects us on the range. All I am saying is, "it's already in there" especially if you dope it first.

Establish your drop minus the software and be sure to write down everything, backing up the computer when it is eventually trued to your rifle system. I like this approach because

Keeping track of your data is one of the more important factors when it comes to successfully engaging targets with a precision rifle. How you keep your information is almost as important as how you got it.

I am looking for patterns. I want to see how the patterns move; it's how Marc was able to create the weaponized math.

A pattern I work with is for a .308 and 6.5 rifle, where a .308 will move 1 Mil or roughly 3.6 MOA per every 100 yards to 800. A 6.5-based rifle will move .8 Mils from 300 to roughly 800 yards. Depending on the targets shot, I can just add a mil and know I will be close to hitting my targets.

At this point in the process, the rifle is set up, the scope is zeroed at 100 yards, and the shooter has data to 1,000 yards. You can go home from the range and clean your rifle.

Cleaning Your Precision Rifle

There is a lot of conflicting information on the topic of cleaning your rifle. For me, I tend to default to the Gale McMillan philosophy that more rifle barrels have been ruined by over-cleaning, versus not cleaning them often enough. Gale

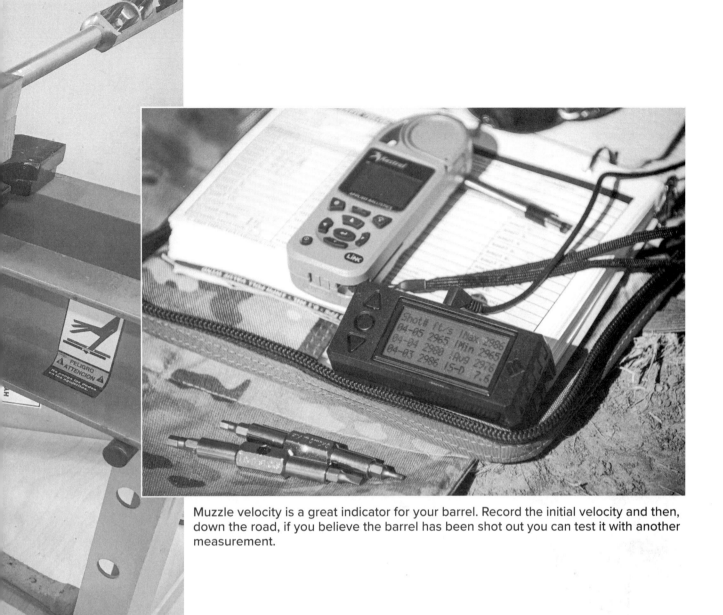

Muzzle velocity is a great indicator for your barrel. Record the initial velocity and then, down the road, if you believe the barrel has been shot out you can test it with another measurement.

Don't be afraid to break down your rifle to the core components to work on it. All riflemen should understand how to disassemble and reassemble their firearms.

McMillan wrote years ago about barrel break-in and cleanup, that much of it was put forth to sell more barrels, not because it worked. His quotes are still all over the Internet to this day.

Both barrel break-in and the related topic of maintenance can be a subject of heated debates by the various camps.

Since I am not a benchrest shooter, I am going to ignore almost all of their thinking on the subject. Those guys will toss a barrel away before ever giving it a chance. Their system

involves an excessive amount of scrubbing, and I can't get behind their methodology.

As time goes by, with the vast variety of systems I do use, I find myself cleaning less than ever before. The key takeaway, if you want to stop reading now, is to let the barrel tell you what it wants.

Much of this goes back to the military. During my service, we were asked to clean our weapons in the worst possible ways. I was probably required to clean twice as much as I shot. What

many people don't realize is, we were not cleaning them because they needed it. We cleaned them because it kept us busy and out of trouble. When you have a bunch of bored 20-something adults hanging around all day, this can become a recipe for disaster if you don' t keep them occupied.

For STA Platoon it was easy, pull the bolt out of the M40A1 and leave the rifle on the rack. Cleaning was easy because it was not dirty in the first place. There were also limitations on the degree to which we could take apart the ri-

fle, so we could not strip it down like an M16A2.

Cleaning should be for a purpose. One of my favorite sayings on the subject is: Cleaning your rifle before accuracy falls off is like wiping your butt before going to the bathroom. Use your imagination on that one.

There are several reasons to clean your weapons system sooner than later. As well, there are other reasons to keep it cleaned and in good functioning order without defaulting to the brush and patch. My main point here is: Don't overdo it, as a little bit goes a long way.

The author uses lighter fluid to flush out his triggers during times when dirt and sand will cause problems with sear engagement.

Good Copper vs. Bad Copper

There is such a thing as good copper inside your barrel. The copper that fills in the imperfections does not hurt accuracy, but can indeed help it. We talk about this much like a cast-iron skillet that has been "seasoned." And when you strip the barrel bare, with a complete cleaning, it might take a few fouling shots to bring it back to status quo. I like the idea of cleaning your rifle and then putting a few fouling shots down the bore to keep in tip-top condition prior use.

Where bad copper fouling comes in, you start to notice accuracy falling off. It's essential to recognize the place your barrel is at during this period. Maybe your groups have opened up, and perhaps you noticed a few fliers entering the equation. That is a message from inside your bore that it's time to clean it. The takeaway from this section is, listen to your barrel. Recognize the signs and act accordingly. For my Accuracy International with custom Bartlein barrel, I will easily go 1,500 rounds between cleanings. It's shot a lot, it's not picky, and accuracy will stay below 1/2 MOA. The custom barrel was not broken in; it was shot and cleaned at the end of the first day. After that, I shot it until I noticed a change, recognizing that change, I then punched the bore and kept a note of the round count.

My cleaning routine is super simple. This would be my big clean, versus the series of small actions I might perform.

1. Start with a wet patch with something like Shooter's Choice or Hoppes #9. I don't get too crazy with the harsh chemicals.
2. With a wet brush (I tend to use nylon, but I am fine with a bronze brush), I make four passes, in fact, you only need to count, 1, 2, 3, 4 in terms of passes and, yes, I go backward. Modern rods will spin freely, so I don't sweat the crowns. Besides most of my current systems have brakes or suppressors, so the crown is out of the picture.
3. Follow with another wet patch to grab the loose debris.
4. The last step, use about three to four dry patches, and you are finished.

It does not take any more than this to clean your bore correctly. If you see someone at the range with a stack of black patches, understand that is their barrel they are eating away. These solvents say they will eat copper, but absent of any real copper in the barrel they are happy to eat stainless steel. Feed the beast, and it will eat, which brings us back to Gale McMillan's quote about ruining a barrel by over-cleaning it.

Carbon Fouling

Carbon is a more effortless clean, but a situation that pushes new shooters above and beyond logic. They scrub and scrub thinking the carbon is embedded in the steel and point to a pile of patches claiming the discoloration is carbon when in fact it is steel. Steel will turn a patch black if you rub it enough.

You can wear out your barrel by over-cleaning it. Harsh chemicals are not necessary, and most shooters do not give the rifle a chance to settle in before immediately reaching for the brush.

I do recommend you invest in a Bore Snake and try using it before and after to knock out the loose carbon versus trying to scrub it after a few rounds fired. I also do not put anything on the snake. I run them clean and dry. When they get dirty, wash them.

For a better carbon cleaning experience, I like to use foaming products like Wipe-Out. These types of cleaners are not as harsh and will let you keep the good copper in place. We don't want to change the barrel physically, the shot does enough of that. When you consider a barrel only lasts a few minutes, I say: why help it speed to its death any faster than necessary? When using Wipe-Out, I place it in the bore and will only let it stay there for 20 to 30 minutes. I have heard of guys letting it sit there for an extended amount of time; I don't recommend it.

For most of my rifles, I never break-in the barrel. I have stumbled on a few that did require it, but those are few and far between. The results have been no different, and to prove this, I bought two identical factory rifles and broke-in one, while ignoring the dogma with the other. You cannot tell them apart. Accuracy, cleaning, barrel life, etc., remain the same. A barrel that needs a lot of break-in was probably chambered incorrectly or by an inexperienced machinist. The movement of the reamer was not consistent, or the speed was incorrect. In 2020, it's not a healthy state of affairs.

In short, it's about time and peace of mind. If you cannot stomach the fact the rifle has been left fouled, do a light cleaning. Understanding why we clean and what we are looking to accomplish. If you are secure in your mind that cleaning is a bit overrated, take the time to read the tea leaves and look at it in terms of accuracy. Shoot enough to register what your particular barrel likes and needs. Treat her like a lady, recognize what she wants, then respond accordingly. If she requests a complete cleaning, by all means, indulge that command. But if she is humming along stacking rounds, why change it because you read somewhere that it needs to be scrubbed every 40 rounds. Trust me a number will appear.

My time is valuable; my barrels are expendable; my accuracy stays within tolerance when

Cleaning the muzzle under the suppressor. Many people obsess over the cleanliness of the crown. Suppressors bypass this point so as not to affect accuracy.

using factory ammunition. I can easily maintain 3/8th of an inch, or better with quality factory ammo.

Lastly, understand your powders. Some are dirtier than others. You need to monitor how your particular loads react. At the same time, all this goes back to listening to your system speak. It will talk to you. The questions are: Can you hear it, and will you respond accordingly?

Cold-Bore Variations

Three variations can show up as a cold-bore shift when starting out with your precision rifle.

- Clean Cold Bore
- Fouled Cold Bore
- Cold Body, Cold Mind

Clean Cold Bore is when the rifle has been cleaned, and it needs to replace the good copper that was removed.

We have good copper in the barrel that fills in some imperfections. Consider the example of the cast-iron frying pan, when it has to be re-seasoned. A clean cold bore is often dependent on how aggressive the shooter was cleaning the rifle.

This is caused by a physical change inside the bore.

Fouled Cold Bore

A Fouled Cold Bore is not a natural condition. If the rifle has been fouled and it still exhibits a cold-bore shift, first look at the Cold Body, Cold Mind definition. Next, consider checking the torque settings of the rifle. We have seen problems in both action-screw torque as well as the barrel-receiver mating.

In this case, there might be stress in the system causing it to shift. Most of the time, you will notice the group walk a bit. If you have a perfect, cold-bore shift with the other four shots grouping together, again see the Cold Body. It's not a natural state.

After checking the system, if the shift remains consider replacing the barrel. You will have to monitor and record this variation for future adjustment.

The author always recommends running a suppressor if you have the ability. The paperwork hassle aside, these are the best muzzle brakes.

Cold Body, Cold Mind

This is essentially a first-round flinch. The body is not prepared for the recoil, and the brain moves to protect itself from the recoil and or sound of the gunshot.

We have tested this and found with dry practice prior, you can inoculate yourself from this first-round flinch. You can also check this issue by taking a second rifle to the range. Fire at least 10 shots with the first rifle then move to the precision rifle with a perceived cold-bore shift.

More times than not, the shift will go away.

Cold Body, Cold Mind is subconscious; it's tough to see you are doing it. Thus, a series of tests should be conducted.

Suppressor Use

Suppressors can also have a first-round pop which will mimic a cold-bore shift. Same basic principle, but found inside the suppressor. If the suppressor is well-used, it's a design problem. If the suppressor is new, try shooting more and fouling it. I had a Gemtech Sandstorm with a first-round pop, and after 500 rounds of carbon buildup, the shift disappeared.

Track Your Rifle

Test and record your shifts, measure the distance and work to remove it. I recommend a paper target that travels with you in order to track the differences and changes. Since you can really only test it once, carry it with you.

10

Arabian Gulf Deployment

The Arabian Gulf float made my USMC time complete. Sure, I initially enlisted because I wanted to be a Marine Scout Sniper. I was able to accomplish that task pretty quickly attending Sniper School as a PFC. The next goal was to move beyond the typical training schedule to one with a little more excitement in the air.

The Iran/Iraq War was in full swing. The United States was quietly supporting Iraq, but our presence was mainly political. When we were crossing the Atlantic, many of us knew where we were going, but the Navy was a bit in the dark. At least the junior sailors must not have been told where we were headed.

To remove a Marine from a tight spot, they used a method called SPIE Rigging. Special Purpose Insertion and Extraction. The Marine hangs from a rope under the aircraft. The author reports it's a pretty fun ride.

When the author's ship arrived in the Arabian Gulf, the USS Stark, which had been recently hit by an Iraqi missile, was leaving.

After a short pause in Spain, we typically took a few days in Rota before heading into the Mediterranean Sea, we had a minor incident aboard ship. One of the sailors, when he realized we were heading into a war zone, decided to jump off the ship. He had a buddy throw a life ring off the boats as he bobbed up and down in the water. Seeing a guy jump a ship is a unique experience. The sailor planned it pretty well. He jumped midship while his friend was on the fantail ready to toss the life ring. The rumor at the time was, if you jumped off a ship the Navy charged you the money it takes to turn the boat around to pick you up. We did a long, lazy circle in order to drag the sailor out of the water. I have no idea if it's true they charge for gas, but it's a good story.

Our first few days in the Arabian Gulf were pretty eventful. We had welded on M2 .50-Cal machine guns and Mk 19 grenade launches to the side of the ship. Every few feet was a gun emplacement for the Marines onboard to man. The Iranians employed a swarm attack tactic, in which they sent several small Boston-Whaler-style boats after ships. These Boston Whalers had ZU-23 anti-aircraft guns mounted on them, so we constantly prepared for the potential of a swarm attack.

Years ago, I was featured in a book and the story I related was about a false-alarm swarm attack. We were having a Steel Beach party on the ship and getting a ration of ice cream. Radar picked up several high-speed boats coming our way, spoiling the party. We had to drop everything and man the rails. Turns out the radar contact was a group of SEALs coming in for a little ice cream themselves. Better safe than sorry.

When we arrived in the Gulf, the USS Stark was just leaving. If you remember the Stark incident, an Iraqi aircraft dropped a French Exocet Missile, which is a fire-and-forget device, which impacted the Stark, killing several crew members. We never retaliated against them, and I can tell you why.

Each night, the Marines had watch on deck. Along with the additional guns we mounted onboard, we ran night vision and kept Marines on deck every night. For me, we had watch four hours every other night. During those nights, we spoke to Iraqi pilots all the time. They could not navigate very well at night. They needed help, so we would position our ship in a place to aid navigation. The Iraqis would fly down the coast, call us on the radio and then we would turn on our lights. This rally point gave them a waypoint so they could bomb Iran. We'd ask them to make their weapons safe before passing overhead, as, in the case of the Stark, the pilot made a mistake.

The Iraqi pilots would fly to a place like Farsi Island, bomb the base there, and return past us on their way home.

This was an active cold war for us; we initially participated without really participating. We would look at the real-time intelligence from the war zone and craft training scenarios around them. Our command was very switched-on when it came to using the information to adjust our training.

The USS Roberts helicopter was transferred to the USS Trenton after the USS Roberts hit the Iranian mine.

The author and his fellow Marines practiced fast-roping all the time. This method allowed them to get 18 Marines on the Sassan oil platform in less than 25 seconds.

Operation Praying Mantis

In April 1988, we were flying to various ships in our battle group only to find out we sailed into a mine field. We had just finished practicing fast-roping onto a moving platform. Today, our platform was the USS Samuel Roberts. It was stuck in this mine field and getting out was not going to be so easy. As it attempted to back out of the mine field, it hit one cracking the ship completely in half, at least it looked that way to me.

We towed the USS Roberts to a port in Dubai, and they allowed us to check it out a bit. The crack I saw was easily more than an inch wide. The Navy was pretty incredible here. Knowing they landed in a minefield, they secured the boat, and nobody died; but the Iranians were gonna pay.

The follow day, we prepared to retaliate against the Iranian forward bases. They used oil platforms to launch their mine-laying activities. These gas and oil platforms (GOPLATS) were the perfect bases to operate from because they were scattered all over the gulf. Prior to any of this happening, we had previously secured the individuals' ammo and explosives in sandbags. So, we had a load-out kit ready to roll, just grab a bag and fill your pouches. The ship was abuzz with activity as we prepared to attack the Sassan and Siri oil platforms.

My first memory of the morning was AC/DC music blaring at 11. *Hells Bells* was echoing throughout the entire ship. I was super happy it was AC/DC and not something like Led Zeppelin's *Stairway to Heaven*. That would have been a bad omen. Hells Bells, on the other hand, was a good musical choice.

My partner Ken was going to be overwatch in the Huey circling us, and I was inserted into Taylor's Stick to hit the main platform in the first assault. We traded in our M40AI rifles for MP5, and I used a CAR15. Marc was slated to be the fast-rope master for our drop, and I was number seven in the stick. We had one platoon of Force Recon guys who would take lead in the assault. The Marines from STA would fill in their ranks with Squad from Bravo Company acting as a QRF.

We had practiced hundreds of fast-rope drops on everything available. We could land 21 Marines on a moving ship in less than 30 seconds. Real-time intelligence guiding our training was about to pay off.

I was on board a CH46, we had several Cobras as escorts and prior to leaving there was

a small Naval bombardment of the area. The brass was trying to convince the Revolutionary Guard to surrender before we hit them, a few did surrender, but that came later.

The ride to the platform was short and fast. It was not like a typical helicopter ride as this one was taken at warp speed in dancing, random pattern. We were coming in just below the decking of the platform and to this day I will never forget the POP up at the end. As we reached the edge, the bird popped straight up in a tail stand. I swear if Taylor wasn't tied in, he was falling out the back. As the CH46 leveled off over the deck, the fast rope dropped, and we slid down it.

For this, we had on Chocolate Chip utilities, the Force Recon guys wore flight suits. We also wore Nomex gloves which are not enough to prevent rope burns, so we wore welding gloves on top. As soon as you hit the ground, you slam

The author and his fellow Marines demolished the useful parts of the Sassan oil platform by laying a generous number of explosives.

Marines from MAGTF 2-88 raised the U.S. flag and the USMC flag on the Iranian radio tower.

your hands down and drop the welding gloves, then in one motion you grab the rifle and go.

I recall seeing flashes and sparks coming from the Revolutionary Guard building in the middle of the platform. It was super-fast and short-lived as the Cobras came between me and the building, immediately slamming two TOW missiles into it.

The place lit up like a match.

We now had a part of the platform on fire and if that fire reached the wrong pipes it could send poisonous gases into the air. It was almost instantaneous that the remaining Iranians gave up, so there not much else to do but sweep up. We had to search every nook and cranny to make sure no one was left on board. At the same time the Marines from Bravo company were assisting in the demolition work, we were laying explosives to blow the platform.

I was moving underneath, as there are several levels to each platform. Meanwhile, everyone topside was combing through the debris for intelligence and swag.

Recently, Marc Taylor was watching a movie, *Body of Lies* with Leonardo DiCaprio. In the movie, there was stock footage of the platform. Apparently, the Navy was filming Operation Praying Mantis and it was included in the movie. We later found it on YouTube. The Marines on the raid hoisted a flag on a radio tower, and one of our guys, "Primo," had climbed up with Haney to affix it along with the Stars and Stripes. The moment was caught on film and you can hear Primo call for Sgt. Taylor to grab a camera.

I had a small Canon Snappy camera attached to my gas mark pouch. I had removed the fake decontamination kit and popped the auto-advance camera into its place. There are a couple

After the raid on the Iranian oil platform, the author and his shipmates had a "Dog and Pony" Show" for the political class. Here is the M19 40mm Grenade Launcher, one of the author's favorite machine guns to shoot.

of variations of the Navy footage out there and in one brief segment you can hear my voice as it's pretty distinct.

With the Sassan oil platform secured, we were headed to the Siri oil fields next.

While all this was going on, the Iranian Navy was not sitting idly by; they were trying to fight back. Unfortunately for them, we had the USS Enterprise in the Indian Ocean supporting us, so their fight didn't go as planned.

Operation Earnest Will, the escorting of the Kuwaiti Tankers had morphed into Operation Praying Mantis, giving the Marines of MAGTF 2-88 a brief taste of combat. This battle turned out to be the largest naval battle since World War II. It sounds crazy as hell in the retelling, as it did not appear that way in person.

Sure, the Iranians shot six Silkworm missiles at us, but they never got close. The Enterprise took care of the remaining ships in the Iranian Navy, while the Iraqis used the diversions to break its navy out of the Tigress and Euphrates rivers. They were also using chemical weapons against each other, but we can't talk about that aspect of the fight. We continued to coordinate our work with the Iraqis in order to prevent the Iranians from getting a leg up.

The pre-raid bombardment of the Siri platform made an attack impossible. We sailed toward them, but never actually put boots on the ground

The author, front row second from left, mixed in with the other Marines from 1st Battalion 2nd Marines just prior to the "Dog and Pony Show" after Operation Praying Mantis. The size difference is black and white, as he was tad shorter than most Marines.

The Navy highlighted the attack during Operation Praying Mantis. Here, you can see the left platform on fire with Marines surveying the ZU-23-2 on the right platform.

After Operation Praying Mantis, Force Recon took the Russian 12.7 machine gun back to the United States and it was placed in the Force Recon Compound on Camp Lejeune.

Several ZU-23-2 anti-aircraft guns guarded the Iranian oil platforms. This particular one was taken back to Camp Lejeune and can be seen in front of the 2nd Marines chow hall.

there. I think the air-burst rounds caught the place on fire, but to be honest, I was on deck sleeping. In anticipation of making another raid, we sat kitted up on deck. With our adrenaline gone there was not much left to do but sleep. The remainder of the day is definitely blurry for me.

We punched back at Iran, but did not escape unscathed. We lost one of the Cobras from the Trenton when it was shot down in follow-up engagement. Captains Hill and Leslie were killed in action during the assault. We had a great air wing with us during our gulf deployment and losing a Cobra hit home. Marines are unique in we can talk directly with our air-wing support. The Cobras and Harriers that work with the ground element move with us even in the field. It's not uncommon to pass through a battalion bivouac to find the air crews and attack aircraft sitting right there with us. Close Air Support is a feather in the Marine Corps cap dating back to the Banana Wars of the early 1900s. As a salute to their work, I say, "Swing with the Wing."

11

Advice on Buying a Scope

You went out and bought a new precision rifle, and you want to purchase a new optic. But there are so many choices, from Athlon to Vortex, Barska to Zeiss. Where do you start? How do you wade through the hype and get down to the meat and potatoes of the questions? Well Sniper's Hide is here to help.

Spoiler Alert: I won't pander to your emotions.

Mission:

What is your intended use? It's that simple. Do you only have access to a 200-yard range, and plan on putting it on your .308? Or are you interested in shooting competitively in Precision Rifle Series (PRS) or F-Class? Just plinking? Because all these details matter. The first thing you need to do is be honest about your intended use for the scope.

To reach 1,000 yards with a .308 rifle, you want at least 40 Minutes of Angle (MOA) of useable adjustment from a 100-yard zero. And trust me you want a 100-yard zero on your rifle. If that means you have a scope with 60 MOA, plus or minus, of adjustment, you are in good shape. You do not need a scope with 32 Mils of adjustments if you can only reach 600 yards at your local range. The long and short of it, the cartridge you are shooting matters too. By understanding your caliber choices, you can determine the best scope for your given application.

Scopes are a telescopic sighting device; glass is secondary to the mechanical operation.

We focus a lot on correctly mounting the optic and setting it up for the individual shooter. It's not a case of just dropping it on the rifle. There is a procedure.

Magnification has very little bearing on how far you are shooting, but it matters depending on what you are shooting at. If you are shooting F-Class on paper, you want to see the X-Ring, so these shooters use very high magnification scopes. But the tradeoff is less elevation adjustment. You don't want a 55x optic for your .338LM if you plan on shooting to one mile. More magnification usually limits your total travel. Most field shooters stick to scopes that hover around 25x or less. Many are shooting

them below 18x, enjoying the increased elevation adjustment. Magnification is a double-edged sword in the field.

Magnification increases problems in the air, like the mirage. Yes, you can shoot 1,000 yards with a 10x scope, but most will use between 12x and 18x to maintain a good field of view and clear sight picture. The days of the fixed 10x are coming to an end. Those scopes are typically used as a byproduct of their owners' budgets. Get a little bit more magnification, so you have

it, but don't overdo it.
You do not need a 32x
scope to shoot 1,000 yards on steel.
You want 25x or less. I love, and use, a ton of
16x scopes. I shoot beyond 1,000 yards all the
time, and the 16x does not hold me back. Lots
of people are magnification whores, and not for
a good reason. Balance the magnification and
have it suit your mission.

Budget:

Super important: How much money do you
plan on spending? What is the top end of your
budget and is it worth holding off a bit to take
the next step up? If your budget is $2,000, you
might want to wait until you have $2,500. If your
budget is $1,500, you might be better served
spending $1,250.

Many leave out the budget constraints and
will let people endlessly talk about scopes out
of their price range. It's sort of like going to the
Cadillac dealer, letting the salesman show you
every bell and whistle and then going out and
buying a Ford Focus. Sure, both cars will get
you from point A to point B, but why waste the
salesman's time on all that Caddy talk? Let's go
straight to the Ford Dealer and start spec'ing
out your Focus. It's a weird fetish to hear about
everything you can't afford.

It used to be the top-of-the-line Leupold

Mk 4 cost
$1,250; now that is a
low-end scope regarding money spent. If that
is your budget, there is nothing wrong with it,
but accept the fact you're now looking at the
lower end of the spectrum and not the higher
end. When everyone was running Leupolds, I
switched to Schmidt & Bender (S&B), and my
budget immediately jumped to $2,000 and up.
Here is a bit of history: I have one of the first
S&B 5-25x PMIIs that hit U.S. shores. New, it cost
me $2,350. Today, that same scope can retail
for as much as $3,800 or more. A few things
changed over the years with them,
but you are not going to see the
difference. I also have a $7,000
Hensoldt 3-26x. It does not help
me shoot any better than my
$2,400 Vortex. In fact, if I walked
down to my local mall and
placed my Vortex Gen 2 Razor
on the table next to my $7,000
Hensoldt, playing the Pepsi
Challenge to see who can pick
out the scope that cost $7,000,
50 percent of the people would be
wrong.

Yes, you get what you pay for, so be

Your budget needs to include a quality optic, such as this Zero Compromise scope.

Today, most scopes look great out of the box. We have higher quality components versus 30 years ago, when most shooters had limited choices for a quality scope.

careful when someone says it's a Giant Killer. The odds are, your $1,500 scope is really only competing with other $1,500 scopes. If it were really a Giant Killer, it would cost the same as the big names. Companies can certainly OEM an optic from the major players, but that does not mean the spec is the same. Quality is not marked by where it is "Made."

You are not going to win by simply choosing a country of origin. Scopes Made in Japan, prob-

Not all scopes are created equally. Focus on the mechanics of the product and not the brand name or the glass. The country of origin has less bearing today than it did 30 years ago.

also marked Made in Japan. Vortex specs them out a certain way, then when they arrive in the U.S., Vortex tears them apart. Yes, that scope is cheaper to get it into the country complete, after which Vortex replaces the internals to ones made here in the U.S. It's not enough to change the country of origin, but it is an important reason why those scopes work so well.

See the Sniper's Hide Legend in the Scopes Forum. Which brings me to glass.

Glass Quality:

As I'm writing this, every damn scope looks good out of the box. Manufacturers have learned enough over the last 50 years to make outstanding glass. The optical prescription and how they spec them is such that we can barely tell the difference when all else is equal.

The glass is subjective. No two users see through the scope the same way. Especially if it was not properly adjusted for the shooter's eye. There are only so many suppliers of raw glass and the difference actually lies in the coatings. The problem with coatings is durability. While your cheap, budget-minded scope, "Looks just as good as my friend's S&B," in two years your coatings will be worn down and not nearly as nice, and his glass will be the same as the first day he bought it. Things like sunlight can wear on coatings over time. So just showing up at the range with a scope can degrade it.

I think people tell themselves how good something is just to justify the purchase they weren't sure about in the first place. After that, it's a case of misery loving company.

Coatings are what gives a scope it's "look," and that look is the same as asking your friend what his favorite color is. They design the coatings and the look for a specific set of results. That usually means outside in the sun, which is one color on the spectrum chart, or to break down shadows so you can see your

ably the most are excellent. majority of great Japan. Nobody or Canon com- all in the specs, same machines hold very respectable tolerances. It comes down to what the vendors want to pay, and how much quality control goes into the scope. An example of this is the Vortex Gen 2 Razor. It's a widely popular, very reliable scope that is plentiful of the bunch, Consider this, the cameras come from bitches about Nikon ing from Japan. It's as they have the we do, which can prey through the camouflage. If you want low-light performance, you get a large objective lens and reduce the power to open up the exit pupil. If you test your scope on 25x at night, you will be disappointed. Try turning down the power. Same goes for the elevation. If you want to see the best sight picture, the erector has to be centered. You cannot crank 50MOA on one scope and compare it to scope that is centered. It's like testing a scope indoors with fluorescent lights when it's color corrected for daylight. All will make a scope look bad. Bay window reviewers are plentiful on the Internet; some of the best-written reviews come from owners of safe-queen rifles.

Glass is discrete and controlled by the Abbe number. Schott, Hoya and Ohara are brands, not a quality value. Each brand has its equivalent model with a matching Abbe number. In fact, there are versions of Ohara glass which outscore similar Schott models. The bird watchers and star gazers have this down to a science. They can tell what lenses are combined in their optics to get the desired effect, and neither favors one brand over another. They understand what the Abbe number means and how the design is impacted by the choices made in optical design.

Bottomline, don't get wrapped up in the glass. The scope companies have taken care of this for you. Today, glass quality is more so a byproduct of your budget than your choice in brand. In many cases, you need a machine to tell the difference.

Choose the features that are important to you; don't let someone else pick your favorite color for you. Instead, educate yourself on the pros and cons of each type of optic out there.

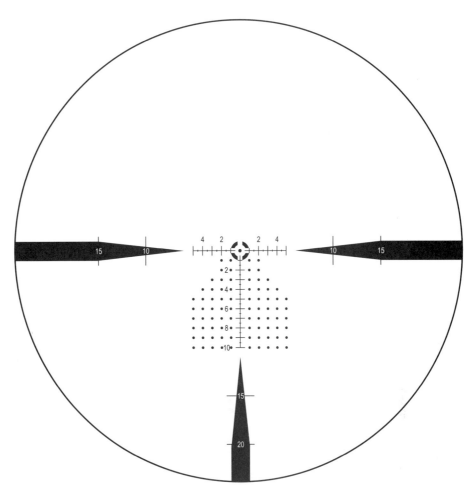

The reticle should speak to the individual and tell a story. Listen to the reticle. Does it whisper or yell?

Features to Look For:

Elevation adjustment is attached to main-tube size. Most common are 30mm to 34mm. The erector inside is the same, so you are not getting more light out a 34mm vs. 30mm. The brightness of the scope is determined by other factors. If you are putting the scope on your .338LM, you want 100 MOA, or more, of elevation. That is equal to more than 26 Mils of adjustment. For Extreme Long Range (ELR) shooting, you want a scope with 28 to 36 Mils of adjustment. If you are using your .308, you can get away with 15 Mils or less. That is about 60 MOA. I do recommend getting more elevation than you think you need; you might decide to swap it over or travel to a location with more distance. Add more weight to total adjustment when considering a new scope.

Zero Stops is a feature definitely worth having. Zero Stops prevent you from being off a turn. Some scopes allow you to set them at a specific point; other scopes are set at the factory. I always like to have a tiny bit, about 1 MOA of down, below the zero stop.

Locks, Brakes, Capped Windage:

This was designed around the military using the Horus Reticle. They are unnecessary for most shooters, but often come on scopes as a default feature. These will be a bit more complicated and will drive up the cost of the scope. In a choice between a S&B Double Turn Turret and a locking turret, I would personally recommend the Double Turn over the locking. But, really, it's not that big a deal. I rarely, if ever, find a need to use the locks for everyday shooting. If I can get a scope cheaper by skipping the locking turret, I will do that.

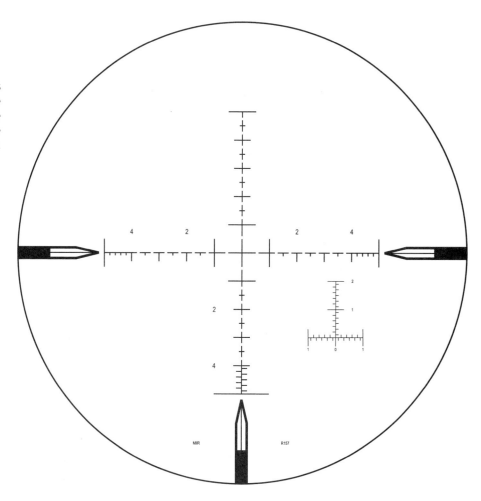

The reticle is one of our points of human contact with the scope. We need to focus more on the reticle choice than the perceived optical quality.

First Focal Plane vs. Second Focal Plane:

The reticles in first focal plane (FFP) scopes appear to get larger when the magnification is increased, and smaller when decreased. This allows the reticle to retain proportion with the size of the target. The result is holdover points remain the same, regardless of magnification.

Reticles in the second focal plane (SFP) stay the same size throughout the magnification. As magnification increases, the size of the target appears to increase, but the reticle does not.

If you are a dynamic shooter, field shooter, PRS shooter, or even a hunter, you want an FFP scope. This might increase the cost. If you plan on shooting F-Class, benchrest, or if you shoot by yourself, you want to get an SFP scope, which is considered a more durable design and will be a bit cheaper compared to an FFP scope. For this reason, you see guys shooting ELR

distances and heavy recoiling rifles using an SFP scope. You can use half the power on an SFP and double the reticle value giving you more range when holding at extended distances.

Reticles, Reticles and More Reticles:

Reticles are like shoes; you get the pair that fits well and is suited for your desired use. You don't buy sneakers to match your business suit. You get sneakers to run in, hiking boots to hike in, and dress shoes to look good, but feel uncomfortable. Same with reticles.

Reticles take understanding and training. We use reticles today like very few did before. The biggest consideration is to match the reticle to the turrets. Mils for Mils and MOA for MOA (more on this in the next section). If you don't need all the clutter, don't get it. Nobody I know of has won an F-Class match with a Horus Reticle holding over. It's a tool. One that might not be necessary for your type of shooting.

Our brains like focus, we like a defined intersection, and the holdover reticles are designed for speed and big targets. Sure, given time and opportunity we can get very precise with them, but they can also block the impact causing us to hesitate and have to think about what just happened. When an expected outcome doesn't happen, some people lock up. Also, under stress with limited training, some people hold the wrong line, repeatedly. Practice is important. But they are just Mils, so they do work as advertised. They also add more money to the scope. The Horus Reticle adds $400 to the cost, that is the license fee which is passed on to the end user.

Look at the schematics of the reticles you are considering, get to know them first and understand what they provide you and what they don't. You have to wear the shoes, I don't.

I trained on the Horus, I have taught others on the Horus, and I personally dislike the Horus. This doesn't mean I can't use it, I just don't like it, never did since day one. I tend to opt for less and do very well with less because I understand both and can use my P4F or MSR in the same manner as my Horus reticles. Sure, I still own them, but I don't need it to hold over, or to be successful when holding. Study the reticles and pick one based on your mission. The one or two stages at a PRS match where there is not enough time to dial can easily be shot with a plain old Mil Dot. Effectively too, it just takes practice. There are no free rides; a Horus will not make you a better shooter.

Mils vs. MOA:

Match the turrets to the reticles. I have written about this in-depth, that they are the same damn thing. If you're going to shoot F-Class you use MOA (Minutes of Angle), if you are going to shoot PRS, use Mils (Milliradians), if you shoot alone it does not matter, just match the turrets to the reticle. For the guys who say: "I think in inches, therefore, use MOA," you're silly. You know 10 pennies are in a dime; well that is a Mil in a nutshell. You cannot hold the difference and you can get one-eighth-inch clicks in Mils, too. The difference between the two is half a bullet width. I promise that you dialing 7.5 MOA is the same as me using 2.2 Mils. We'll both hit center of the same target. Your DOPE is your DOPE.

However, let's dig deeper into the Mils vs. MOA discussion without getting wonky.

This debate is never going to end, but we should agree on the facts. Every day we see the uninformed arguments how one angular unit of measurement is better than the other. The truth of the matter is, one is not better, they are just different ways of breaking down the same thing.

Personally, outside of the disciplines like benchrest shooting and F-Class, I think Minutes of Angle should be retired. We have bastardized the unit to the point people have no idea a true MOA is not 1 inch at 100 yards, or 10 inches at 1,000, but 1.047 inches at 100 and 10.47 inches at 1,000. If you round this angle, you create errors at the longer distances. Today we shoot a lot farther than before, and five percent of error compounding at an extended range will cause a miss. In fact, this is one of the main reasons your ballistic software does not work. You default to MOA when in reality your scope adjusts in Inches Per Hundred Yards (IPHY).

Shooter MOA or IPHY is not a true MOA, and yes it does matter when companies mix them. Having someone question how IPHY is different when they don't understand we don't use 1 MOA or even 10 MOA to hit a 1,000-yard target is frustrating to explain. If we consider a .308 as a point of reference, we are looking at almost 17 inches of variation between the two units of adjustment.

We can quickly point to the adoption of Mils here with the military to demonstrate the ease of use, but then the Americans reading this will argue how they think in inches and yards as if Mils only work with the metric system. Mils are base 10 and, unfortunately, Mr. & Mrs. America thinking in fractions is nowhere as simple.

Note that 3,600 inches is 100 yards and 1/1000th of that is 3.6 inches, and adjusting in .1 Mils means we moved the bullet .36 of an inch per click at 100. See what we did there? We moved the decimal point. Some people believe a MOA is a finer unit of adjustment. Failing to realize: .3 Mils is 1.08 inches at 100 yards. Contrary to popular belief, you can get a Mil-based scope that moves the reticle .18 of an inch per click. Mil-based scopes usually adjust in .1 Mil increments; however, they do make scopes that adjust in .05 Mils.

While Milliradians were added to the metric system many years ago, it was never designed to be a metric-only unit and works outside the metric system as this is an angle. Every angle has a linear distance between it. You should be ignoring this fact and using the angle versus picking a linear value to adjust your correction. If I am shooting 873 yards away, saying the bullet is six inches off the target is neither honest nor accurate. You're guessing. In your mind, it

looked six inches away, but what if it was nine inches? Using the linear value is more work. Why not just adjust the angle?

Minutes of Angle started out like that too, but, unfortunately, companies took shortcuts and ruined it for everyone. It was easier to manufacturer 1-inch vs. adding in the .047 of an inch. Long range back in the day was between 400 and 800 yards. Read any old textbook on ballistics, and it rarely goes past those ranges in the examples.

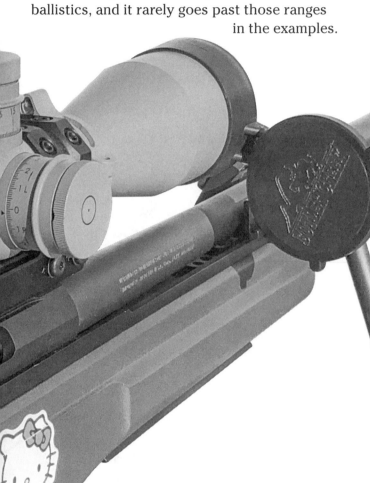

A scope can follow you as your shooting progresses. It's better to invest more in the optic up front than to constantly chase the next best thing.

Today, we are shooting beyond 1,000 yards, so it matters more than ever. You have to take it into account.

Defaulting your program to MOA when you are using IPHY is a significant point of error. JBM Ballistics online is a great place to demonstrate this, as you can include both MOA and IPHY in the output. The same amount of adjustment is accomplished with two different values. Mix these numbers, and the result is a miss. Did you dial 40.1 or 38.3 MOA? I highly recommend you map and calibrate your MOA scope to confirm its actual value. It works both ways, not every MOA-based scope is True Minute of Angle (TMOA), some are Shooters Minute of Angle (SMOA). The compounding error is a lot bigger than .47 of an inch.

One is not more accurate than the other. I can hit the center of any target using either unit of adjustment. Using JBM, we can see that both correctly move us to the target. The difference is less than a bullet width. I have no trouble zeroing or hitting the center of a Shoot-N-C target.

Which unit of adjustment is right for me?

This is the ultimate question. It should not be up to someone else to answer it for you. Communication is your number one consideration.

What are your friends and fellow competitors shooting?

You want to be able to communicate and understand what a fellow competitor is talking about when he walks off the line. You can convert using 3.43, by multiplying or dividing the competing unit of adjustment

against the other. That will give you a direct conversion.

12 MOA / 3.43 = 3.5 Mils

4.2 Mils x 3.43 = 14.4 MOA

Next, you have your reticle choices. You will find more versatile options when it comes to Mil-based scopes versus MOA scopes. That is changing a small amount as manufacturers adapt. But a reticle with 1 MOA hash marks is not as fine as a scope with .2 Mil lines in it. You now have to break up an already small 1 MOA into quarters. The Mil-based scope is already breaking up the Milliradian for you.

Pick the reticle based on your initial impression, as well as your use. You don't need a Christmas-tree reticle to shoot F-Class. You don't want to use a floating-dot benchrest scope for tactical style competition. Put your intended use into the proper context.

A lot has been written about the nuts and bolts of Mils and MOA. You can dig deep or understand we are using the angle and there is no need to convert to a linear distance. A Mil is a Mil, and a MOA is a MOA (unless it's not because you didn't check). Today, I don't even teach, one inch at 100 yards, two inches at 200 yards, five inches at 500 yards. It's an unnecessary step and confusing to a lot of people. Also, it's not right: that is IPHY, not MOA.

We match our scope reticle to our turret adjustment, so at the end of the day, "What you See is What You Get." It matches what we see in the reticle so we can dial the correction on the turret. A super simple concept that allows the shooter to use the calibrated ruler three inches in front of their nose. That calibrated ruler is

Scopes are the weak link in our rifle system and can be prone to mechanical issues. Selecting a brand with a better mechanical track record is recommended over saving a few dollars.

called a reticle, taking away the need to think about the adjustment. You just read it.

If the impact is off in any direction, you measure with the reticle and then translate that reading directly to the turrets. Remember: 1 Mil is always 1 Mil, and 1 MOA in any direction is a 1-MOA correction on the turret.

If you have not made the change to Mils, consider it. You will find it's much more intuitive. You do not have to be a resident of Germany to understand it, and you do not have to use it with meters. All my data is in yards, and Mils directly translate to whatever range you use.

The mission of Sniper's Hide is to uphold the traditions of those who came before us by expanding on the science of long-range shooting while developing the art of Precision Rifle Marksmanship.

What is the Best Scope Out There?

Every day, the question is: "Who makes the best scope?" Scope A or Scope B?" Well, if there was one scope that solved it all, we'd be using it. You'd find it under "What the Pros Use," except every pro cannot be sponsored by one scope company. When you see a scope in the list that doesn't quite work this way, it's probably a sponsor's optic being used by a very good team. Doesn't make it better, just makes it sponsored. It also proves that a $1,500 scope will not hold you back when shot against a $3,000 scope. That scope is not doing something different at a lower cost; it's doing the same thing. Scopes are sights and are not spotters. We need the internals to track and repeat correctly. We try to eliminate the need to use customer service by

picking a scope with a better track record, but still, there is no guarantee of perfection.

The scope is your weakest link next to the actual bullet. It's a mechanical device subject to potential failure. If two out of every five sold need repairs, but the company is super nice about it. Do you still want it? Imagine traveling to a precision rifle competition, $500 airfare, $500 for the room, rental car and ammo prep, only to have the scope go down on day one. You get back on Monday, call the company, and the representative is super nice about checking it out or even replacing it. That doesn't replace the time and money you wasted. Look at track records versus customer-service praise. If nobody can answer a customer-service question, it's because more people are not using the customer service from that company.

What is your shooting mission: plinking, paper, steel, competition or real world? You pick the optic to suit your mission.

I have used everything from the Weaver to the Hensoldt, and all scopes in between. Each one has its place, and some are more user-friendly than others. The features I like are not the same as the features someone else will like. You have to define your mission to figure out where you sit in that spectrum.

Do your homework, ask smart questions and don't let others pick your favorite color for you. Spend your money wisely observing the features you need versus what other people are selling you. Look at the context of your shooting when making this decision.

The final decision matters, because you have to live with it.

12

Wind, The Great Equalizer

On the range, people describe the wind as the great equalizer. Next to your drop, drift from wind is the second most important consideration for the long range precision rifle shooter. Unlike drop, which is predictable, the wind is a constantly changing factor.

So how do we get a handle on the wind? What are some tools, tips and tricks we can use to manage this element of long range shooting?

Starting out, we are going to look at the wind in two ways: the science department and the art department. By breaking it down this way, we'll begin to understand the complexities of reading the wind out in the field.

The wind is dynamic; it does not move in a straight line or at a constant value. We use the tools available to determine an average based on our observations.

This is where the art and science of long range shooting meet. How the wind acts, how terrain affects it, and how we can estimate it in order to put rounds on target.

Science Department

What wind is most important?

This is probably the number one question asked by a new shooter, and even some very experienced shooters. The answer will vary depending on who you talk to and how detailed they want to get. The short answer is, "all of them." However, we want to get a little more precise than that, because just saying all of them doesn't help you become better shooter. So, where do we start? Well, of course, we start with you, the shooter.

Wind at the Shooter

There are several reasons we can look to wind at the shooter as the most important. The first being, the time of flight. Understand once the bullet is blown off course it stays off course and will never return. Wind at the muzzle has the

Corrected Wind Speed for Angle

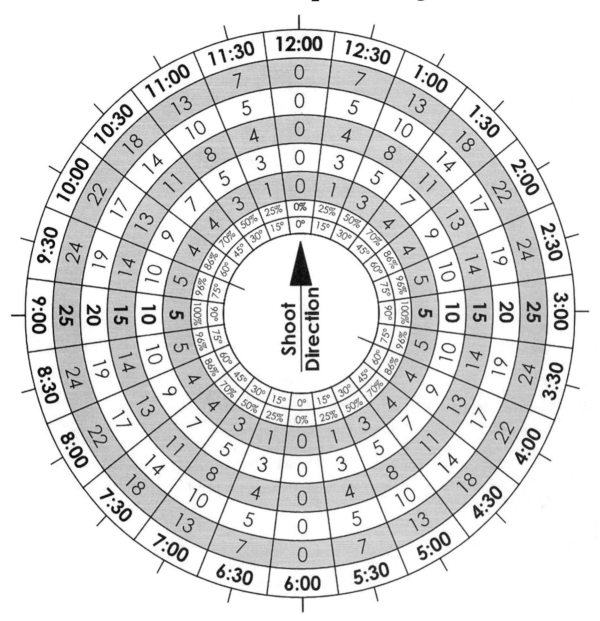

Sniper's Hide member "JackMaster" created a series of wind charts and this new Rose to determine the deflection at an angle to the shooter.

longest amount of time to move the bullet off target. The flight of the bullet is angular. Distance and time increase that angle away from the intended target.

The next reason is a bit more physical. It is the only place along the bullet's path you can actually measure the wind to better than 1 mph. This is important because even a 1-mph error, especially at long distances can be the difference between a hit and miss. A 1-mph wind blows a 175-grain SMK from a .308 10 inches at 1,000 yards. I call it the science department because it is here. We can hold a Kestrel Wind Meter in our hand and read the actual wind speed with a scientific instrument.

Then we have the shooter. It all has to start somewhere, and that place is with us. The moment we hit the range or enter the field we begin analyzing our surroundings. We are using our sense of touch; we feel the wind on our bodies.

The wind is the great equalizer. Using a local wind meter, we can determine the speed at the shooter. Wind at the shooter is the foundation for all calls.

Our sense of sight, we see what the wind is doing to objects around us. Our hearing, we can hear the changes in the wind with our ears. The wind gusts resonate, so we can use that information. Combine these factors and this is why we call wind at the shooter the science department.

Reading the wind over time to better than 1 mph helps us establish a baseline. A foundation for all our wind calls moving forward.

The only place we can do that with any chance of accuracy is at the shooter. Understand everything else is just a guess. We'll discuss how to fine-tune that guess, but first let's start by analyzing the conditions at the shooter.

Kestrel Weather Meters

I am huge advocate of technology. I believe

it helps us, especially if used correctly. That doesn't mean I don't have low-tech backups just in case. It just means I feel you are better off with technology than without.

I recommend investing in some kind of wind meter. I personally recommend the Kestrel brand of weather meter. Long range shooters default to the Kestrel 5700 with Applied Ballistic Software included, or today you can purchase the Hornady version with their software installed. For those who have software and just want the weather meter functions, be sure to order one with density altitude included as that is a defining feature of the models designed for the shooters. We want access to the Density Altitude, not every meters includes this function.

The Kestrel Weather Meter is the easiest way to begin calibrating your body to what the wind is doing. Not just at the shooter but downrange as well.

You start the moment you step out into the field. Feel the wind, see what it is doing to objects around you and listen to the gusts. Immediately a number will enter your mind. Once you have that number, take out your Kestrel and compare that to what the meter reads. The more you do this, the better your estimates will get. You can even carry one on your morning walks. As you move around the neighborhood, estimate the wind speed from various angles and compare them to the Kestrel. What we are doing is building our personal database. We are matching those values to our senses in order to fine-tune them. This helps us develop our skills, but there is more needed when retrieving a number on the firing line.

Prior to shooting, even before you set up, take the Kestrel and establish a baseline read-

ing. This reading should be done for a minimum of two minutes. What we are looking to establish is an average wind, plus we want to see the highs and lows. We are looking for hard numbers here. The Kestrel will register to within a one-tenth of a mile per hour. We are looking at getting as accurate as possible, as this is our foundation for all our calls moving forward. Now understand, as the ground heats up, you might have to take these readings several times a day. Still, we want to start out on the best foot possible by reading the wind with a meter.

What we have is a solid way to learn and understand the wind by comparing our calls to the meter. Sure, we can look downrange, estimate a call (guess), and then shoot. Work the data back and tell yourself how close you were based off the impact. This trial-and-error method takes a lot of time, and even more shooting. By starting off at the shooter, we can then verify our call right there with the Kestrel with the necessary level of accuracy.

As our experience grows, so does our ability to estimate calls downrange with greater accuracy.

Finally, shooting at night. Our sense of sight is greatly diminished when shooting at night. So, we have Night Vision (NV) capable Kestrels. These allow us to read the wind at the shooter under the cover of darkness. Our calls down-

A wind meter should be a basic requirement to learning the wind. Embrace technology, but understand the "why" behind it.

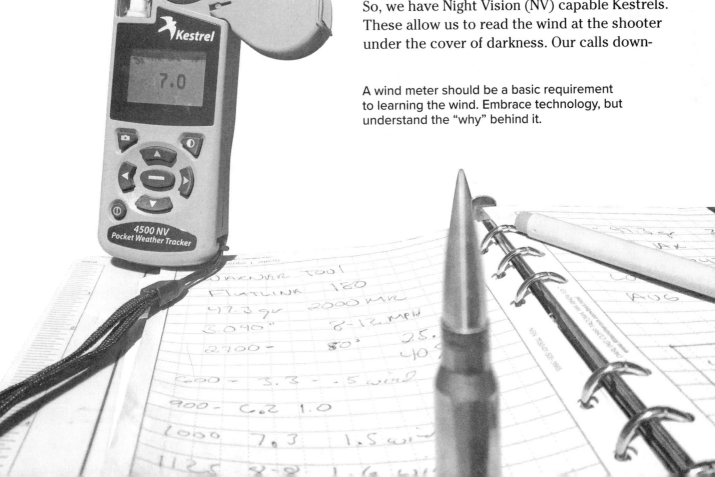

Robert Brantley, a winner of the King of 2 Mile ELR event, is doping the wind with his hands. There are a lot of different methods that yield success. Develop a plan and stick with it.

range are basically using a single sense. What we see downrange in terms of movement. If we ignored everything we are told at the shooter, we still only have our ability to see movement as our sole sense to rely on for our call. You can't see mirage. You might not be able to judge movement that well 600 meters away in pitch black. We need to fall back on the wind at the shooter and our use of a NV capable Kestrel.

Basically, the Kestrel puts everything we need to start in the palm of our hand. It's foolish not to embrace it. Plus, with the Applied Ballistics Model we can combine it with our ballistics software.

The Argument Against Wind at the Shooter

We established that wind at the shooter is the best place to start, however there are always exceptions to the rule. There are times when wind at the shooter will not work. Some of the drawbacks to using wind at the shooter are:

Our position is blocked from the wind. It is possible our position is not open to the prevailing winds, a prime example of this is having the shooter inside a structure. So, we will be forced to look downrange. In this case, we have to rely on our experience to project what we know; to use what we can see downrange. How are things like trees being affected? That is our only source of information, the visual indicators.

Downrange is where our final focus is. We want to use our initial call based off the wind at the shooter. But adjustments to that call might be based off what is observed downrange. That is where we are looking. In this case, hopefully we are just favoring slightly because we found a solid average with the Kestrel at the shooter. It's a common practice.

Max ordinate, when shooting beyond 600 meters, the bullet is arcing. A 175-grain SMK will be traveling approximately 15 feet above the line of sight for a 1,000-yard shot. Because the wind is experiencing less friction higher off the ground, it might increase in speed beyond what is read at ground level. Still we can base that call off what we know from what we read at the shooter.

Limitations of the Science Department

Many shooters point to the conditions down-range, and this is where the science department has its limitations. Because the bullet will be affected by wind during the entire flight, conditions read at the shooter can be too small a piece of the puzzle. This is where the art of precision rifle shooting comes into play.

We cannot read the wind to better than 1 mph out to distance. As well, the wind does not flow in a straight and even manner. We have to use our experience to figure out the changes based off what we see. It becomes highly subjective at this point, as no two people will read the conditions the same way.

Shooting is a cause-and-effect activity, if X happens, Y will be the result. Wind at the shooter might only give you one branch of the X while the conditions downrange fill in the other three branches.

But it is possible to calibrate and condition our senses to educate our guesses. After all, everything we can't read with a wind meter is just a guess. Some shooters have educated their guesses, but that takes time, especially for guys who are used to shooting on one particular range.

Robert Brantley is shown doping the wind prior to his turn shooting the King of 2 Mile. Wind speed is determined by what we see, feel and hear.

The more experience we have shooting, and reading the wind, the farther downrange our accuracy will become. This not only applies to our shooting, but to the wind calls we make. You cannot buy success. You can fool yourself and lease it, but you cannot outright buy it with the latest gadget or by using a wind-cheating caliber. At some point, nature will throw a curve at you.

Educate yourself, focus on the fundamentals, success will follow.

I find using ballistically superior calibers a double-edged sword, especially if you live in an area with relatively light winds, where for a majority of your shooting you are never holding off the plate, or just using the edge of the target as your aiming point. How successful will you be when traveling and being faced with heavier winds?

Most people underestimate their wind calls. It's not uncommon for people who are using the trial-and-error method to walk shots in. This is definitely one approach, but not always a very effective one. Recording your data can help expose faults in your calls. If you see a pattern appear where the first shot on a target always has you underestimating the wind, you might have to recalibrate your senses. It's possible your 8 mph is really a 10 mph and your 5 mph call is closer to 7 mph. Your data book will help you answer this question and allow you to diagnose your calls.

Part of the science department is using technology. JBM Ballistics online is a free resource that will give you everything from drop to drifts in printable charts. I use JBM a lot as it has an extensive bullet library and is easy to use.

The Science Department Math Class

OK, the Sniper's Hide shooting mantra is W.T.F., this stands for Wind, Target or Trajectory, and the Fundamentals of marksmanship.

WTF is your pre-shot checklist to engage a target at long distance. Everything else is really just noise or varying degrees of noise. We can beat the science of a shot to death with a ton of calculations which have very little bearing on the shot. Let's consider spin drift, as this is the only time I will mention it without snickering. For me, I turn any addition of spin drift off in my software. I don't use it. The concept was never mentioned in Sniper School and I managed to graduate that course. So, why am I bringing it up? Well, a lot of people have made a ton of money off the idea that spin drift is going to get that first round hit on target. No, doping the wind within 1 mph of actual is what is going to get the hit. Spin drift, realistically, is only 1 percent of your elevation. If you are shooting something super slow, with an aggressive twist rate, you can slide the needle closer to 2 percent, but, realistically, do I really need to sweat something that is 1 percent of the problem?

Anecdotally, I can relay this important story to you regarding spin drift. We were at Gunsite attending its XLR Course, shooting targets to beyond 2,000 meters. This was a private class with a bunch of students from Alaska in attendance. Several of us were shooting 300 Norma rifles, so pretty consistent. I was calling shots for the guys and we were hammering the target when a third shooter appeared. At this point, we had the wind locked on, 6 mph coming from the left put all of us on steel. Shooter three steps up and after his first shot, my next wind call put him on the wrong side of the target. I hate being on the wrong side of the wind, makes no sense to me and calls into question my reading of said wind.

I asked the shooter what was dialed on the scope, and he told me, .8 Mils of spin drift as required by the software. .8 Mils! "What the heck are you doing with that much dialed on?" I told him to remove it. As soon as he did, he hit the target. One of the instructors asked why I had them remove the spin drift from their rifles. "It was wrong," I said. Let's look at the math and calculate an actual number. So, we did the math, looked at everyone shooting the same caliber, and to our surprise we had a new number.

At 2,000 meters in a 6-mph wind, we estimated the spin drift to be .3 Mils at this distance for this rifle and caliber combination. Note: .3 Mils is a lot different than .8, and this highlighted in it in real time. So, for this reason as well as

It's not uncommon to see 12- to 18-mph winds during the author's precision rifle classes. Students come from all over the world to dope these winds.

countless others, I ignore this prospect of the equation. I will simply say, not everyone agrees on this part of the science and many are using flat-rate values to give you something rather than doing nothing.

Dope the wind. Don't mess with my wind call.

Wind is first, because the wind is everything. If you followed the process outlined earlier and doped the rifle to distance, you included every drift imaginable to the data. Then, you are going to take that data with all your drifts included and true your computer. Well, you just trued your computer to data that includes it, so why add an extra layer on top? Most software is already doubling that 1 to 2 percent, so we have too much there. Just turn it off and focus on the wind drift. That would be my advice. When you can hit a .25 MOA sized target on command at distance, you can think about turning it back on.

We have worked super hard over the last two years to simplify the wind. We are teaching stu-

dents in this method every month and trust me it works. In fact, it works so well you're going to question it after reading this passage. We have created dedicated wind targets just to teach and test this theory. It's moved beyond the discussions of "how I dope the wind," to, "this is how you dope the wind." Full stop.

Last piece of setup: The people reading this who are shooting milliradians, or Mils, are going to have a much easier time with all this than the MOA people. I will definitely write about using MOA to dope the wind, but doing it in Mils is 10 times easier because Mils are Base 10. If you have not realized it by now, I hate MOA and think it should be retired, or at least left to die at the feet of the F-Class or benchrest crowd. If you are not shooting Palma with iron sights or some other type of NRA Paper event where the targets are calibrated in MOA, you need to immediately switch to Mils. Just take your MOA data, divide it by 3.43 and convert it all to Mils and enjoy life.

The BC Method of Doping the Wind

Why have G1 numbers lasted so long, if G7 has been around since the 1940s, you ask? Because the numbers in the G1 ballistic coefficient (BC) have value. That first number in the G1 BC is your wind speed.

Most examples of wind drift are demonstrated using a 10-mph base wind from 90 degrees. This is pretty common and yet has no value to us whatsoever. Sure, we can divide up the number 10 very easily, ask the guys using Mils, but for a point of reference, it's just a random number. How about we calculate the actual miles per hour your rifle lines itself up with organically? That number is based off the bullet you are shooting. The bullet has a published ballistic coefficient based on its average performance. We use this number to choose a bullet, the higher the ballistic coefficient, the better the bullet should perform downrange. Now understand, ballistic coefficient numbers are in part, muzzle-velocity dependent. We have to look at a combination of the number as compared to the velocity in which it was pushed.

Using MRADs (Mils), we can line up the drift column of wind to .1 increments per every 100 yards. This makes doping the wind much easier because you have an actual value to start with. The number is not a guess, but a verified piece of information being applied to the shot we are taking. The idea here is to simply count, and not do the long-hand math of the past. We don't need software to inform us, we simply determine the bullet's mile per hour base wind and add it to the conditions.

The drift column for every rifle will look like this:

100 = .1 Mils
200 = .2 Mils
300 = .3 Mils
400 = .4 Mils
500 = .5 Mils
600 = .6 Mils

We are going to stop there because after 600 yards specific calibers will begin to deviate in a small way. The faster and flatter your rifle shoots, the farther out this chart will line up.

Based on the first number of your G1 BC, this is the answer. We just need to solve that wind-speed question.

Say I am shooting a .308, 175-grain SMK going 2,650 fps. The advertised ballistic coefficient for this bullet is .505, but most use a corrected value of .485 to .496. If we look at the first number that is a 4, giving me a 4-mph base value. If we want to get hyper accurate, we can say we have a 4.8 or 4.9 wind speed, but 4 works well and most targets can absorb the rounding error.

What this tells me is, I have a 4-mph rifle. Moving forward, I want to work in multiples of 4 mph and not 10 mph.

A key element in shooting is communication. We say in the Marines: Shoot, Move, Communicate. Part of our job is simply to communication between shooters. Picture this scenario:

I am at a PRS event, step up to a stage and do quite well, exaggerate and say I hit nine out of 10 targets. In this case, I am shooting a 6.5CM with 130-grain PRIME Ammunition. As I walk back to my gear, a shooter on deck asks me my wind call. I tell him, "I held .7 Mils," and continue on my merry way. That shooter starts his run using my wind call of .7 Mils and misses the target every time. As he wanders off the line, he is muttering how I lied to him. No, I didn't lie, I was just using a different bullet and caliber than he was. What I should have said to him was, "I doped the shot using an 8-mph wind." The wind speed will translate to every rifle, but my wind hold is subject to my system.

The BC method of doping the wind works, and it does so the first time. Reading online questions about the wind, I often see the response:

"Grab a case of ammo, and go shoot in the wind, that will learn ya."

Yes, shooting up a case of ammo with a focus on what the wind is doing will teach you something. What, I am not sure. Probably just reinforce a lot of bad habits. But understanding your rifle system's miles per hour is very straight forward.

Before you even hit the range, you have a plan and answer. We have taken most of the guesswork out this, so it's not voodoo, it's sci-

Emil Praslick, of the U.S. Army Marksmanship Unit (AMU), is a true professional wind caller behind the spotter. Yes, it takes years of experience, but you can learn faster today than in the past.

ence. At this point, I just need to know my wind brackets then do simple addition in my head.

At 600 yards, with a 4-mph wind is the first bracket, so that means a .6-Mil hold. If the wind speed is 12 mph, I am in bracket 2, so the wind hold is 1.2 Mils. If the wind increases to 18 mph, I am in bracket 3, so I am needing a 1.8-Mil hold. Because this is using one-tenth Mil increments, we can estimate other speeds and be within a one-tenth again. An 8-mph wind is a .7 to .8 hold; both will get the job done. We can nudge it one-tenth, or just add .2 Mils to our 6-mph hold, as 8 is 2 miles per hour faster, either will work.

Engaging an 8-mph wind with a .308 rifle at a 400-yard target, my first thought WTF, is dial on .8 Mils for my first shot.

We talk to a lot of really accomplished competition shooters, and you'd be surprised to hear their wind-hold methods.

Bob: *"What are you doping the wind at?"*

Frank: *"Edge of plate. Spot my hit or miss and adjust.*

You'll get more edge, or plate, holds than any other value, regardless of what the actual conditions are doing. Instead, try doping the wind with an actual value. That is what we use the Kestrel Weather Meter for, confirming the wind speed.

Target Error Budget

Wind is dynamic. We have to be vigilant to stay on top of it. It's why we ask you to register the average wind speed, along with the gusts and the lulls over a two-minute period. We want to understand how the wind is flowing. Wind does not flow in a straight line, it's not consistent through the flight path of the bullet, it changes. Using the target size, we can look at the average, and where a gust or lull might fall on it.

Looking at the size of the target, we can overlay these estimates onto the steel. Most plates will be about .5 to .8 mils in width. If we have a base speed of 4 mph with gusts up to 6 mph, the plate will absorb both of those values. We can adjust the .4 hold on one side of the plate and place the .6 hold on the other side of the plate. We are then bracketing the target to absorb any error in reading the conditions to the target.

In our classes, and I have to admit I stole this Emil Praslick of the U.S. Army Marksmanship Unit (AMU), we try to keep the students on the "pro" side of the target. The downwind side is our pro side, with the upwind side being the amateur side. Cut the target in half and look at the wind direction. Most new shooters underestimate the wind. Experienced guys call wind on the pro side. With this method, we see a majority of the class hitting on the pro side every time, and it's a great feeling.

I wish this was harder to write about, but it's not. You wind call is nothing more than the following, based off the first number of your G1 BC:

100 = .1 Mils
200 = .2 Mils
300 = .3 Mils
400 = .4 Mils
500 = .5 Mils
600 = .6 Mils

This value will change by 1 mph per every 4,000 feet of density altitude you move. So here in Colorado, I have a 5-mph rifle, the same system will be a 4-mph rifle in Florida. It easily travels with you and adjusts on the fly. Roughly 200 fps of muzzle velocity changes will have a similar effect.

We recommend once your ballistic calculator has been properly set up and trued, you turn to the wind and test this using a full value. Caveat, of course, is to make sure the additional drifts are turned off as they will corrupt this information. We just want the pure wind call versus one that includes the flourishes. Pull up the HUD in your software, dial the wind to match the first number of your G1 BC and confirm it is .6 at 600

yards. After that you can be secure in the fact your wind will be correct in the App.

"X-mph Gun" Rules

Standard Elevation is 2,000 feet above sea level (ASL).

Standard Velocity is 2,800 fps.

For every 200-fps increase, your mph increases by 1 mph.

For every 4,000 feet of increase in elevation, your mph increases by 1 mph.

To determine your "base" mph, multiply your G1 BC x 10.

Example: G1 BC of a 175-grain SMK equals 0.485 (Litz) x 10 equals 4.85 mph.

Now 4.8 mph is correct for 2,800 fps at 2,000 feet ASL.

Now, for 2,950 fps at 1,000 feet ASL.

Example: 150 fps increase, 200 fps jump per 1 mph, equals three-quarter mph increase.

1,000-foot decrease, 4,000-foot jump per 1 mph, equals one-quarter mph decrease.

Adding it all together we get:

4.85 mph plus three-quarter mph minus one-quarter mph equals 5.35 mph

You then can choose to round to 5 mph for fast and easy numbers.

Now the standard numbers for any given mph range are:

100 yards = 0.1 Mils
200 yards = 0.2 Mils
300 yards = 0.3 Mils
400 yards = 0.4 Mils
500 yards = 0.5 Mils
600 yards = 0.6 Mils

For many modern calibers you can extend this out to 700 yards, but 600 is standard value across the board.

MOA Variation on Wind Math

I really hate to write about the minute of angle (MOA) wind strategy because there really is nothing intuitive about it. We worked pretty hard to try and simplify this method as well, and to be perfectly honest, it's a bit all over the place. We have stumbled upon various methods that will work, but in my mind, they require more effort than any Mil version of the math. Fractions just suck. They don't work as well as Base 10.

To start out, we have the British Method, which goes back a lot of years. The British Method is another one of these caliber- and bullet-specific formulas where everyone just ignores the limitations. Even the USMC long-hand math formula you can find written in every copy of a data book is caliber-specific. The funny part is the constants. We use a caliber-specific constant then when we need to change it, the math says we have to know the hold to solve for X. Well, if I knew the hold, I would have used it.

The British Method is based off a full value wind at 10 mph making it a bit easier to adjust the wind value when it is not exactly 10 mph.

So then using 10 mph as our base wind, you use the following shortcut. Our base wind speed in this case equals 1 MOA per 100 yards.

Here is an example of the British Method in practice.

Range 600, velocity 2-3mph =1.5 MOA
Range 600, velocity 5 mph = 3 MOA
Range 600, velocity 10mph = 6 MOA
Range 600, velocity 20 mph = 12 MOA

The baselines for the wind are as follows:

2-3 mph = Light Winds
5 mph = Medium Winds
10 mph = Base Wind
20 mph = Heavy Winds

To convert any MOA-based solutions to Mils, you can divide your MOA answer by 3.43. This is the correct conversion factor when going from MOA to Mils or back. I write this because I want you to sell your MOA-based scope and buy an MRAD version. Convert your data and be a happier shooter.

Sniper's Hide Forum Method

As I noted, we put the call out to the Sniper's Hide forum members to fix the math with MOA. We received at least three variations on the formula to simplify the MOA wind calls. None of them are that simple, but they will work. Even in writing this down, I don't find it very intuitive at all, so why am I including it? Well, to demonstrate to everyone that Mils are easier, of course.

MOA Wind for Base Wind Value equals (50 percent Target Distance)/100.

Base Wind Calculator:
- Add your G1 and G7 BCs together
- Example: 140-grain ELD equals .587 plus .301 equals .888
- Move decimal right one place (.888 equals 8.8 mph base)
- Correct for altitude by subtracting/adding .5 mph per 1,000-foot change away from 2,500 feet.
- Example altitude corrections: 0 feet equals minus 1.25 mph; 500 feet equals minus 1 mph; 1,000 feet equals minus .75 mph; 4,500 feet equals plus 1 mph; 5,500 feet equals plus 1.5 mph.

In other words, take half the distance and move decimal left twice. This is just like converting IPHY or SMOA corrections.

Example: 800-yard target equals (800/2) equals 400/100 equals 4 MOA wind hold for a base wind.

Example: 140-grain ELD at 1,000 feet equals 8.05 mph base wind

400 yards equals 2 MOA per 8 mph (AB says 1.8 MOA)

600 equals 3 MOA per 8 mph (AB says 2.85 MOA)

900 equals 4.5 MOA per 8 mph (AB says 4.7 MOA)

Now for crosswind constants:

Full Value = 1
Three-Quarter Value = 0.9
One-Half Value = 0.7
One-Quarter Value = 0.4

For another example, if we have a 12 mph, one-quarter value wind at 700 yards: 12 mph multiplied by 0.4 (one-quarter wind constant) equals 4.8 mph. So, you would use your 700-yard, 5-mph wind value hold of 0.7 Mils. (*The 0.2 mph will be impossible to account for because wind is a fluid, and nobody is capable of shooting a noticeable difference that the 0.2 mph could give in theory, so we ignore it.*)

Step 0:

Have students figure what "wind cheater"

value their gun/cartridge is.

Step 1:

Determine your base wind-hold number is at distance (5 mph): use 1/3 MOA for each 100 yards, and round to nearest .25 MOA and add an extra .25 MOA starting at 700 yards for rounding errors.

Step 2:

Figure out the "real wind factor" by dividing the observed wind value by the "wind cheater" factor (e.g. 10 mph wind (full value) divided by 5 mph wind cheater value equals 2.0 real wind factor).

Step 3:

Multiply the numbers from steps 1 and 2 (base wind-hold number by the real wind factor) to get your wind dope).

Example:

Step 0:

5 mph rifle

10-mph right quartering crosswind (3/4 value)

700-yard target

Step 1:

Determine your base wind-hold number using 5 mph. Use 1/3 MOA for each 100 yards and round to the nearest .25 MOA (*in other words, instead of .1, .2, .3 Mils at each 100 yards use 1/3 MOA and round to nearest .25 MOA*) giving us the following values:

200 yards = 2 times 1/3 = .75 MOA

300 yards = 3 times 1/3 = 1.0 MOA

400 yards = 4 times 1/3 = 1 and 1/3 or 1.25 MOA

500 yards = 5 times 1/3 = 1 and 2/3 or 1.75 MOA

600 yards = 6 times 1/3 = 2.0 MOA

700 yards = 7 times 1/3 = 2 and 1/3 or 2.25 MOA plus .25 MOA (extra) = 2.5 MOA

800 yards = 8 times 1/3 or 2 and 2/3 or 2.75 plus .25 MOA (extra) = 3.0 MOA

900 yards = 9 times 1/3 or 3 MOA plus .25 MOA (extra) = 3.25 MOA

1,000 yards = 10 times 1/3 or 3 and 1/3 MOA or 3.25 plus .25 = 3.5 MOA

Step 2:

Get your real wind factor: 10 mph times 3/4 equals 7.5 mph; 7.5 mph (observed wind) divid-

ed by 5 mph equals 1.5 real wind factor.

Step 3:

Multiply the 700-yard base number (2.5 MOA) by the real wind factor of 1.5 to get 3.75 MOA.

This shows what I wrote previously: When you dropped the base wind 1 mph to a "5," every single yard line lines up with .3 (1/3 MOA) multiplied by the yard line.

100 yards: 0.3 x 1 = 0.3 MOA

200 yards: 0.3 x 2 = 0.6 MOA

300 yards: 0.3 x 3 = 0.9 MOA

400 yards: 0.3 x 4 = 1.2 MOA

500 yards: 0.3 x 5 = 1.5 MOA

600 yards: 0.3 x 6 = 1.8 MOA

700 yards: 0.3 x 7 = 2.1 MOA

800 yards: 0.3 x 8 = 2.4 MOA

900 yards: 0.3 x 9 = 2.7 MOA

1,000 yards: 0.3 x 10 = 3 MOA

We can sum these different approaches up in the following ways:

1. Base wind equals 0.3 (1/3) MOA per 100 yards, equals 3 MOA at 1,000 yards
2. Base wind equals 0.5 (1/2) MOA per 100 yards, equals 5 MOA at 1,000 yards
3. Base wind equals 1 MOA at 500 and .25 MOA adjustments up and down per 100 yards, or, can be figured by two multiplied by first number of yard line divided by 10, so just move decimal to left one place.

There are a few different ways to get you to your base wind, but for the average shooter here with a ballistics program, it isn't any harder than just plugging in the wind and finding the one that gets you there.

The methods for finding base wind to be considered:

Method for number 1 above: First number of G1 BC minus 1 mph seems to work.

Method for number 2 above: First number of G1 BC plus 50 percent, or first number of entire G7 BC multiplied by three.

Method for number 2 above (alternate): G1 plus G7 divided by 100 at 2,500 feet ASL.

Method for number 3 above: First number of G7 BC plus 1 mph.

100 = 0.5 MOA

200 = 1.0 MOA

300 = 1.5 MOA

Students in a precision rifle class held in Colorado dope the wind on the line. The author sees an average of 12- to 18-mph winds in his classes. Students learn to shoot in the wind; not to stop and wait for it to slow down.

400 = 2.0 MOA
500 = 2.5 MOA
600 = 3.0 MOA
700 = 3.5 MOA

That is a ton of a math and none of it lines up as easy as the BC method using Mils. I hate to sound like a broken record, but Mils are just easier. It's straight forward. We just count, and the math is no more complex than adding two plus two equals four.

Most will default to the British method, or use the USMC formula, ahead of time with Excel and make a chart you can reference. I think if I was an MOA shooter needing to dope the wind, I would put extra effort into my ballistics calculator. I would try to find the mph wind speed that gives the best solution with a pattern I can follow.

Even today in classes with students shooting MOA rifles, we do everything in Mils and then just translate it to MOA for them. We are doing basic conversions in our heads and passing along the corrected information. But we start with Mils first, and begrudgingly speak in MOA after.

The Art Department

Once we get past the muzzle, everything else downrange is the art department. I call it the art department because it is subjective; no two people read the conditions downrange the same

way. Let's look at the elements for reading the wind downrange and how these elements will affect our shot.

Wind Midrange

We have already noted that wind across the entire flight of the bullet matters. Each cause has an effect. We need to account for as many of these as physically possible. Once you move beyond the shooter, everything gets much harder, as we can no longer consistently estimate the wind speed and even direction down to that 1-mph threshold we are looking for.

The more experience you get, the farther downrange you can successfully estimate

your calls.

Looking at the midrange wind, this is where a lot of high-power shooters turn for information. With a square range situation there are less obstacles to deal with, and many of these shooters will stick to a single range, or only a handful of ranges. They learn to account for any hiccups in the terrain that their particular range might have. It's their home-field advantage that helps with their success. Calling wind midrange works for this particular style of shooting. Generally, they are not dealing with unpredictable scenarios; it's pretty consistent how wind blows across a square range. There is, however, one important element to midrange wind we want to look at and that is max ordinate.

Robert Brantley, at the King of 2 Mile event, where the wind was determined off the clock. They had a plan going into the final stages and executed it perfectly.

Max Ordinate

Maximum ordinate is the highest point the trajectory reaches between the muzzle of the weapon and the target. Why is this important? Well, because of wind gradients. We want to know how high above the line of sight the bullet is traveling so we can consider the increase in wind speed the bullet will experience. Basically, as the vertical height increases, the horizontal wind speed will increase due to less friction from the ground. The higher the bullet is above the ground, the more wind velocity the bullet will be subjected to.

In the past, people rationalized the changes to the slowing of the bullet. However, we know the bullet is not going "that slow" to be overly affected. Yes, it is going slower, but it is still supersonic, and the ballistic coefficient is giving

A target at 4,000 yards as seen through the author's spotter. The wind was read using the mirage as it was focused on at different distances. Max Ordinate was 1,500 feet above the line of sight.

Using weighted wind flags, the author can get a rough estimate of the windspeed on his range. These are golfing flags he uses to determine wind speed.

an overall average, which accounts for this slowing. What actually happens is the bullet is subjected to higher wind speeds, which effect the shot. In some cases, the changes can be quite significant.

Locating midrange for your shot is quite simple. Most people use the halfway plus 10 percent solution to establish where max ordinate will be. After finding out where max ord will be for your shot, you can then subtract the Mil reading for the shot distance, from the Mil reading for the max ord range and that difference above the line of sight is where the bullet will be flying.

A 1,000-yard dope equals 11.2 MRAD minus 3.9 MRAD (550) equals 7.3 MRAD.

Looking at this in the reticle, you can begin to see where your bullet is actually flying for the shot being made. Well above the ground.

Now a midrange call will work very well for a

Competitors at the Sniper's Hide Cup have to determine the wind in a variety of conditions where the indicators are not always in the correct position. Terrain will move the wind in strange ways.

shooter working inside 600 meters. Why? Because the height of the bullet is not enough to get effected by max ordinate. Extend that same shot out beyond 600, 800 even 1,000 meters and max ordinate becomes a factor that a midrange call might not be able to account for.

Midrange calls are a very good average; you can look at them like the Rule of Thumb formulas. They will give you a single place to look and one number that might not be off enough to miss the target. Using a ballistic computer with

multiple winds enabled, the shooter can read the wind, note the value at midrange and then increase the wind speed with the understanding that the bullet will be affected by the wind-gradient increase. An example of this: You are making a 1,000-yard shot; the wind read at the shooter is 8 mph; and we know by observing the wind we have at least a 2-mph swing, so we dope the midrange call as 10 mph. That little increase in our call is often enough to fix any errors from attempting to estimate a downrange call by visually noted objects being moved by the wind alone.

Difficulties With a Midrange Call

Let's face it, wind is invisible. Sure, we can see what it is doing to objects downrange, but those objects are rarely calibrated. So, calling wind downrange presents a lot of trouble, especially to new and inexperienced shooters. You'll always hear old-timers talk about what they see

Wind flags can point in different directions due to localized effects caused by terrain. Here, one flag appears to point in a different direction than the rest.

on the ground, the grass moving, the mirage. We need to recognize all this, observing what is being done under the bullet. If the shot is going beyond 600 meters, odds are the bullet is a full wind gradient over that, so the value needs to be increased. By understanding this, we can dope the wind at the shooter, observe the mid-range direction and changes and then add to our initial call based on that information.

Another problem arises when looking for this call in the field. When the shot is going across a canyon or from ridgeline to ridgeline with a valley below, the shooter might be several hundred

Emil Praslick, AMU wind coach, is working the Applied Ballistics crew at the King of 2 Mile event. It was interesting to watch him call wind for the shooters in his squad.

feet above the valley floor, so we have nothing but empty space. Add to this the bullet is still above the line of sight and you won't have a mirage between the shooter and target, no change in air layers to cause it. So how do you use a midrange call in this case? Well, you can't. Which is why knowing about the wind gradients and increase in horizontal wind velocity is important. You can estimate a call based on this knowledge even though there is nothing to observe.

If the terrain and the shot give you information midrange, use it, but know what it will do when that information is missing.

Downrange Wind Observation Values

Here are some common wind speeds for downrange observations. People will key off trees, grass and dust, and over the years they have provided a rough value to these observations. However, understand these are highly subjective and not accurate to within our goal of 1 mph accuracy. I am including these references points only as a historical reference, as I don't think I have ever used these numbers to success. I would much rather have a Kestrel in my hand.

0 to 3 mph: Wind barely felt on face and smoke lightly drifts

3 to 5 mph: Wind felt lightly on the face and ears

5 to 8 mph: Trees and leaves in constant motion

8 to 12 mph: Raises dust and loose paper

12 to 15 mph: Small trees sway

15 to 20 mph: Small trees and bushes are in constant motion

20 to 25 mph: Large trees sway

As you can see, these are very coarse, rough estimates for the wind. I highly recommend you calibrate your own observations backed up with actual readings from a wind meter. We want to build a personal database by training our observations. You can even write down what you see or take a picture of a wind flag on your local range and place it in your data book. This is much easier to work with than the common observations above. A 5-mph swing is a pretty rough estimate.

Square Range Wind Flags

If you are shooting on a high-power range that employs the use of wind flags, you can estimate the speed based on the angle of a calibrated flag. The formula for this is simple:

Angle divided by four equals wind mph.

A flag that is blowing at a 60-degree angle from the flagpole would be a 15 mph. They also sell calibrated flags for golfing that would work well for a shooter on a firing line.

These are outdated practices to base your wind off the flag angle. But flags are helpful in calibrating your senses and matching them up to a Kestrel. It's giving you a great visual on the highs and lows, but nobody is going to calculate the flag angle to determine the wind speed. This is 1978 thinking, but here we are repeating it.

Mirage

Mirage is a naturally occurring optical phenomenon in which light rays are bent to produce a displaced image of distant objects. Hot air rising and cold air descending causes turbulence or waves. When looking at distant objects with a telescopic sight, we are then magnifying the effect. A shooter can use the mirage to his advantage or, in some cases, be hurt by the effects seen through the scope. Over magnifying it a bad. Power down.

Using mirage to determine wind direction and speed is a very good way to determine values. Mirage will be affected by the wind sooner than the objects around it because it is so much lighter, as the hot air is being carried up. If you have fishtailing winds that are constantly changing direction, the mirage is the best indicator to tell actual direction at the time of the shot. Changes that might be slower to observe are, generally speaking, real time with mirage.

Finding the mirage is simple: Focus on the target and then bring the focus back roughly one-quarter turn. That should give a view of the mirage in front of the target. Also look for straight lines.

The frequency of the mirage, how fast it is moving and how wide the waves are can help determine wind speed. Look at the mirage as fake water. It will flow just like water in a stream. This flow will first give you the direction of travel then the speed of the flow or frequency will give you the speed. We base the flow off a boil. In a no-wind condition, the mirage will appear to boil straight up out of the ground. The angle off center is the flow. The slower the wind, the less the angle and the wider the waves will be. The heavier the wind, the tighter the frequency and the more horizontal the flow will appear.

Like many things here in the art department, using the mirage to your advantage takes practice. You have to go out and actually shoot in it at the same time noting what you are seeing on target versus what you are seeing in your scope. The nice part about mirage is, especially with a scope using a side focus, the shooter can observe and shoot at the same time.

Disadvantages of Using Mirage

There are some disadvantages to using the mirage. First off, mirage is not always present. You need roughly a four-degree difference between the air layers. That usually means we are observing the mirage on the ground, where we have already established that we are not shooting straight across, but well over it. So, we have to be aware of max ord when looking at the mirage.

With heavy winds, mirage just lays over. Mirage is very effective under 10 mph, but over 10 mph it becomes difficult to discern 12 mph from 15 mph, as it just appears to lay over. It still helps with direction, but speed becomes less precise.

On hot days with a heavy inferior mirage, the target image will be carried away from its actual location. Picture a pencil in a glass of water. In a heavy mirage, the target image will be carried down wind and appear to shimmer and move. In order to focus on the actual target image, we first want to power down our optic. Remember, we are magnifying the phenomenon. So, if you are attempting to shoot on 25x, consider dropping that to 12x. You'll reduce the amount of potential error. Next, we want to look upwind. The target image will peak through the waves on this side and always return to its original location here. If the target is really dancing in the scope, look upwind on lower power to find its true location.

Don't get fixated on using the mirage. We want to use as much information as we can, so use it, but don't rely on just this one effect.

Without a boundary layer, the mirage will not be present. One tip to use is finding a straight line out at distance. The mirage will run across that line and it will help you. In the field, this might be difficult to find, but anything that gives you an indicator is a good thing. We want as much information as we can muster. Rocks are an excellent boundary layer; you can pick up mirage off them.

Snell's Law

Every so often we see a weird mirage effect that completely upends our thinking. It happened to me in Alaska recently, which made me take a hard look at the atmospheric conditions that cause the issue.

It was September 2018 and we are shooting during the Alaska Precision Rifle Class Reunion at the Upper Susitna Range near Talkeetna. A crisp morning at about 45 to 50 degrees, we had a few scattered clouds, but otherwise a perfect morning. I had my 2013 Accuracy International AX rifle chambered in .308 and I immediately went to 1,000 yards. Up in Alaska at this range there is next to no wind, maybe 3 mph, but, for sure, very little. I was impacting one round after another when everything started to change.

It was a rolling situation echoed down the entire firing line. Hit, hit, miss high, miss high, miss high. What the hell was going on? We went from hitting on command to missing .5 Mils high in a nanosecond. Come up .5 mils and you go right back to hitting the target again. This lasted about 30 minutes before the sun moved out of position and the air was sufficiently warmed up.

Enter Snell's Law.

"Snell's Law (also known as Snell-Descartes Law and the law of refraction) is a formula used to describe the relationship between the angles of incidence and refraction, when referring to light or other waves passing through a boundary between two different isotropic media, such as water, glass, or air."

That is the Wikipedia definition of the effect.

We see it when cold air gets trapped under warmer air as it inverts the way we naturally see light and objects around us. We are designed to see objects at distances through warm air under cold. When those layers invert, it changes how we perceive objects. I had a minor grasp on the concept until seeing a documentary on the Bermuda Triangle. In this part of the show they had videos of sailboats moving across the air, they appear to be hovering about 200 feet above the water. This was Snell's Law at work: Phantom ships floating over the water, not on it.

There is a calculator for figuring the Snell's Law effect, but I don't think we have the right information to use it. A lot of times, this is confused with lighting effects on the scope. But the reticle is not really three dimensional and it's covered by the scope tube. It's not like smudging your iron sights which are 3D objects where the sunlight can work on it. Iron sights are subject to changes in lighting, scopes not so much. If the changes affect our vision, they will affect the scope, but 3D objects have an additional layer of reflection.

If you see these changes, believe the bullet and adjust. I wish I could say how and when it will appear, but I cannot. We don't see it happen in Colorado, it's too dry. Where I tend to see it is in locations with a heavy water content in the air.

Wind at the Target

Wind at the target is good to help fine-tune your call because that is where our final focus is. When we shoot, we should put 100 percent of our attention to the sights on the target. This means our focus is downrange. It gives us the opportunity to favor any significant changes we see. We can then use our reticle to hold as we know it has the same value as dialing. If the shooter, prior to breaking the shot, observes something that indicates a big change in the wind, he should react using the target wind observations.

Wind at the target is a place a lot of people like to use because they feel the bullet is moving the slowest. However, like midrange, the bullet is not moving "that slow" and when we look at it from the point of time of flight, it has the shortest exposure to the effects of the wind. As we noted previously, the BC is an average accounting for the entire flight. Attempting to sidetrack that number by saying the bullet is moving slower goes against this average. Yes, you can band your BC in a ballistic computer, but most wind calls use one number. Only ballistic programs with multiple wind zones can narrow down varying speeds across the entire range. Everything else is a single number average, so there is no need to weight the call at the target.

We use several senses to determine the wind speed, direction and any changes. We see the effects it has on objects around us. We hear the increase and decrease in speed as well. We feel it on our body. All this helps us establish a call. When we understand wind across the entire bullet flight matters, we have to understand how we use these senses to adjust. Wind at

the target is the hardest to successfully call to within 1 mph, which is our target goal. Any less than that can mean a miss, and it's really not easy to determine this across a long distance. Wind does not move in a straight line, nor does it move at one constant speed. We want to hone our senses and build a personal database where we can recognize these changes in time in order to make an on-the-spot correction. Wind at the target is a very useful tool here.

Another good tip for the competitive shooters out there: Watch the splash of the bullet to see what the wind is doing to the dust. If you are on a line with other shooters you can hesitate and observe their splash to see if the wind is changing. I often use the splash observed to fine-tune my downrange wind call. That splash has value in not just correcting for the shot, but for determining wind speed and direction. In fact, Field Firing Solutions has timing utility to estimate the dust movement.

Effects of Terrain

Terrain can have as much effect on your shot, even more than just the wind alone. Wind is water, or you can say, wind can be visualized like water. Picture a river or stream, add in obstacles, rocks, branches, and it creates turbulence. Terrain features in the path of the wind will do the same thing. This turbulence can throw off your shot in an unexpected way.

Have you ever been on a high-power range with a row of flags every 100 yards? Have you ever noticed one flag blowing in the opposite direction of the rest? That is due to some terrain feature or obstacle redirecting the wind. There was not some odd spike in the prevailing winds going in the wrong direction. This was caused by a terrain feature, maybe a berm in or around that one flag. It's what we call a local phenomenon and it was isolated to that one spot. Unless the terrain feature was significant in size, and wind is very strong that day, in 95 percent of those cases you can ignore that one flag. Tip: Move to the center of the range.

Individual ranges have their quirks and there is no discounting that time and experience

Sniper's Hide field matches use natural terrain as the obstacles. Here the wind is truly the great equalizer because the rolling hills move it in all directions.

will help overcome the unpredictable changes presented. It's why the old-timers on that range can call it so successfully. Experience. Look for the root cause, something physical in the wind's path. The transition from woods to field can be the culprit; maybe a set of hills funneling the wind. When you recognize the effects of terrain, it helps refine your personal database to make the correct call.

Thermal Effects

Heating and cooling of the Earth's surface has a major effect on the wind. This heating and cooling also causes turbulent flow accounting for unpredictable changes in the wind patterns. We see the greatest influence of this in the early afternoon. We can see increased wind speeds and changing directions due to the area one might be operating in. We have a friction layer across the Earth that extends roughly 2,000 feet above the surface. Changes in terrain can affect the depth of this friction layer.

Mechanical Effects

Mechanical effects are when the winds encounter something solid, like terrain, trees and other obstacles, even buildings. This causes the wind to increase or decrease in speed and can cause them to change direction.

These two effects are very similar to each when viewed from the shooter's perspective. They have the same effect on the bullet, but are caused by two different things.

Winds ebb and flow, creating gusts. I picture the waves of the ocean crashing on a beach. Imagine that effect on the bullet as it passes through the wind. I use this information as a foundation for my holds. There is a high, low and average wind speed.

When I plug these numbers into my personal database or ballistic computer, I can then determine what effects my bullet will encounter. Just like the values at the shooter, midrange and at the target matter, so do the changes in speed experienced during the time of flight.

Wind Eddies From Both Mechanical and Thermal Effects

Every solid obstacle in the path of the wind will create an eddy, with its speed based on the size and composition of the solid object. They can change the wind's direction as well as effect whether they are horizontal or vertical in nature. A dust devil observed in an open field is an example of a vertical wind eddy.

Here is your visual representation on why a wind flag might be moving in a different direction relative to the rest of the flags on a square range. It's because of the eddy current created by solid objects in the wind's path.

Wind Gradients

As you rise above the Earth, the wind experiences an increase in speed. This is due to the reduced friction from the surface. Roughly every 14 feet, we have a new wind gradient. The problem with this gradient is, we can't see it. The mirage has to have a difference in temperature between layers in order to be visible, so once off the ground, the mirage will no longer help. Knowing the maximum ordinate of your bullet will help you determine where the bullet

Terrain is a giant obstacle out West. We have to determine more than one direction for the winds being split by canyons, on top of adding in elevation effects due to winds climbing the hills.

will be flying. We know at longer distances it's no longer moving across the ground, so using the mirage can cause an underestimation of the wind speed.

A good way to look at the gradient effect is to use the gusts you read on the ground. If the gusts are 2 mph, you can expect the increased effect from the gradient to be close to that value. A lot of times for a shot where I know the

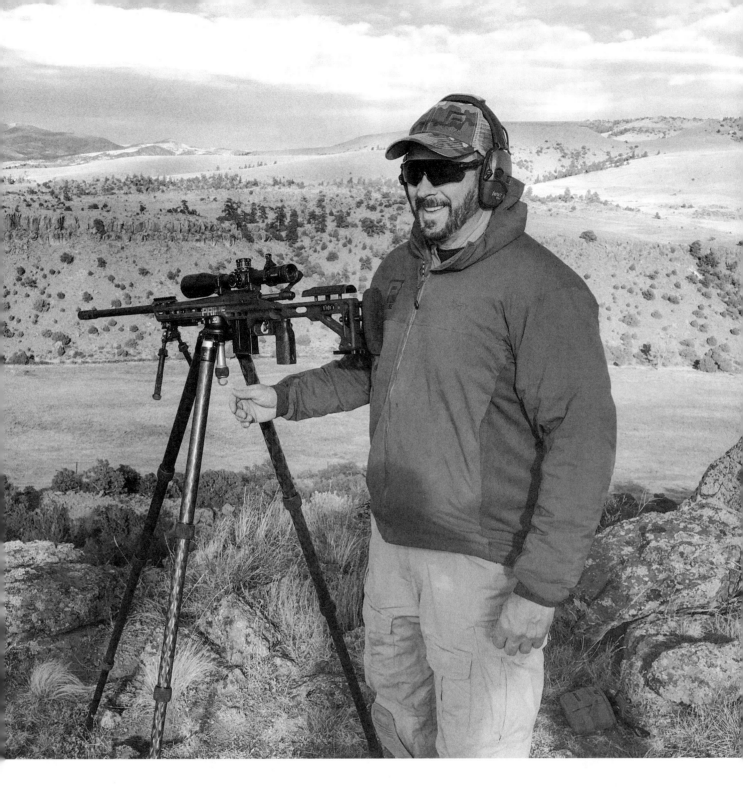

bullet will enter the next wind gradient, I increase my wind call to compensate.

The topography of the land controls the wind flow. Both regionally and locally. We are most concerned with the local variations caused by the terrain around us. The field shooter must have a good understanding of the obstacles in the flow pattern in order to account for them. Vegetation moving 1,000 yards away from the shooter's position might not give you an accurate representation of what the wind is doing, at the same time, neither will the wind pattern at the shooter. By observing, analyzing and recognizing the terrain features around us, we can make better estimates at distances.

The reference material used in this section was derived from wildfire material put out by groups like the Smokejumpers. For the men and

women who are tasked with combating wild-fires, wind is one of their biggest threats. Studying their material on the subject will help the field shooter become more proficient at recognizing the wind patterns at distance.

Having a Plan to Engage the Wind

When it comes down it, having a plan is the most important tip we can give you. Sure, we can easily shoot as much as possible in the wind and use trial and error to solve the problem. But this is a long and time-consuming method. The old hand at your local range used years of experience to figure it out. But we have the tools available today to get the job done sooner, and more effectively.

Before you head to the range, have a plan.

Trajectory μCard - Wind Only						
Range	6.0 mph		12.0 mph		18.0 mph	
(yd)	(mil)	(MOA)	(mil)	(MOA)	(mil)	(MOA)
100	0.1	0.3	0.2	0.7	0.3	1.0
200	0.2	0.7	0.4	1.3	0.6	2.0
300	0.3	1.0	0.6	2.1	0.9	3.1
350	0.4	1.2	0.7	2.5	1.1	3.7
400	0.4	1.4	0.8	2.9	1.2	4.3
450	0.5	1.6	0.9	3.3	1.4	4.9
500	0.5	1.8	1.1	3.7	1.6	5.5
525	0.6	1.9	1.1	3.9	1.7	5.8
550	0.6	2.1	1.2	4.1	1.8	6.2
575	0.6	2.2	1.3	4.3	1.9	6.5
600	0.7	2.3	1.3	4.6	2.0	6.8
625	0.7	2.4	1.4	4.8	2.1	7.2
650	0.7	2.5	1.5	5.0	2.2	7.5
675	0.8	2.6	1.5	5.3	2.3	7.9
700	0.8	2.8	1.6	5.5	2.4	8.3
725	0.8	2.9	1.7	5.7	2.5	8.6
750	0.9	3.0	1.7	6.0	2.6	9.0
775	0.9	3.1	1.8	6.3	2.7	9.4
800	0.9	3.3	1.9	6.5	2.8	9.8

Wind charts are an excellent way to reference the wind speeds measured with a Kestrel.

Some ranges have no wind indicators. It's important to use a weather meter to dope the wind speed as nothing on this range tells you the true story.

Prior Proper Planning Prevents Poor Performance

We have all heard this. I can't think of a clearer case where this statement is true. The more you do before you get the range, the more successful you will be.

Use the tools we have available, like software to determine what method you are going to use.

If you do plan on using a formula, do the math before you get on the range. If you intend to do long hand math on the firing line, you have already lost the race. Create a table designed around your bullet and muzzle velocity. Even if you will be using a handheld ballistic computer, input the values and save the drop tables before you arrive on the range. Don't get distracted by trying to shoot and diagnose the computer data at the same time.

Step One: Read the Wind at You

By starting off with a wind reading at the shooter, you develop a baseline for all calls. You can then take these same readings and apply them to your downrange observations. By doing this, you give those observations actual value. Don't believe you can accurately determine the wind speed 1,000 yards away by looking at the trees moving. All you can say is, the wind is blowing and whether it appears to be blowing faster or slower than the last time you looked. I recommend at least two full minutes of observation using a Kestrel or similar wind meter.

Step Two: Find the High, Low and Average Speed

During our observation of the wind meter, what we are looking for is an average. We want to know the high, which is the gusting value, the low, where it drops off to, and the average velocity.

The gusting value is your high. For example, if the gust is going to be 12 mph, we would note that value. When we see, feel or hear the wind speed increase we now have a number.

The low, is where it drops down to. Rarely does it go to absolute 0 mph, usually it's a pretty consistent number, like 8 mph, in this case. Here is where the call of 8 to 12 mph came from, people would note the entire swing. For us, we want to dope the wind to within 1 mph if at all possible. That is the goal.

As we observe the wind meter, an average number will appear, say 10 mph for this exercise. So, we know with the ebb and flow happening 10 mph will put us right in the middle. This is where we start off doping the wind.

Step Three: Assign a Hold Value to the Wind

This is the important part: We want to assign our hold to the values we have recorded. Here are our assigned values at 800 yards:

8 mph: 5.3 MOA or 1.5 Mils
10 mph: 6.6 MOA or 1.9 Mils
12 mph: 8 MOA or 2.3 Mils

Now we have a hold for the wind based on the actual speeds observed over the 2-minute period.

Holding vs. Dialing your Dope

Before we proceed, we have to answer a question. Do we hold, or do we dial for the wind? The answer is, there is no real answer. We have pros and cons for both methods. Holding is faster, more dynamic in nature and can be every bit as precise as dialing. The downside is people under pressure will sometimes hold the wrong direction. And when holding in combination with elevation, those unaccustomed to it will feel they are holding out in space. The latter is just a matter of practice, but not everyone is set up to invest that much time into the process.

Dialing brings us closer to the center of the reticle, gives us a clearer aiming point and takes the windage out of the equation. The downside is, it's slower and can be something left on when it needs to be removed. Shooters can also dial the wrong direction as with the reticle hold, but given time and opportunity has easier user interface to work with. With a second-focal plane (SFP) scope it is often necessary as the reticle is only accurate in value at one magnification.

In the field, as well as during tactical type matches, holding is much more common. We use first-focal plane scopes, so the values of the reticle are always correct, and it's much more dynamic like the situations where it is used. It allows for rapid transitions from target to target as well and is flexible with direction.

KD Shooters will dial more often because they are on a known distance range with targets employing scoring rings. They will dial their average and then based on their sighter rounds, will adjust the windage knob and then hold the small changes observed. Since the targets have scoring rings which equal an MOA value, they can simply use them to adjust with. Their scope is usually higher magnification and SFP so it's more intuitive to dial.

Holding is a skill set that requires practice; in the field it is one of the most valuable tools in the shooter's toolbox. As part of your prior proper planning, if you establish solid drops for your elevation, the only question becomes the wind. Then quarter the target using the wind hold with the elevation dialed on.

At ELR, or extended long range, distances, it is often important to use a combination of holds and dialing to keep the shooter in the center of the reticle. It would not be uncommon to find yourself at the edges of the reticle at extreme distances. So, dialing in the average and holding the gusts is a great way to stay centered up. The closer you can stay in the center of the reticle, the better your changes are of observing any adjustments you need to make with the shot. Naturally our eyes are drawn to defined intersections. It makes our brains more comfortable to be in the middle. As well, this is usually the sweet spot of the optic. Once I am starting past 3 Mils or close to 10 MOA, I want to be dialed in back to the middle.

Learn both, and don't be afraid to experiment.

Step Four: Understand the Holds

Now that you have established a value in Mils or MOA for the wind speeds recorded, you can easily see what the difference is. As you focus downrange, if you perceive any change off the average speed you can make the appropriate adjustment on the fly.

As an example, we have 1.9 Mils dialed on the rifle and we are holding center of the target. We know during the gusts we need to add .4 Mils to the hold in order to account for the 2 mph increase in wind speed. If the wind dies down as we are getting ready to fire, we can move in the opposite direction and reduce the hold to 1.5 Mils. Since we observed the wind never truly dies down to 0 mph, we can avoid the pitfall of holding too little. Before we start shooting, we have established the values and the correct holds. This will eliminate a lot of the trial and error previously used to learn wind reading.

At 800 yards according to our ballistic computer, the 2 mph changes, both increasing or decreasing, require a .4 Mil or a 1.4 MOA adjustment.

What you see or hear happening in terms of the wind is instantly given a value. So, if your

Spend two minutes determining your wind speed before calculating the high value, average value and low value.

final focus is at the target and you can see the changes taking place in the scope, this can be in the form of mirage or vegetation movement, you can make the correct adjustment in real time with an actual value.

Step Five: Stick to the Plan

New shooters often second-guess themselves. Using the tools available to us, the ballistic computer, and Kestrel, we can have confidence in the shot. It's important to stick to the plan established ahead of time. Don't second-guess yourself when practicing this. We understand for many people shooting is a recreational activity. However, we want to learn something and the only way to learn is to have a plan. By sticking to this plan, we can move to the next and final step.

Step Six: Record and Diagnose

Even with ballistic computers and iPhone apps, our data book is still our most important resource we have available. Better record keeping means better results. D.O.P.E. translates to Data On Previous Engagement. When we know what worked before, we can repeat that success when we see it again. If you never take notes, you have no way of improving. By starting off with a plan, and sticking to it, we have laid the groundwork for immediate improvement. It's no longer a question of what worked, we have all the information at our fingertips. You read the wind, assigned a value, and shot that value based on your personal observations. If you hit the target, you know why. If you missed the target, you can go back and look at what might have gone wrong. Did we miss a terrain feature, was it a fault in the fundamentals of marksmanship, was there an error without data given to the computer? It streamlines the process and simplifies the possible answers.

If we trued the computer and know our elevation is right, what are the reasons why our windage could be off?

How big was the target? If we are shooting at 600 yards on a .75 Mils (2.5 MOA) wide target, and the wind changes we predicted only give us a .3 Mils change from average to gusts, did we induce the mistake to take us off the plate? Use the target size to help diagnose where the error could be.

Remember this, in our data books we only want to record true statements. So, using a separate notebook to include our starting point, then transferring the correct information to our data book cuts down on the erroneous information. We can also print a page from JBM to take the range to use as our starting dope, then add in the verified data off that sheet to our data book. This will assist in truing the calculations at a later time.

Don't fight the software on the line. Focus on the fundamentals and understand it's about the process not the gadget.

Use the tools available to record and monitor the wind.

Believe the Bullet

No matter what we do to combat the wind, at the end of the day the bullet has the final say. It's always right, which is why we repeat: "believe the bullet."

You might have the perfect solution in your head. You can be absolutely convinced the ballistic computer is right. But nothing trumps the bullet. Once fired, we have no control over its flight path. At that point, it's all exterior ballistics. If you're straight back behind the rifle,

if you are following the bullet's path through recoil, and you're able to see the results of your shot, the bullet will give you 100 percent of the necessary information to hit the target. Even if you screwed up your fundamentals, the answer is, screw them up again and do what the bullet tells you. In short, believe the bullet.

This comes down to the fundamentals of marksmanship. They are the foundation on which everything in shooting is built. We tell people to eliminate the angles, get straight back behind the rifle and this will give the shooter

the ability to correct for themselves. In most cases, you won't need a spotter again.

The old idea that the spotter is the senior man and a necessary part of the sniper team is becoming outdated. Why, with such a small team, would you take 50 percent of the group out of action, when you can line up and correct for yourself?

How to do you put into practice this concept? Very easily, if you can start off with a range that is at least 400 yards in distance. The best case, your steel target will have a raised berm behind it to give you an indication of the bullet's strike in the form of splash. This will allow the shooter to see the strike through the rifle scope and then measure the offset and correct using the reticle.

The reticle is a calibrated ruler. If you use a scope that has matching adjustments, a Mil reticle with Mil-based turrets, you have the recipe for success. Don't fear MOA shooters; you can do the same thing with a MOA reticle and MOA turret.

Try this: Hold center on your target with no wind dialed or used, fire your first shot and see the result in your scope. Measure the distance with the reticle, and simply move the reticle that distance to put the strike in the center of the target. One-shot corrections become very easy.

With the wind coming from right to left, you can see the bullet impact or splash is 3 Mils to the left of the target. The next step after spotting the shot through the scope is to adjust and fire. In the field, this is the quickest and easiest way to correct. It's the same thing a spotter is telling you, only you can see it and adjust in real time. No spotter necessary. The reticle is a calibrated ruler that is valid at all ranges. Slide the main crosshair of the reticle into the wind and move it the observed 3 Mils in distance so that mark on the reticle where the splash was is in the center of the target and fire.

This can be accomplished with a MOA scope as well. In fact, you can do it with a duplex scope if you are able to superimpose the shot splash on to the target. The sub-tensions of the reticle just help us measure the distance more effectively.

This is also how you can accurately determine the wind with just one shot. If you know nothing else before the first shot is fired, after observing the impact like above, you have 100 percent of the data you need to dope the wind.

The Reticle is a Ruler

The reason we use scopes with reticles that have graduations, is to assist the shooter measure and adjust. These reticles are essentially calibrated rulers. They work at any distance thanks to the angular unit of measurements. Both Mils and

MOA are nothing more than angles. While many will talk about the linear value or the ability to range, the fact is, they are angles.

It will automatically account for the distance if you use the angle. In other words, 1 Mil is 1 Mil, doesn't matter if you are viewing this at 100 yards, 633 yards or 1,760 yards. If you see the distance from shot to impact is 1 Mil, the answer is 1 Mil. This holds true with a MOA reticle also. If you see the impact is 2 MOA from center, you dial 2 MOA or hold, the answer is the same.

Once we wrap our heads around this, adjusting for the wind using the reticle becomes much easier.

While technically correct, we should not use the often taught: 1 MOA equals 1.047 inches at 100 yards, 2.094 inches at 200 yards, 7.329 inches at 700 yards. Teaching this as anything more than reference material is doing a disservice to the shooter. It's an angle. We want to match the turret to the reticle and use the angle, thus eliminating the need to worry about the linear value. There is no conversion, it's WYSIWYG (what you see is what you get).

Take the shot, observe the impact, adjust and follow up with the correction in place. When you are done, record the correction necessary to hit the target under the conditions at the time. This is what establishes your DOPE, or data on previous engagement. So, your wind call is not in inches, but in your actual dope. It's much more efficient to say your dope is 1 MOA, instead of calling as 10 inches.

This is how we shoot and needs to be how we speak.

For the Mil Reticle with MOA Turret Group

I have mentioned several times, that for today's scope-buying public, we want to match our reticle to our turrets. However, there are still a lot of you out there using a Mil-type reticle and MOA turrets. This type of scope does require a conversion if you want to match what you see in the reticle to your turrets.

In order to convert your MOA or Mil adjustment to the other, you need to use 3.43. That is

The author uses a custom wind-chime-style target to help students understand their holds. Each colored target is .2 Mil wide, with a 1 Mil total. It helps them correct their misses.

the number, plain and simple.

If you have 12 MOA and want to know what that translates to Mils you take 12 divided 3.43 and you get 3.5 Mils. If you want to work in the other direction you would take 3.5 Mils and multiply by 3.43 and get 12 MOA.

Once in the field, we don't want to do any form of math or work with fractions. We want to simplify the process as much as possible. So, in the field, we would use 1 MOA per every .25 Mil observed.

.25 Mil seen in the reticle: Dial 1 MOA on the turret

.5 Mil seen in the reticle: Dial 2 MOA on the turret

.75 Mil seen in the reticle: Dial 3 MOA on the turret

1 Mil seen in the reticle: Dial 4 MOA on the turret.

We have rounded up the value to make it much easier to work with on the fly. It's another one of those Rules of Thumb that helps the shooter get by under field conditions.

It's much easier to break down the old-style Mil-dot reticle into quarters than to try and

figure out the tenths. With practice, you can do it, and it's important if you are going to range targets using the reticle. But for wind holds and calls, it's easier to use quarters.

This method will also help Mil shooters translate their information to an MOA shooter, and vice versa. If you are shooting with a friend who is using a method of adjustments different from yours, you can convert on the fly using these values for ease and simplicity.

Is one method superior than the other? Well, I think so, but that is a discussion for another day. It really depends on your shooting discipline to say which one is better. I have my opinion, others have theirs. For the tactical shooter, you will find more and more are using Mils so consider your needs before buying. At the end of the day, if you buy a scope with matching values you'll be that much ahead of the game.

Understand this, Mils are not metric only. You can use yards and inches just as easily as you can with a MOA scope. There is no difference as far as your dope is concerned. Saying you need 12 MOA at 500 yards is not easier than saying you need 3.5 Mils to hit the same target at 500 yards.

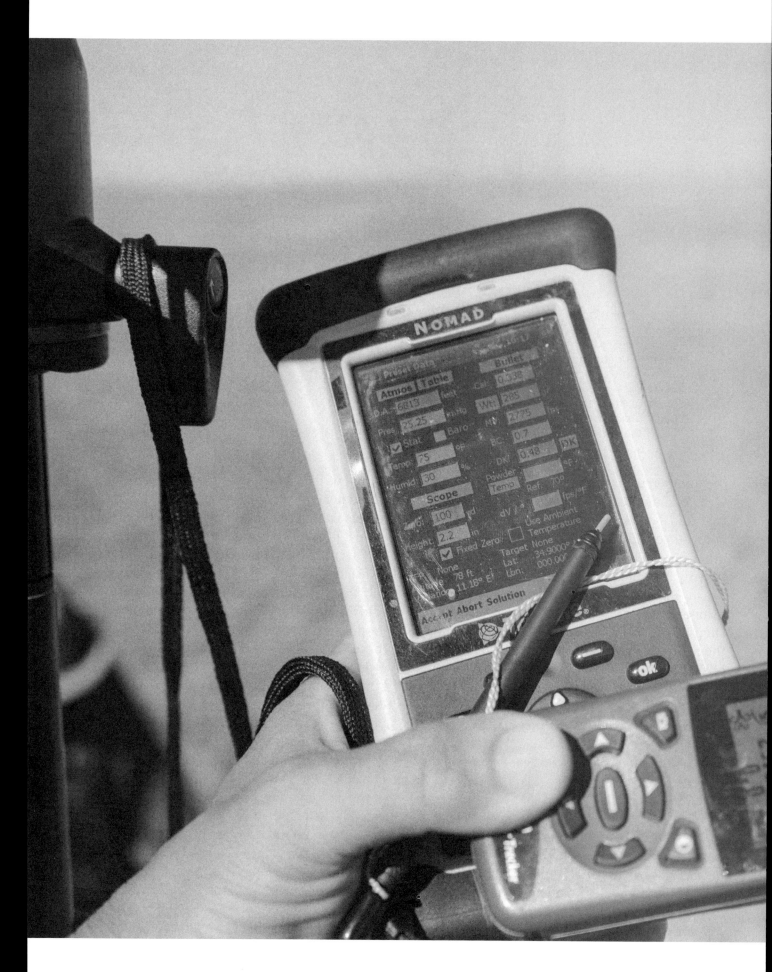

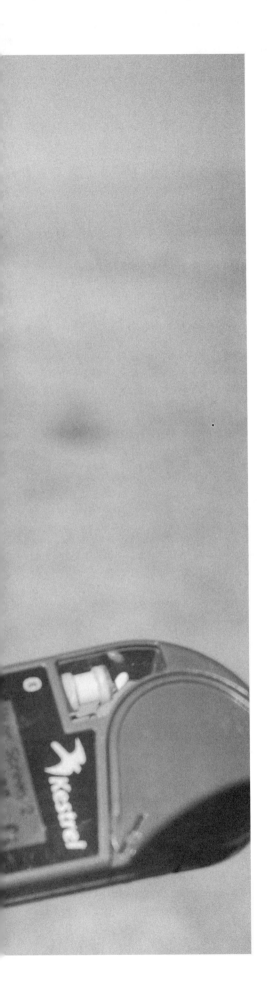

13

Ballistics Calculators

I have a love-hate relationship with ballistics calculators. I think they are an extremely valuable tool for the precision rifle shooter. Many of the modern changes we enjoy when shooting a precision rifle came because of the introduction to ballistics calculators. They allow us to visualize so much with our trajectory and data, creating the charts and graphs we have today that grew out of ballistics calculators.

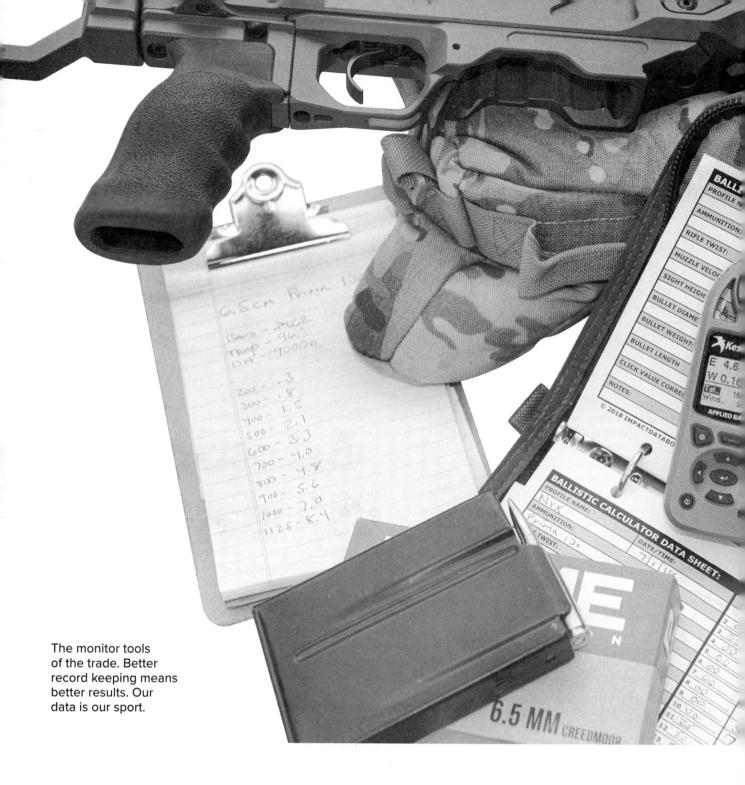

The monitor tools of the trade. Better record keeping means better results. Our data is our sport.

The part I hate is twofold.

First, I hate that some people want to bury their heads in their phones, hoping to align the rifle to the predicted solution. And second, I hate the anecdotal comments on how great they work for the uninitiated. Sure, some of their ranges go only to 400 yards, but they can be the loudest proponents of the use of software out there.

I was on the ground floor of their inception. When I worked at Rifles Only, we had a two-point connection to ballistics software. One of the first programs on the market was from Gerald Perry and it was called ExBal. This was a very good program and later it would be brand-ed by Nightforce as its software solution. Gerald Perry was a ballistician who lived close to Rifles Only in South Texas. He would often visit the

Back in the day, they used to tell you to grab a case of ammo and just go shoot in the wind. Instead, understand how and why the wind moves your bullet and you can save a lot of time and ammunition learning to address the wind.

range and talk ballistics with us.

The next program was Precision Workbench, or what is now known as Field Firing Solutions (FFS). FFS comes from Lex Talus, who is actually a lawyer named Blaine Fields. He was contributing member of Sniper's Hide and used Lindy Sisk of Rifles Only to help beta test and craft the program. Lindy is one of the smartest guys when it comes to the math behind precision rifle

shooting. He is a long-time instructor at Rifles Only and really has few equals in this space.

At the time, the military just started using the CheyTac A, B, C, ballistics software used for the .408 platform. It was in its infancy, and the computers needed to run it were quite expensive. Most of these programs ran off a Trimble Nomad, a big heavy Windows mobile device that is about the size of a brick.

TERRAPIN X

2114 yd
My measured distance

Wed Nov 14 11.20.03 2018

The 1-mile target on the author's range, with next to no wind indicators between him and the target. In this situation, the bullet is easily 45 feet above the line of sight, so watching the grass has very little value.

We also had the Horus system on the PalmPilot devices at Rifles Only. Jacob Bynum was the original instructor for the Horus system in the early years and Rifles Only was the key training facility for the system. The Horus system was easier to use, but the other programs were more robust and feature-rich. One of my favorite features of ExBal was the "shooter drift" dialog. Instead of trying to find a fake, flat-rate value for spin drift, Gerald recognized there was Shooter Drift included in the solution. You would find the best day possible, go to 600 yards and shoot a no-wind group. The offset from center left or right became your shooter drift offset to count-

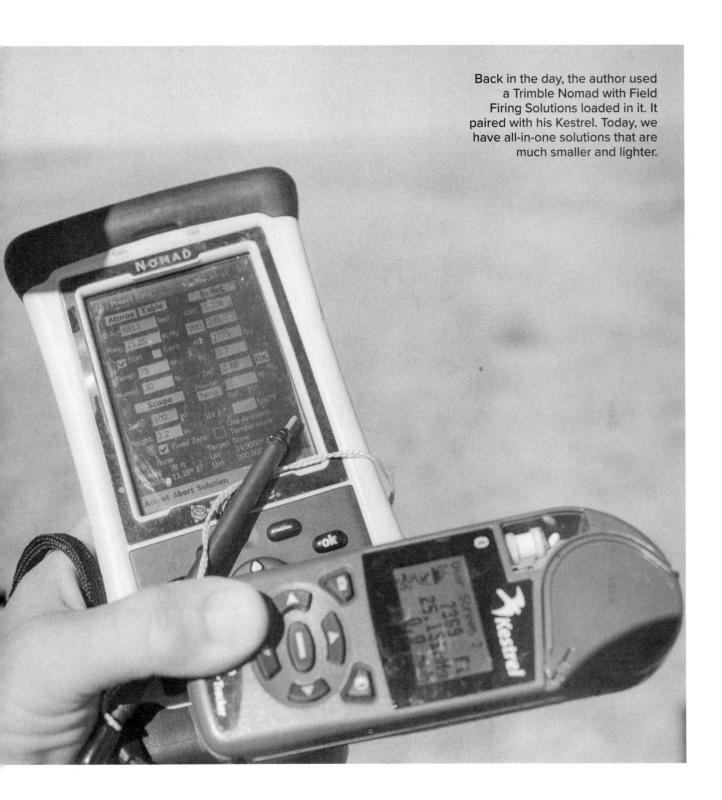

Back in the day, the author used a Trimble Nomad with Field Firing Solutions loaded in it. It paired with his Kestrel. Today, we have all-in-one solutions that are much smaller and lighter.

er the influence the shooter put into the shot. This was a pretty neat feature and a much more honest representation of how we shoot.

About this time, Sniper's Hide was getting even more popular on the Internet. One day I noticed a ballistic software company from Argentina was using my images off the site and I contacted them. This was first introduction to Patagonia Ballistics and Gus Ruiz. He is a ballistician from South America who created Loadbase, which became ColdBore 1.0, which is also the engine behind Desert Tech's TRASOL.

These gentlemen were the early pioneers of commercially available ballistics software. They

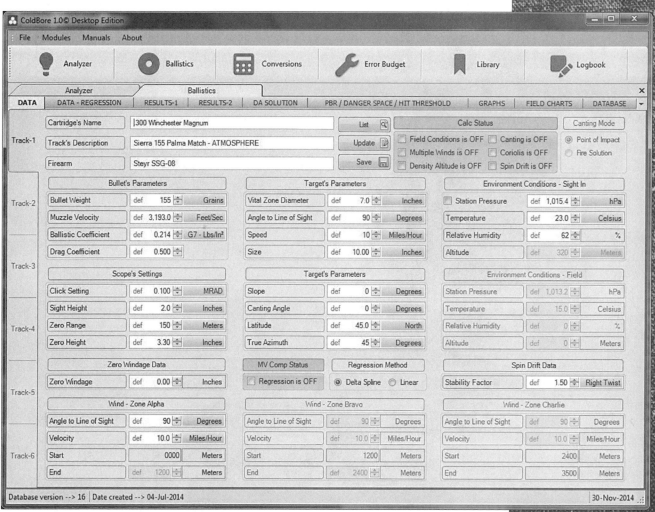

Ballistics computers share a lot of similar inputs. However, the engine that drives them can be different based on the understanding of the methods used. ColdBore uses a modified point-mass method that goes beyond most apps.

harnessed Windows mobile devices which ran the software. I continue to use both Field Firing Solutions and ColdBore today and will often find myself defaulting back to the older programs instead of opening up my phone.

History aside, ballistics calculators are powerful tools when used correctly. They crunch the numbers and do all of the long-hand math

instantaneously, giving the user an actionable call immediately, in the palm of your hand.

You can find a ballistics computer almost everywhere. There are several apps available for your iPhones, Androids as well for Windows-based PDAs. One of the better ballistics calculators is online for free. JBM Ballistics has an excellent ballistics engine and will allow you

Many products put shooters' heads into their phones. We want to use technology in a way that does not compromise our shooting mindset.

to print drift and drop charts for any number of bullets found in its extensive ballistics library. Even if one is not there, you can add it manually. I use JBM more than any other program on my desktop. I can immediately check data thanks to this giant library of information.

I hate the fact that people will jump into their phone before understanding their rifle or the fundamentals, but they are extremely effective when used correctly. Remember with any software, Garbage In, means Garbage Out. If you are winging the inputs, you cannot expect 1-MOA accuracy out of the software. I like to say in class, they are tools, not toys. Just because they exist on our phones does not make them a game.

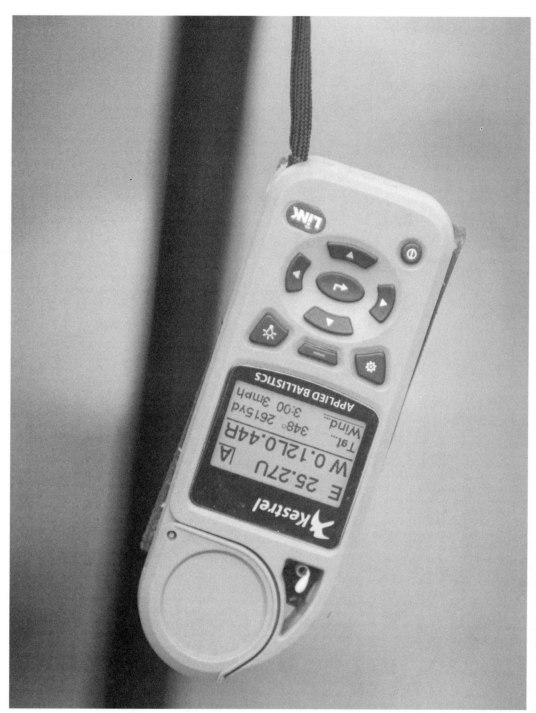

A single-device solution, like a Kestrel with Applied Ballistics installed, can be a very useful tool. Don't chase all the software. Learn one and stick with it. Constantly having to learn a new device can be confusing.

Much of the underlying software used to predict a solution comes from the military. Recently, Hornady released a new app called 4DOF. The ballistic program with four degrees of freedom used to power this app was written in 1966. We have a couple of different models, 3DOF, 4DOF and 6DOF. You will find them under the Point Mass formulas, and the 4DOF can also be found under Modified Point Mass. None of it is new,

only the UI and method of delivery has changed. We have taken the artillery model and scaled it down for the precision rifle shooter.

My favorite conundrum with an app is when shooters will download more than one. Prior to sending any rounds downrange, they are working the apps in order to see what the predictions look like. Immediately when they fire up the second program and repeat the inputs, they are on the Internet screaming about the differences between the two. Of course, if there are differences, we have authors adding in their own interpretations of the formulas. We read about every kind of phenomenon out there, and the writers of the software want to address them, but the software is incapable of doing so correctly. This means flat rates and shortcuts to fill in the missing blanks.

Trust me when I report, none of the ballisticians we read about agree with each other. There are always varying levels of disagreement between the camps. McCoy is the standard, Pejsa contradicts, while Litz promotes, Boatright models. It's all very disjointed, but in a way the end-user benefits. If these guys agreed on everything, life would be extremely boring.

Key Inputs for Ballistics Calculators

Many of the ballistics calculators out there share a common interface. If you can learn to use one effectively you are well on your way to learning the others. Understand some are feature-rich and some are more basic, but they all require similar input data. The key pieces of data you need to start are:

- Bullet Weight
- Bullet's Ballistic Coefficient
- Muzzle Velocity
- Atmospheric Data
- Sight Height/Scope Over Bore
- Twist Rate

Today, many programs require bullet length, azimuth and latitude to account for drifts. They use the twist rate and bullet length to account for spin drift, and latitude and azimuth to target for Coriolis. As noted earlier, I turn these off, as they are incorrect.

The biggest error in data inputs I see comes in the shape of the form factors. Most software gives you the option to use G1 or G7 and people having read on the Internet they need to use G7 will change the form factor without updating the ballistic coefficient value to correctly model the new form factor. Believe me, I would not steer you wrong here. It does not matter if you use G1 or G7, this should not matter in the least unless

the program was written to add value to one over the other. Sure, if you are using Applied Ballistics, I would recommend you default to G7 first as he puts value on it over G1, but any other programs, which ever one works for you, works. As a side note, Field Firing Solutions, one of the most often used programs for shooting extended ranges, does not even work with G7. You cannot use G7 or those values as the program, like Patagonia Ballistics, is not G-dependent.

G-dependence, as in saying G7 is better than G1, is beginning to die off. Going back to Hornady, because its 4DOF app uses Doppler radar models, it uses an Axial Form Factor in place of a G-Curve. There is no BC, which means if a couple of programs can be written without the emphasis on a certain form factor, the others can be written that way, too. I predict BCs will be used as historical data in about 10 years. We will move completely away from their use.

I use G1 80 percent of the time when inputting my data. I don't care, and personally I have a lot of G1 numbers memorized so they work for me. Don't let the marketing hype fool you, the program can work equally effectively with either model.

I think I own pretty much every piece of software out there. While I try to default to the Pejsa-based models, I have no issue using a Kestrel with Applied Ballistics in it. The key to any software is how you true it up. We want to universally true it and not just true it to one location. Some are similar, but this can be different depending on the program.

Truing Your Software

There are a million ways to skin this cat, and most of them will work. What we have found is, universally, this method allows us to stay consistent among the programs and work using practical ranges. Some truing methods require shooting beyond transonic ranges. For magnums and sporting 6.5 calibers, this could mean 1,400 to 1,600 yards away. Yes, my personal range goes every 100 yards to a mile, but not everyone has access to unlimited distance.

Chronographing, in recent years, has become a love-hate endeavor. Because software will change the number to true, we find using drop is more desirable. But we still want a chronograph in our toolbox, as there are other values to the information beyond software.

We start at 600 yards; this has been tried and tested many times over. We started out at 300 yards, then moved to 800 yards, finally landing on 600 yards as a happy medium. It's here we can use a similar method and it will work pretty darn well.

In the past, we said chronograph your rifle first. In a class of 10 or more students this is a bit time consuming. After we chronographed everyone, we'd insert the information into the software and immediately it would change the number. So today, we skip the chronograph and go straight to steel.

I want to record my 600-yard drop and make

sure I have point of aim, to point of impact on target. We watermark the plate and verify the ranges. With this information we can start to true the computer. I will repeat this a couple times, so bear with me: We cannot true the rifle to the software, we have to true the software to the rifle.

With all the initial inputs added, you should have a base prediction, and odds are it does not match. To align the 600-yard drop to the computer you simply adjust the muzzle velocity up or down until it does. Using 25 fps, plus or minus, should move the solution by .1 Mil. I get that you spent a bunch of money on your

The author uses custom-made targets to true his software. The belt on this IPSC target is .2 Mils wide at 800 yards. Hitting point of aim, point of impact takes the guessing out of the math.

chronograph and now I am saying the data you collected is not being used. Yes, the software will change it.

Once the data at 600 yards is lined up using your muzzle velocity, you can fine-tune it at distance. Understand muzzle velocity in your program changes everything, so now that we have the short ranges trued up, we have to adjust the longer ranges. We do that with BC. Any variation at 800 to 1,000 yards will be tweaked with a simple BC change.

Ballistic coefficients are dynamic; they are like a fingerprint to your rifle system. Yes, we use an average value and that works really well. But we can and should tweak this value using software to align it to our rifle system.

We start off by changing the middle number of the ballistic coefficient. We have three numbers to work with, adjusting the middle number first is the best starting point. When it comes to this adjustment, a little will go a long way. Adjust the numbers in small doses.

These two changes should be enough to work across the board. However, we have a weak link in our system that needs to be addressed. Our scopes are one of the biggest potentials for error when it comes to software. Scopes are mechanical devices and subject to error. We have to do a tall-target test, or tracking test, in order to confirm the adjustments. Several companies, including Sniper's Hide, sell tall targets for testing tracking on our optics. In our PR-2 classes in Alaska, we test every student's scope for tracking and record the information, building a database. We have found a majority of scopes that cost less than $2,000 have at least a 1.5- to 2.5-percent error in movement. That might not be a lot, but consider the spin-drift discussion online. If they are getting so worked up over 2 percent of drift, what does a 2-percent tracking error do?

Testing your scope using a tall-target test it is very easy. I built a fixture to hold the scopes in place. The fixture weighs 30 pounds, so when

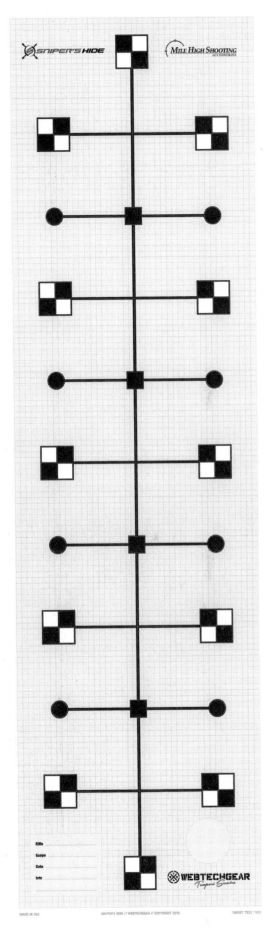

Sniper's Hide sells a tall target to test scope tracking. It's one of the biggest errors the author sees in his system, next to shooter error.

Always read the manual for new software programs and learn to set them up properly. Just because they exist on our phones does not make them games.

you adjust the scope nothing moves. You can use a tall target or just mount a 4-foot level at 100 yards on the target and test that way. The level will allow you to do the same test without a purpose-built test target.

Placing the reticle at the top of the level, you dial your elevation up, which will move the scope down, and you can measure the move-

ment. Both Field Firing Solutions and ColdBore have utilities for testing scopes. Most will do the work manually and calculate the movement with some simple math. For ease, I know 13.3 Mils is the right answer for traveling a 4 feet level from top to bottom.

Testing a scope is simple, but often overlooked. We want to believe because we spent

the most money we could afford, the product is spot-on. But, the reality is, the odds of it being perfect are against you. Suck it up and test your scope.

Doping the wind to within 1 mph across the entire path of the bullet to the target is the goal of the precision rifle shooter. This is a lot harder than it sounds. From a practical standpoint, it's not possible because the wind rarely cooperates, but this is the mantra we strive to achieve.

Today, with software, shooters can get a leg up on the competition by letting the software control the wind call for them. This is not a great learning tool, but it can give you effective downrange results if you set up the computer correctly. Just like your elevation, you have to

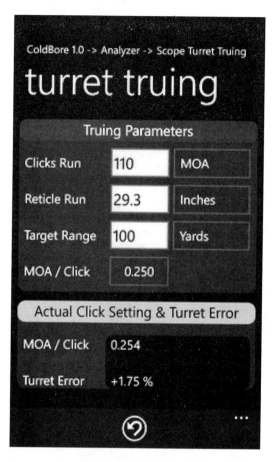

ColdBore 1.0 -> Analyzer -> Scope Turret Truing

turret truing

Truing Parameters

Clicks Run	110	MOA
Reticle Run	29.3	Inches
Target Range	100	Yards
MOA / Click	0.250	

Actual Click Setting & Turret Error

MOA / Click	0.254
Turret Error	+1.75 %

Your software should have the ability to adjust your turret inputs to fix any common errors in scope tracking. The author finds 2 percent is a pretty common error to see in most midrange and lower-cost scopes.

look at the wind holds and true those results.

How do you true the wind? Well, the wind adjustment is controlled by the bullet's ballistic coefficient. We shortcut the term ballistic coefficient by saying only BC. This is the first piece of information needed to set up your ballistics computer. You can find the BC in several places. Some bullet manufacturers put the numbers on the box; if not, you can do an Internet search to get the correct information.

These BC numbers tell the software how well

the bullet performs. What is the rate of drop and the amount of drift of that particular bullet? The higher the number, the better the bullet will perform. It takes a bit of distance for the full effects to kick in, so you want to shoot the rifle to distance.

There is a lot of bad press out there regarding ballistic coefficient numbers. Many people feel the figures are overinflated to market a particular bullet, or that the manufacturer is somehow manipulating this to increase sales.

Sniper's Hide, along with Marc Taylor, designed a fixture to test scopes without the human influence when adjusting. This 30-pound fixture holds the scope while the turrets are tested.

The fact is, BCs are rifle-system dependent. You have to true the BC for your system because the value is just an average based on the tests conducted. Most manufacturers test their bullets at 300 yards. This is the shortest range you can use, which will give you a pretty good number. But that number is based on the rifle system it is shot from and the barrel used. It's an average to give the shooter a starting point. It's not wrong; it's just not specific.

The main problem is, it's not easy to cor-rectly change a ballistic coefficient. You need a velocity downrange to do it right; and by down-range, we mean 800 yards or more. It will not work close in, so shooting through your chrono-graph at 800 yards is not going to happen with-out specialized equipment. You can do it from the drop, and you can use software to adjust it via the trial-and-error method.

Let's cover that last method, as it is the easiest way to do it for the average shooter out there. We know we can true the software by

ColdBore 1.0 -> Ballistics -> Tools

true zero reticle

Ruger KM77RP (22") - BARNES TSX-BT

True Zero Range
205
Meters

METERS

Tgt Range
175

Meters

+ **−**

POI Center
1.0

Inches

+ **−**

Just because you are within one-quarter inch of center does not mean your zero is at that range. A true range zero utility can be useful in solving complex ballistics problems.

Regardless of the reason the author is on the range, he is always recording the data as it presents itself to him. He carries him Impact Databook no matter where he goes.

changing the muzzle velocity. That is the default way for most software, but it's unnaturally bending the curve. Chronographs have gotten better, we have the LabRadar and the MagnetoSpeed, and their numbers are outstanding. Gone are the days of sky screens and faulty readings, so why start off changing these measured values?

We want to start off adjusting the BC first and then make minor tweaks to the muzzle velocity if necessary. A host of variables affects the BC, so we want to begin by adjusting this number first.

Before I get too deep, I have a wind class, and in this wind class, we use the mph of the rifle.

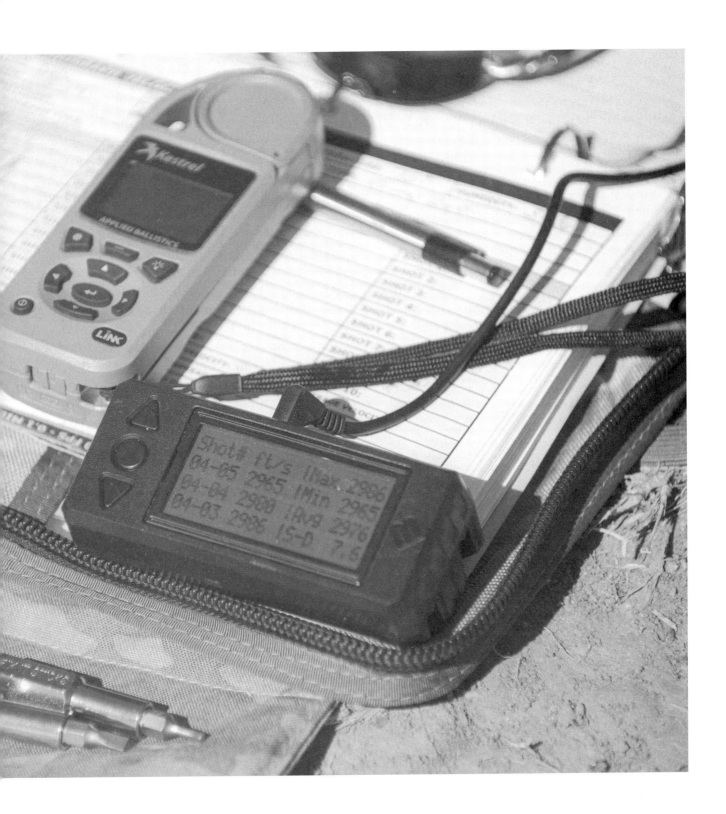

It's a value based on the bullet shot, and we get this value from the G1 BC. I use G1 BC numbers in most of my software. I don't subscribe to the idea that you need to use G7. Then again, most of the software I run is not G-dependent. The first number in the G1 BC is, in fact, my mph value. So, if I am using a bullet with a BC G1 of .583, that means I have a 5-mph gun. It's simple, what that means is, for every 5 mph my bullet will follow this pattern:

100 yards: .1 Mils
200 yards: .2 Mils
300 yards: .3 Mils
400 yards: .4 Mils

500 yards: .5 Mils
600 yards: .6 Mils

Beyond 600 yards is a small variation in the numbers, but trust me, it is minor. We use this method every day in precision rifle shooting, and we have values for those shooting MOA-based scopes, but that is a bit more complicated. For a 10-mph wind, you double these values; it's quick, simple and does not require long-hand math.

When you tweak the software, you want to align these numbers to match the above. So, 500 yards should read .5 Mils for a 5-mph wind. One of the reasons we like Mils over MOA for shooting is the wind call is easier to work with.

Now don't get me wrong. You are not adjusting the BC so much that you are changing whole numbers. Your .58 BC is not going to become .6, but it might be .56 versus the .58 you read off the box. That will help align the ballistic curve in your software. It's a better method than starting with the muzzle velocity. We have productive conversations in the Sniper's Hide Forum as well as some very easy to follow videos on the subject. Once you are exposed to it, a light bulb will instantly go off in your head. It's the simplest wind method you have ever used.

Take your rifle system, fire a group at 800 yards. Then, before changing the muzzle velocity to line up the curve, adjust the BC numbers in a small way. Get the curvature to match at this distance and if you notice any errors in your short-range data, change the muzzle velocity to line it up and complete the curve. It will most likely be a small change, roughly 25 fps, maybe 50, but not much more. Changing the verified muzzle velocity beyond 100 fps risks some potential errors.

Finally, recognize that ballistic coefficients are manipulated by velocity. The more speed you have, the higher the BC number. So, if you are shooting a cartridge designed around 2,800 fps and your rifle system is only shooting that bullet at 2,650 fps, it's not going to have that advertised BC. It will then become a lower number. Understanding this part of it will help you adjust the value. Look at how your velocity changes the BC value. Then, start by moving the middle number up or down based on that speed. It's pretty simple once you get the hang of it, and

The Newcon laser rangefinding spotter. Today, we can combine devices, such as a rangefinder with a spotting scope, so the shooter has to carry only one optic.

...OR DATA SHEET:

DATE/TIME: 7 1 18			TRUE DOPE		
			MIL	MOA	WIND
	2	00	.3		
	3	00	.8		
BULLET BC:	4	00	1.5		
	5	00	2.1		
ZERO RANGE:	6	00	3.3		
	7	00	4.0		
DENSITY ALTITUDE:	8	00	4.8		
	9	00	5.6		
TEMPERATURE:	10	00	7.0		
	11	25	8.4		
STATION PRESSURE:	12	50	9.9		
	13	25	11.5		
HUMIDITY:	14	30	13.0		
	15	00	13.8		
AZ / LAT:	16				

WIND: ☐ MPH ☐ KPH
☐ 1-3 ☐ 1/4
☐ 3-5 ☐ 1/2
☐ 5-8 ☐ FULL
☐ 8-12 ☐ HEAD
☐ ___ ☐ TAIL

LIGHT:
☐ BRIGHT
☐ HAZY
☐ OVERCAST
☐ NIGHT

Only verified data should be recorded and kept for future reference. When you are trying to determine the correct data used, avoid recording false information.

you'll find your software, and your wind calls, will be much happier.

Kestrels

Given the choice, I would much rather carry a dedicated unit like a Kestrel with software in it, versus using my phone. Our phones are not really field-worthy. They are slow, want to go to sleep too often and require a password to unlock. For these reasons and others, I prefer a Kestrel. Does not matter to me, Hornady 4DOF or Applied Ballistics, they both work exceptionally well and let you pull both weather conditions and give ballistic predictions. I need both, and because one device will do both, it's the

smart choice.

I true the Kestrels the same way as mentioned above. Yes, they have processes they recommend for truing the unit, but we find our small hack is a better method. Using the advertised methods, I have found when traveling and having density altitude swings in excess of 5, 000 feet, the computer needs to be tweaked again if we follow the instructions. By using the above method, we can travel from the mountains to sea level without having to constantly chase the model.

The Caveats to Consider

The question continually comes up about lining

BALLISTIC CALCULATOR DATA SHEET:

PROFILE NAME:	DATE/TIME:
	7/1/18

AMMUNITION: Primr 130

RIFLE TWIST:	BULLET BC:
8.0	.583

MUZZLE VELOCITY:	ZERO RANGE:
	100

SIGHT HEIGHT:	DENSITY ALTITUDE:
2.5	8000

BULLET DIAMETER:	TEMPERATURE:
264	85

BULLET WEIGHT:	STATION PRESSURE:
130	25.12

BULLET LENGTH	HUMIDITY:
1.3㎞	50%

CLICK VALUE CORRECTION:	AZ / LAT:

NOTES:

TRUE DOPE

		MIL	MOA
2	00	.3	
3	00	.8	
4	00	1.5	
5	00	2.1	
6	00	3.3	
7	10	4.0	
8	00	4.8	
9	00	5.6	
10	00	7.0	
11	25	8.4	
12	50	9.9	
13	50	11.5	
14	35	13.0	
15	00	13.8	
16			

WIND: ☐ MPH ☐ KPH
☐ 1-3 ☐ 1/4
☐ 3-5 ☐ 1/2
☐ 5-8 ☐ FULL
☐ 8-12 ☐ HEAD
☐ ☐ TAIL

LIGHT
☐ BR
☐ HA
☐ O
☐ N

Record your ballistics data using the original information as saved via hard copy. If you use only a computer, you risk losing your data, so have a backup copy.

your dope to your software. The problem is, people go out to the range with software in hand and then can't quite understand why it is not matching up, or they have troubling "truing" it after the fact. Not all, some find it pretty straightforward, but the forum is full of people commenting about ballistics software errors.

There are several reasons why software might not line up correctly, but part of the prob-lem is using the software first and not doping the rifle before exploring the ballistic solvers. When using the software before shooting, I call anything the computer spits out as "Try Dope," because you are just trying to hit the target, not much more. It's not 1-MOA accurate. Remember, manufacturers drop data was designed to get you on an NRA 6x6 target board; it is up to the shooter to fine-tune that drop to hit the center.

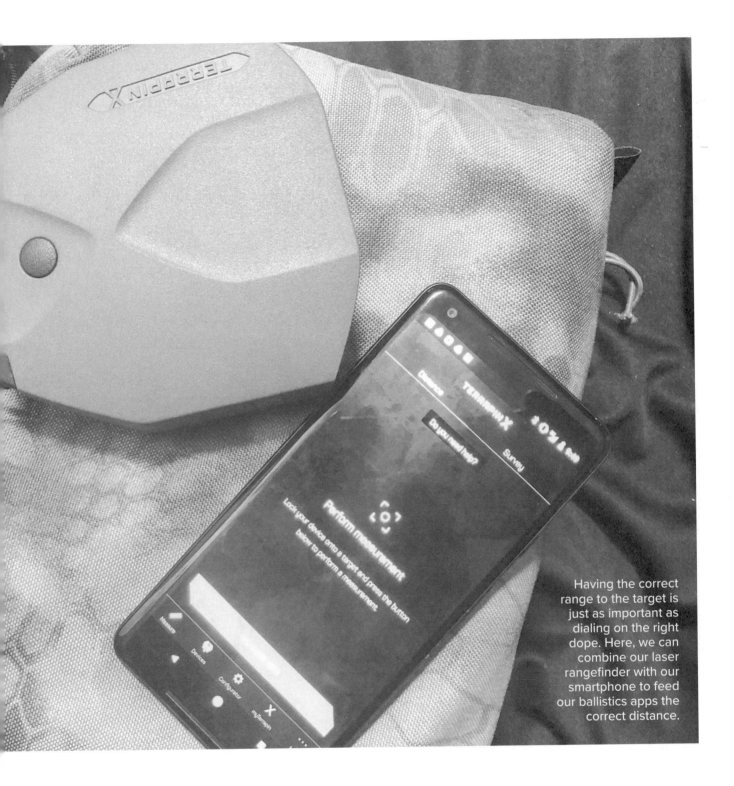

Having the correct range to the target is just as important as dialing on the right dope. Here, we can combine our laser rangefinder with our smartphone to feed our ballistics apps the correct distance.

We never questioned it; we just knew we needed to put in the effort.

My argument has always centered around the human factor. Regardless of what the Doppler radar says, what the computer model says, the human element has a much bigger say as to where the shot hits. I have heard several times that what someone saw in a fixture was not what happened when they put a shooter behind the rifle. It comes down to recoil management. This is why one shooter will hit using Solution A, and the next shooter needs Solution B or C. How individuals manage the recoil and exactly where that barrel is upon release of the bullet affects hits on targets. It's why your zero and your friend's zero are inches apart. No software

Tom Manners is transferring his ballistics data to a hard copy to use on the firing line. Not wanting to be distracted with too much information during the King of 2 Mile event, he is using what is needed only for that stage.

out there considers you; it only finds an empty, near-perfect world.

The next problem is the promotion of "drifts." We have a lot of new data that points to a series of drifts that can affect the placement of the shot. The development of these is a relatively new phenomenon. When I went to Marine Sniper School in 1986, we didn't worry about spin drift (wasn't even mentioned). We didn't worry about Coriolis, crosswind jump, or any of the other examples we see today. Baron Roland von Eotvos, who the heck is that guy? In all, we have about four drift factors that are discussed, and some people start employ-

The author's 300-yard truing bar. These targets are scaled to be .2 Mil tall at their respective ranges.

ing a correction for them as close as 400 yards. Am I saying they don't exist? No, but I am saying they are being blown out of proportion. I think much of it used to take the blame away from the shooter. Here is why:

If we gather our dope by walking out our shots, actually shooting each yard-line distance and recording the data and include everything, including the drifts. There is no such thing as a no-wind day. If you experience one, consider yourself lucky, but practically, no-wind days don't exist. So, under normal circumstances, we zero and dope our rifles with everything already included. Then when we go to our "Data on Previous Engagement (DOPE)," and it's taking into account these factors. If today I am shooting to 1,000 yards and used 7.4 Mils to hit center along with .75 Mils of wind for 5-mph breeze, that assumes all the drifts and drop data. If conditions change because of the location or atmosphere, a computer will help account for it rather than the old, outdated rules of thumb, but hitting the target usually happens. We see this every week in tactical rifle matches around the country. Guys travel from their home location to ranges 500 miles away and hit. Why do they hit? They practiced and recorded their dope. Talking to several high scoring PRS Shooters, they strive to nail down their data, so elevation is a given and the only question becomes wind. In known-distance courses, they consider this information their zero data. They essentially re-zero the rifle for each yard line.

Wind is the most significant drift factor we have and actually will offset some of the other drifts. It depends on the direction, and speed, but it will cancel out or increase several of the other factors. So, it's essential to understand

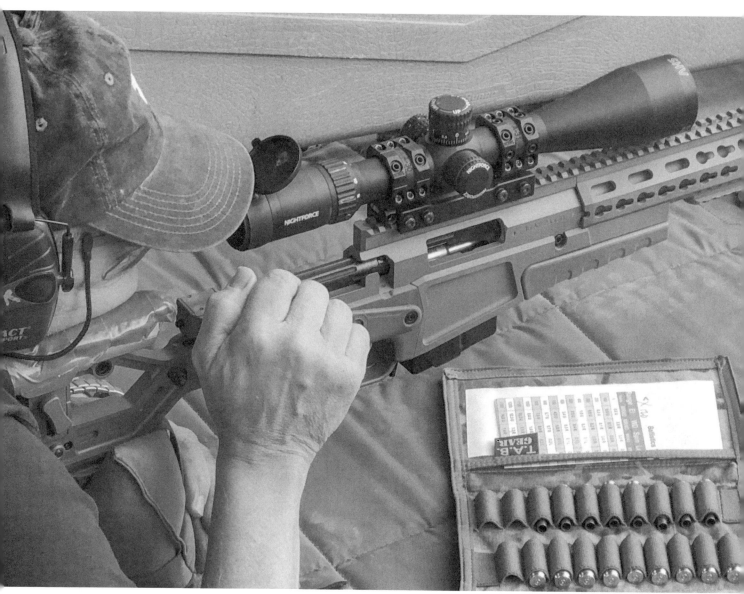

Marc Taylor keeps his current data with his handloaded ammunition. The data matches his load, so nothing else is needed.

the wind. No dispute, you need to know what is going here as it can control so much of how we hit the target. That includes elevation changes. To expand, it's not unheard of to have a terrain feature in or around a specific yard line that causes an elevation issue. So, even if everything with the computer lines up, your 700-yard dope is off because the wind changes the flight path to hit that one target. It often has people scratching their heads. A shooter is everything but "X-range" perfect? Odds are it's the wind.

Still, if we recorded our data, we know what the wind was doing. If we doped the rifle in a

5-mph wind, going to an 8-mph wind is not like starting from zero. While they might say an 8-mph wind will move the impact .1 Mils up or down, it's only 3 mph more we are dealing with. We already accounted for 5 mph, so why add 8 mph on top of the 5?

If you're modeling the shot on a computer, I can see the importance of all this. But it's not the same as shooting it. Not to mention we miss out of adding our own spin to the bullet. Weak fundamentals will not line you up with the model. If you are adding .2 Mils of trigger hook to your shot and you want to call it spin drift, well

Rifle:									
Ammo Mfg			Temp		Press				
Bullet Mfg			Hum		B.C.				
Wt	Fps		Elv		DA				
Dist	Drop	Wind	Wind	Ranging	Dist	Drop	Wind	Wind	Ranging
Yds		mph	10mph	10 in	Yds		mph	10mph	20 in
100				2.8	950				0.6
150				1.9	975				0.6
200				1.4	1000				0.6
225				1.2	1025				0.5
250				1.1	1050				0.5
275				1.0	1075				0.5
300				0.9	1100				0.5
325				0.9	1125				0.5
350				0.8	1150				0.5
375				0.7	1175				0.5
400				0.7	1200				0.5
425				0.7	1225				0.5
450				0.6	1250				0.4
475				0.6	1275				0.4
500				0.6	1300				0.4
525				0.5	1325				0.4
550				0.5	1350				0.4
575				0.5	1375				0.4
600				0.5	1400				0.4
625				0.4	1425				0.4
650				0.4	1450				0.4
675				0.4	1475				0.4
700				0.4	1500				0.4
725				0.4	1525				0.4
750				0.4	1550				0.4
775				0.4	1575				0.4
800				0.3	1600				0.3
825				0.3	1625				0.3
850				0.3	1650				0.3
875				0.3	1675				0.3
900				0.3	1700				0.3
925				0.3	1725				0.3

Spin Drift = 1% come up

AeroDyn Jump= wind mph/100 (10mph=0.1)

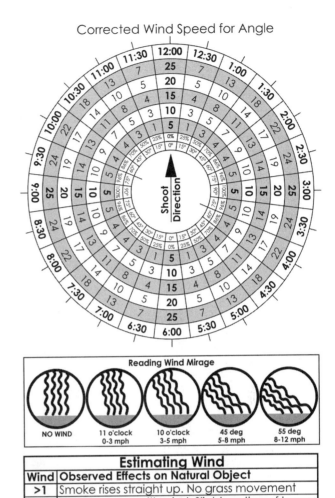

Corrected Wind Speed for Angle

Reading Wind Mirage

NO WIND	11 o'clock 0-3 mph	10 o'clock 3-5 mph	45 deg 5-8 mph	55 deg 8-12 mph

Estimating Wind

Wind	Observed Effects on Natural Object
>1	Smoke rises straight up. No grass movement
1-3	Smoke moves with wind. Slight motion of leaves
4-7	Wind just felt on face. Tree leaves in motion
8-12	Leaves turn. twigs and tree tops in motion.
13-18	Small Branches move. loose dust blows around.
19-24	Large branches and small trees sway
25-31	Whole trees in Motion. Hard to walk

Sniper's Hide member "JackMaster" created this blank chart as a download for Sniper's Hide members to use. Charts and graphs like this make pairing the data to your rifle system easier.

OK, I suppose you can. But are we really talking about the same thing? Why did I not use any, and you are using .2 Mils? Why is my wind call 1.5 Mils to hit the target and you are using 2 Mils to hit the same target? Happens every week. Maybe it's rifle cant?

Spin drift has recently been boiled down to roughly 1.25 percent of your elevation used in the shot. This is important to note. Many programs will apply two to three times this amount of correction.

The point is, while all these effects exist, they are not equally distributed among the shooters.

We all release the shot in our own way. Before you go adding all the drifts to your ballistic solver, try doping your rifle first without any software. Develop YOUR dope to distance and record everything, then true the software to what you shot, rather than worrying about what the computer said before your first round went downrange. It only takes an hour. And I once recorded a video in 50 shots. Now I can go back and line up the computer at my leisure. I think you will find the variations are much smaller than you might think. Solid dope is hard to argue with as we all know the bullet has the last word.

14

Practical External Ballistics

I am not going to dive into the deep end when it comes to external ballistics. We have three different ballistics variations we can look at:

Internal Ballistics: What happens to the shot after the firing pin strikes the primer, but before the bullet leaves the barrel.

External Ballistics: What happens after the bullet leaves the barrel and before it hits the target.

Terminal Ballistics: What happens when the bullet hits the target.

Solid bullets are expensive, but the benefits extend well past what most people understand. Solids push the boundaries by squeezing every micron out of the bullet design.

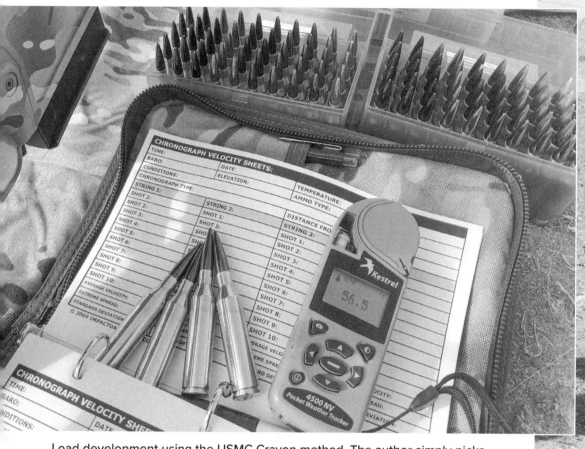

Load development using the USMC Crayon method. The author simply picks the correct color and that is his load for this rifle.

Internal ballistics deal with the bullet before it leaves the barrel. Here, we focus on the variables we can work with like external ballistics.

Internal ballistics can focus around the gunsmith's work on the barrel; how straight the chamber is and how square to the bore. We can combine this to include discussion on the bullet's runout, how concentric it was assembled and how the bullet is pointed in the chamber. If you have a factory rifle with factory ammo, we really can't do much about it. So, the discussion of internal ballistics is often reduced to runout and primers.

For me, the discussion of internal ballistics has focused on using left-hand, gain-twist barrels. I love gain-twist barrels and use them whenever I can. Bartlein barrels has reinvented the way we look at this turn-of-the-century revolution. I call it a revolution because back in

the day, left-hand, gain-twist barrels from Harry Pope (born in 1861) were considered the best competition rifles of their day. Bartlein, with its CNC-controlled, barrel-making machines, has changed how we look at this practice. I could spend two chapters writing about Bartlein barrels, but it would be extremely boring. If you want to know more about gain-twist barrels,

research Harry Pope and Pope rifles. The NRA has a lot of them in its museums.

Terminal ballistics is all about energy on target. Hunters focus on terminal ballistics as do those who work with their rifles in harm's way. We need to know how much energy the bullet is going to place on the target and what that will do upon impact. We can look at both energy and

Reloading is a way to boost accuracy out of your precision rifle. It's a great way to learn more about the type of shooting you are engaged in.

shot placement, or, as some do, using energy when placement is less than optimal. If you are a hunter, there are scales for how much energy is necessary to put down a particular game animal based on its size and weight.

External ballistics is very important to the long-range shooter because of parasitic drag. The farther we shoot, the more drag is placed on the bullet. Our ballistic coefficient is how we represent performance of a bullet, and high-

lights the effect drag will have on it.

The BC of a bullet is used to translate the effects of:
- Shape
- Area
- Mass
- Muzzle Velocity
- Air Density

A bullet is subject to gravity the moment it leaves the barrel. It's design, the shape, area and

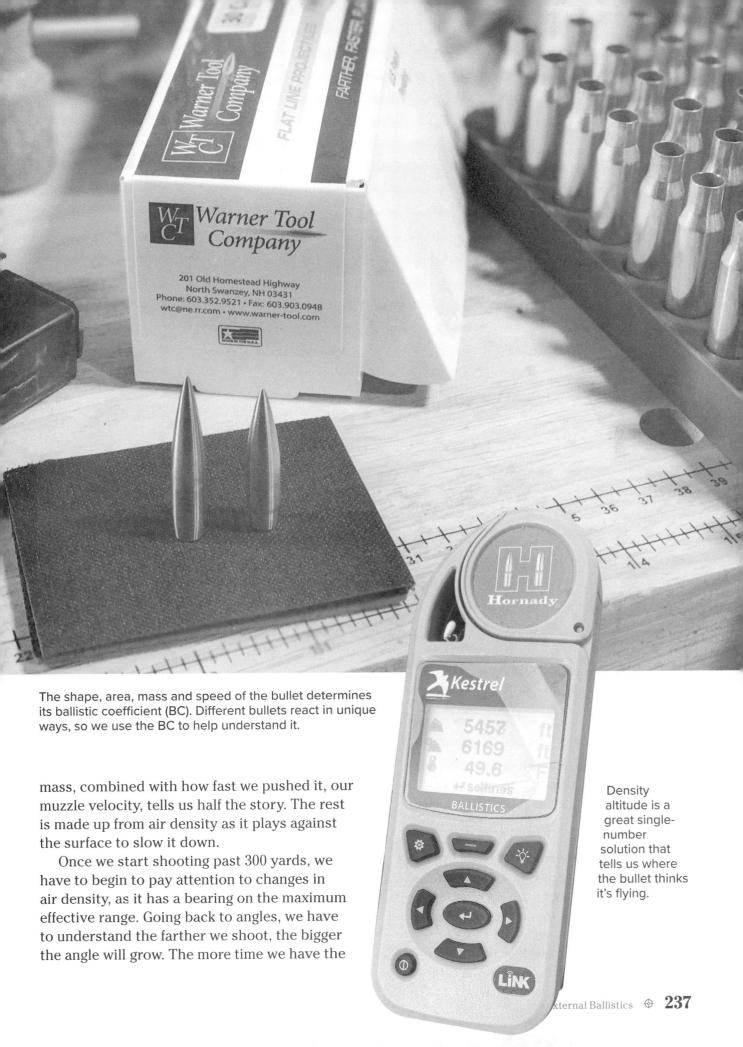

The shape, area, mass and speed of the bullet determines its ballistic coefficient (BC). Different bullets react in unique ways, so we use the BC to help understand it.

mass, combined with how fast we pushed it, our muzzle velocity, tells us half the story. The rest is made up from air density as it plays against the surface to slow it down.

Once we start shooting past 300 yards, we have to begin to pay attention to changes in air density, as it has a bearing on the maximum effective range. Going back to angles, we have to understand the farther we shoot, the bigger the angle will grow. The more time we have the

Density altitude is a great single-number solution that tells us where the bullet thinks it's flying.

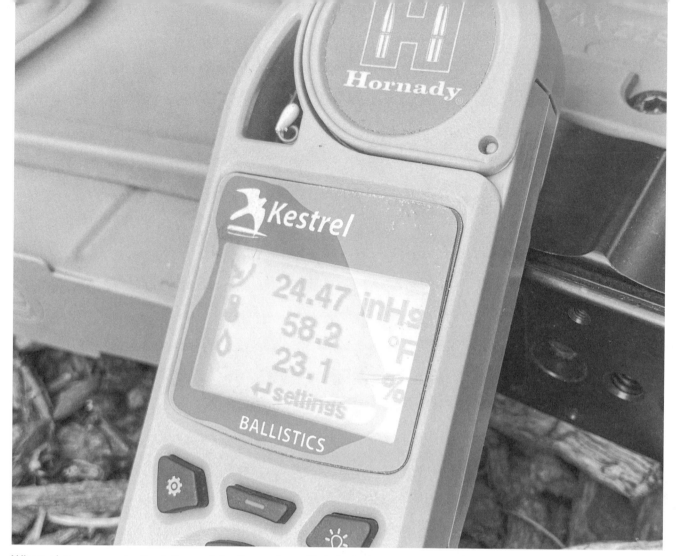

When given access to the full raw data, the author will default to using that versus using just density altitude.

bullet exposed to the air in flight, the more it will slow down. Time of flight is a guiding factor for a lot of the math we work with.

There are three factors we have to look at when it comes to air density:

- Barometric Pressure
- Temperature
- Humidity

Density altitude is a combination of barometric pressure, temperature and humidity. It is a one number representation of these three factors combined. They are combined using a weather service formula which is not necessary to break down. Density altitude tells us where the bullet thinks it is flying.

The reason we write where the bullet thinks it is flying is a very important distinction. As an example, my home range is in Colorado. The physical location is 4,500 feet above sea level,

which gives me an advantage in the air-density column. When we combine the other factors, humidity, and, most importantly, temperature, it raises the density altitude to 7,000 feet, sometimes more than 8,000 feet, above sea level. I might be standing at 4,500 feet, but the bullet is operating as if it is being shot at 8,000 feet.

Density altitude is the only time we need to consider humidity, which has a strange reputation with precision rifle shooters. They like to mention it as often as possible as if they're related, but humidity is not a factor to worry about.

What we do need to report about humidity is humid air is lighter than dry air. Yes, several of the military manuals have it backward. Humid air is lighter because of the addition of water vapor. Why are the clouds in the sky? Because wet air is lighter. Unless you are talking about density altitude, get humidity out of your vocabulary.

I use it as a weather gauge when meeting new people. As soon as they start rambling about calculating the humidity for a shot, I am gone. We have nothing left to talk about.

Density altitude works the same way in shooting as it does with flying an aircraft. Think about a military shooter being ferried by aircraft to a hide site. He can ask the crew chief what the DA is and that crew chief will know.

My range is 4,500 ft, and my average summer density altitude reading is 8,000 feet. I have a place I shoot at 9,000 feet and even in October the DA is closer to 12,000 feet.

Because I have a Kestrel, I use the actual air-density factors, barometric pressure, temp and humidity and only record my DA in the logbook. Using the Impact Data Books Shooters Diary Page, I asked Tony G. to remove humidity and replaced it with density altitude. I tend to use DA for field expedient and raw data when time and opportunity permit.

It's worth knowing and understanding density altitude as it's a quick reference to use when considering air density. It's all about simplifying the process, and density altitude is a great single number representation of the air density.

Altitude

For shooting, altitude is a factor of barometric pressure. We have two types we can look at: station pressure, or barometric pressure.

Barometric pressure is a value that has been corrected for sea level. Sea level is represented by 29.92 inches of pressure at 0 feet above sea level.

Station pressure is not corrected for altitude and includes the altitude in the number. Here in Colorado my standard pressure would be

The Hornady app with Doppler radar tracked the author's rifles to 2,000 yards and beyond, providing him verified data to 1,500 meters for later use.

Altitude for shooting is a function of barometric pressure. The author uses station pressure, which includes the changes for altitude.

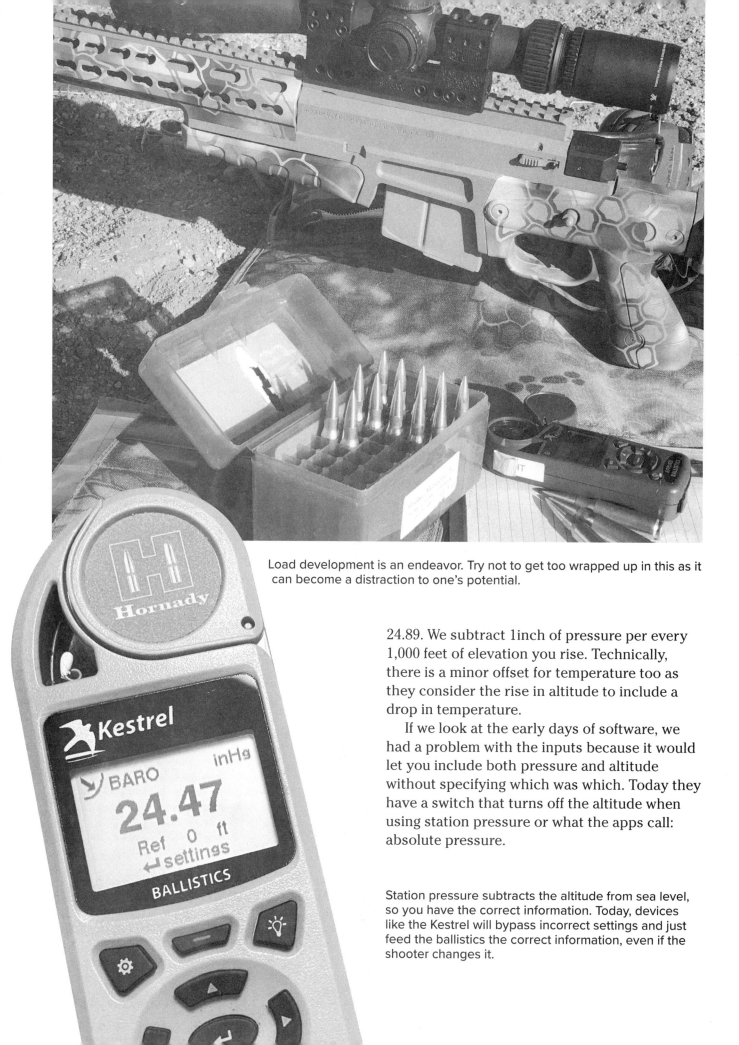

Load development is an endeavor. Try not to get too wrapped up in this as it can become a distraction to one's potential.

24.89. We subtract 1 inch of pressure per every 1,000 feet of elevation you rise. Technically, there is a minor offset for temperature too as they consider the rise in altitude to include a drop in temperature.

If we look at the early days of software, we had a problem with the inputs because it would let you include both pressure and altitude without specifying which was which. Today they have a switch that turns off the altitude when using station pressure or what the apps call: absolute pressure.

Station pressure subtracts the altitude from sea level, so you have the correct information. Today, devices like the Kestrel will bypass incorrect settings and just feed the ballistics the correct information, even if the shooter changes it.

Combining altitude with absolute pressure will double the value. If I said to the software, my pressure is 24.89 and then also added in 5,280 feet above sea level, the computer would think I was shooting at 10,000 feet above sea level. We already included the altitude because we subtracted the elevation per 1,000 feet in the station pressure.

The takeaway with pressure is, the weatherman uses barometric pressure. He assumes you know where you are standing. Shooters use station or absolute pressure, which combines the altitude.

Temperature

Temperature is our most important air density factor, next to changes in altitude which will affect our station pressure. Temperatures constantly change. We go from cold in the mornings to warmer in the afternoon.

Temperature is again about parasitic drag. The hotter it is outside, the more excited the air molecules get. When they get excited, they move around and spread out clearing a path for the bullet to fly through. When it's cold outside they huddle together and get in our way. Cold air is dense and will slow down the bullet down.

I recommend staying on top of the temperature throughout the day. Sure, depending on how far you shoot, the offset might be only a click or two, but trust me it can add up fast.

This is the beauty of the Kestrel handheld weather meter; it does the work for you. We don't have to monitor the changes in conditions if we use a Kestrel. Another great feature is even if you change the settings on the weather side and mess it up, when you are using the ballistics computer features, it will bypass your changes and pull the correct data.

Shooting at the Hornady facility, testing the author's personal rifles over the company's Doppler radar app.

Field shooting includes a lot of difficult terrains, like here in Hells Canyon, Idaho, where the angles can be very steep.

The question often asked by new users to software is what information to input. Do we pull the raw data, our station pressure, humidity and temperature or can we just use density altitude?

There is an argument to be made for both. In some software, I like the simplicity of using the density altitude, other times I am more apt to use the raw data derived from my Kestrel weather meter.

When I use just the DA, I find I am educating myself on the conditions. I can remember my dope based on a DA number. We all have busy

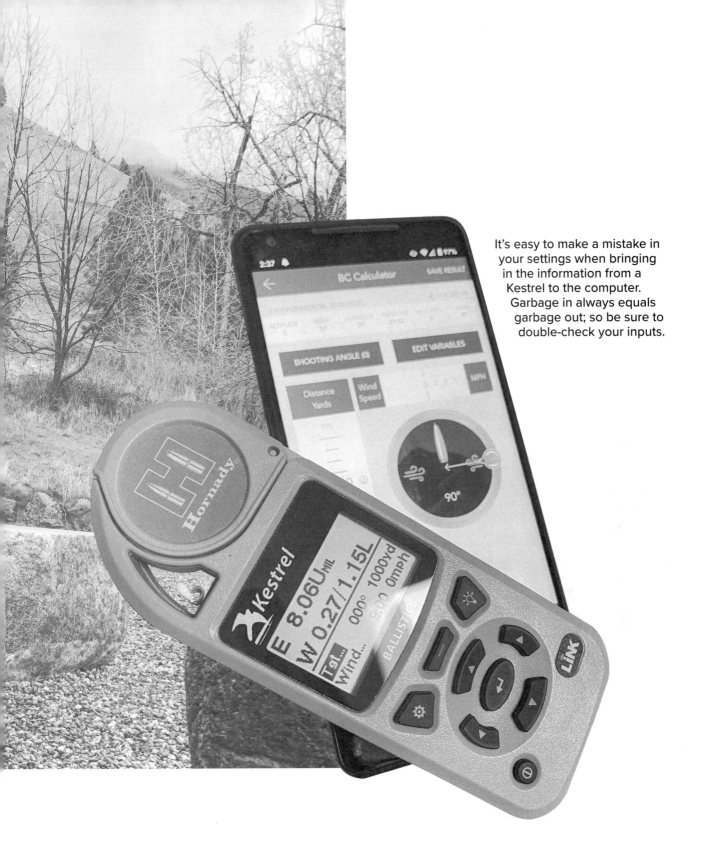

It's easy to make a mistake in your settings when bringing in the information from a Kestrel to the computer. Garbage in always equals garbage out; so be sure to double-check your inputs.

lives, the less clutter the better. But I still want the education.

If I am shooting in Colorado at my home range, with a density altitude of 8,000 feet, my 1,000-yard dope with a .308 rifle and 175-grain bullet would be 9.7 Mils or 33.25 MOA. If I was

to magically travel to sea level, that same shot would require 11.4 Mils or 39 MOA of adjustment, a pretty significant difference. It's also important to note, the shot at sea level would be in the transonic zone and not supersonic.

Our goal as precision rifle shooters should

be to engage targets while supersonic. Yes, we shoot beyond transonic into the subsonic region all the time, but accuracy becomes a question mark when we cross into these regions.

This is what air density does to our shot. So, to recap, when shooting, a bullet likes the following conditions:

- High Temperatures
- Low Barometric Pressure or High Altitudes
- High Humidity

These are the most favorable conditions when it comes to shooting at long range. We can throw in angles, but that is a whole other topic for discussion.

It's all part of our dope. We match up the conditions encountered when we hit a target at a known distance under the same conditions and apply it.

Tools of the trade. We have rifles, scopes, chronographs and more. Precision rifle is very gear-driven.

This is a great example of data the author displays during his classes to help new students understand how to record and monitor all this information.

200 - AVG .4 Mil

300 - AVG 1.0 Mil

400 - AVG 1.8 Mil

500 - AVG 2.4 Mil

600 - 3.2 AVG Mil

710 - 4.0 AVG Mil

800 - 5.1 AVG Mil

900 - 6.0 AVG Mil

1000 - 7.1 Mil

1125 - 8.8 AVG Mil

1255 - 11.2 Mil

1325 - 11.7 / 11.8 Gm / 12.8 Gm

1425 - 127 Mil / 14.0 6.5 Gm / 13.1 Gm

Mils
.1 - 1.0

Temp 65°
Hum. 65%
Bar 2542
D/A 6000ft

Shooting a precision rifle is a journey; one without end. Record the information gleaned on your journey so you can always keep improving.

15

Distraction-Free Shooting

A lot of our head goes into shooting a rifle. The human factor is the most significant variable we have to combat. Followed closely by the wind, it's the number one factor. The fundamentals of marksmanship guide us in so many ways and deviating from them can cause both vertical and horizontal variations in our shot placement.

I recently taught a private lesson for a gentleman who shoots for a living. He ran into an incident where his confidence was shaken and he needed a refresher course.

Immediately during our fundamental evaluation, I noticed one of the problems, and the effect was his initial zero was off by 1.5 inches from the center. He was hitting low left of the target. We worked together, and after only 40 rounds, we were ready to leave. So, before going, I had him check his zero, which was right back to the center of the three-quarter inch dot he was shooting, and we never adjusted his scope. That mental mistake was costing him 1.5 inches at 100 yards.

We must get out of our heads sometimes. If you shoot alone, as many do, you can end up making numerous adjustments on the fly, never stopping to analyze the cause and effects. So here I want you to take the time to shoot distraction-free for a few series. Put down the phone, move the target back and paint a dark neutral color, or better yet, put it on paper where you cannot see it, and focus on your fundamentals.

Paper beyond 400 yards is the best solution; this way, you get a mix of elements at play, and you should not be able to see the holes appear.

Start by doping your rifle, both windage and elevation and do this based on your routine wind calls. In other words, don't do anything differently. It's best if you engage in this drill first thing, so the calls are not only blind, but cold.

Next, focus on the target and shoot your group, slow fire. Concentrate on body position, use of the support hand with the rear bag and, most importantly, trigger control. If need be, record your "call" for each, but if you break position, be sure to reset it properly and don't just roll into the next. Then, go downrange and analyze your target. Look at the group, determine its center, and see how that measures up to your point of aim. Look at the horizontal spread and distance from the center. Are the groups moved with the wind or against it? Does the group appear open and strung out, or tight and just compensated for by the wind call? All this information should help build confidence and fine-tune your dope.

If steel is all you have, make sure you paint the plate a color where the shot groups don't show up as well. Sure, you'll still hear the hits, but try to refrain from making those micro-adjustments that center you up.

Don't be afraid to mix up your targets. Paper does not lie, so include a mix of steel and paper for maximum results.

The author's 18x32 1-Mile Target with a group from his 6.5CM rifle. Hits on target can help decipher any errors in our fundamentals.

We adjust on the fly a lot. We blank out our minds and fail to see. When you first arrive at the range and begin that initial shot series, concentrate on the moment. Go through your checklist and remember W.T.F.

Putting It All Together

Let's look back at the process.

First, we set up the rifle to the shooter. We adjusted it the same way we would adjust the seats, mirror and steering wheel of a new car. We are spending as much time as necessary to properly fit the rifle to our particular body type.

We want our head in line with the scope. We want the sight picture to have edge-to-edge clarity in the optic. We adjust the length of pull so our hand can easily manipulate the bolt and trigger when our head is lined up behind the scope.

The bipod is adjusted and tightened down to mitigate canting the system. We have the reticle aligned to the fall of gravity with a plumb line, and our head is straight. The shooter is up on his elbows and the rifle system is leveled to his body type. Not just front to back, but side to side; our shoulders are relaxed and square. All this is done before ever hitting the range.

We bore-sight the rifle, and then begin the process to zero the scope. We establish a solid point of aim for a point of impact for a 100-yard zero. We want to zero at 100 yards to eliminate any wandering during travel. Changes in conditions and wind will have a minor effect with a 100-yard zero. Once confirmed on paper, we want to reset our turrets to read, 0 on elevation, and 0 on windage, as we require a repeatable reference point.

Zeroing completed, we then want to dope out the rifle shooting every yard line available, recording the information as it unfolds. We want to adjust the center of our groups to the center of our reticle on target and not the drop needed to hit that particular target.

With our data written down, along with the atmospheric conditions at the time of shooting, we can then align the computers to match our rifle system. Using the muzzle velocity dialog in our software, we adjust it plus or minus to match the 600-yard data recorded. Once that is trued to our shooting, we can check the longer ranges, 800 and 1,000 yards. If the curve is not correct, we tweak the ballistic coefficient to bend the curve at distance, while leaving alone the shorter ranges which are adjusted with the muzzle velocity.

If the conditions are saved alongside the dope, our software should be aligned and ready for use. We adjust the software last so not to distract from our shooting. We need to focus on the fundamentals and execute the firing task in a consistent manner. Any changes, no matter how small, will cause noticeable deviations in precision.

Our goal is to focus on the fundamentals to ensure precision, and diligently record our data for accuracy on target. Once the initial work is complete, you can then start moving around and engaging targets under the various conditions you might find yourself.

W.T.F. is our checklist to hit targets at long range. We start out by looking at the Wind. The Wind is our wildcat, the ever-changing factor that must be managed for each and every shot. The Target we are shooting requires the proper Trajectory. What is the distance and what do we need to hit it? This information should have been gathered after zeroing. Finally, it's about the Fundamentals of marksmanship. Sure, with a decent amount of money we can buy a hit, but the fundamentals transcend a dollar value. Every sport we participate in has its own variation of the fundamentals of marksmanship. The best players are the athletes who can execute those fundamentals under quickly changing and adverse conditions. What is the advanced-marksmanship class? It's the fundamentals executed faster and from alternate positions. In this regard, every sport is the same.

There is no voodoo. People selling you voodoo are just lining their pockets. Nobody alive today invented any of this. At the very least, they rediscovered an old way of doing things that applies to our modern equipment. I love this stuff. I have been doing it for a very long time and, believe me, the shortest route to success is through the fundamentals. We live in a world with a lot of really good, bad shooters out there.

Seek out competent instruction. It's not always easy to do it on your own.

Guys who have adapted their bad habits and can manage success. Sometimes it's through superior equipment, other times it's through endless repetitions. Doing the same thing over and over has an impact, even if you are doing it wrong.

Just Go Out And Shoot!

There is nothing that I can recommend that will replace going out and just shooting. The key element to that is engaging in perfect practice and not just repeating the same mistakes over and over again hoping to eventually get it right.

I don't care what level of equipment you are using. It can be a surplus Mauser with ammo from 1987. Proper execution of the fundamentals is not dependent on how much money you paid for something. It does not cost any more to do it right.

I do recommend you go out and shoot. I recommend you enter at least one competition a year and participate. Just about every state in the country has a precision rifle match. If you bought a Tikka Tac A1 and you want to shoot a local 600-yard F-Class competition, do it. You will learn more in that one day of competition than reading any number of articles, including my own on the Internet. Putting the theory into practice cannot be overstated. Get out and shoot and enjoy yourself.

Have realistic goals in mind, and if those goals cannot be realized locally, travel. Take a class, attend a big national competition, preferably one with a train-up included.

I did not get to where I am today alone. There was a lot of support along the way. Often, we overlook the help while in the moment, but looking back, I had a lot of people helping guide me on this journey.

This is a journey and it never ends. Precision rifle thoughts and theory moved at a snail's pace from the 1900s to 2000. After 9/11, all this changed and changed very rapidly. Every month we have a new piece of equipment or a technique has been modified to work under the situations we find ourselves. There are CNC machines to cut options and accessories in real time. Software gives us long-range solutions in

Guiding students on their precision rifle journeys is the author's job. He and his fellow instructors spend time arming students with the tools necessary to be successful.

The friends you make in class carry over to competition and all types of recreational shooting. The author loves to see students branch out.

On the range instructing is the author's happy place. He enjoys seeing the successes of his students.

the palm of our hand. If you have not figured it out by now, I will just say it: I am a super fan. I love this stuff and breathe it every single day.

Whether I am on the Sniper's Hide website writing about precision rifle in the forum, or producing the Everyday Sniper Podcast, it's all precision rifles, all the time. I am hoping it translates to the end-users out there. If I saved you a bit of time or little money, I see that as a job well-done. We don't need to go overboard to be a successful shooter. It only takes knowledge.

I enjoy traveling around the world talking precision rifles. I look forward to seeing all of you at a range sometime in the future. Until then, thanks for everything.

16

Sniper's Hide History

Most people know the name Frank Galli from my website, Snipershide.com. It's been in existence since 2000 and just how I went about setting it up is a story within itself.

In the summer of 2000, I was going through a divorce. In November of that year, my divorce was finalized, giving me new options to fill my time. A group of us were using a few different website message boards to discuss long range shooting. Forums did not really exist like they do today, but instead these were extensions of the old BB Boards. The conversations were one long continuous conversation.

There were about 10 of us who messaged

nightly about all things long range, however, as soon as shooter, 12, 15 and 20 showed up, the site would crash and be down anywhere from 12 to 24 hours. On the night of my divorce, I purchased the domain Snipershide.com. With this domain in hand I grabbed a copy of Microsoft Frontpage and began to create the first version of the Sniper's Hide website.

Of course, this version of the site didn't last long. It was too hard to follow these threaded conversations, so I need an alternative. I began researching forum software and settled on a turnkey package from UBB, and this forum version of Sniper's Hide appeared in May of 2001.

UBB Threads took the site to a whole new level. At the time, there as two different sniper sites on the Internet that people were using. The first was Sniper Country, which had a similar threaded layout to my MS Frontpage attempt. It had long running conversations with some really good people dropping nuggets, but at the same time it was hard to navigate. The next was Sniper Paradise. This was a true forum and the new

Sniper's Hide was very similar. I reached out to Sniper's Paradise at the time, Thomas B. owned it, and I explained my site would follow an USMC model versus his Army-centric writings. Shortly after we came on the scene, Thomas had a personal situation that was played out online and effectively killed his site until years later when someone would buy it. Sniper's Hide was growing, and things were about to change in a big way.

A squad working the problem at the Sniper's Hide Cup. During matches, shooters have to find the targets, range the targets and engage them. Instructors give shooters a bracket to work within and then put them on the clock.

Author Frank Galli shooting a Ruger RPR in .223 at a local one-day competition. While most shooters know Frank from the Internet and his Snipershide.com website, he tries to get out and shoot as much publicly as possible. He believes it's important to maintaining his edge.

The terrorist attacks on the World Trade Center in New York City on Sept. 11, 2001, hit in a big way. I was in Connecticut at the time, dating my current girlfriend and we traveled to NYC on Sept. 10 to Manhattan to visit her brother. We spent the day and night there until heading back to Connecticut around 11 p.m. We both remember it vividly because there was a killer thunderstorm taking place. The city was awash in color the entire trip home and I recall it being a particularly violent storm. Upon hearing about the first plane hitting the towers, we attributed it to the storm that evening.

With the United States on a war footing, Sniper's Hide was now in a position to discuss all things shooting, sniping and their military applications. Our membership skyrocketed during this time.

The author, left, at Rifles Only with two long-time friends, Jacob Gottfredson and Pete Carpentier of Texas. Pete is a former Army Sniper; and Jacob is a Special Forces operator from the Vietnam days, and an accomplished writer.

Rifles Only Years

In 2003, I was contacted by Jacob Bynum of Rifles Only, which is a training facility in South Texas and, at the time, was aligned with Sniper Paradise. Precision rifle competitions were getting more popular, with Rifles Only being the center of that activity. As Sniper's Hide was rising, Jacob wanted to host a Sniper's Hide

match at his facility. Earlier in my history, I was trying to work with Bobby from the Badlands in Oklahoma. Badlands was a rival to Rifles Only, however I could not get along with Bobby. I worked to host an event with him, forwarded my Course of Fire suggestions and without notice he dropped the talks and held his own event without Sniper's Hide.

Jacob had a wedding in New York, so he

The author at Rifles Only with members of the USMC Shooting Team.

bounced across the border into Greenwich. It was an easy sell for me to hit South Texas. In fact, I attended a Rifles Only Sniper Paradise event. I was immediately hooked on this style of shooting. It was fast, it was dynamic, it was nothing like what I had experienced in the military. I spent additional time working with Jacob because I felt they were doing things in a way the military never imagined with a precision rifle. The slow, methodical shooting we engaged in was quickly replaced by this fast, dynamic style of shooting developed in South Texas.

I quickly started working nearly full time at Rifles Only. Jacob was scoring more, and more contract-instruction work from the military. It started out with one class a month, in short order it grew to three weeks on, one week off, for close to 10 months a year. I was living in the cottage on the range, and later, in a fifth-wheel camper. I quit my full-time job and focused on

this and my website Sniper's Hide.

I think we fundamentally changed the way people shot a precision rifle. Jacob was ahead of his time with lining students up straight back behind the rifle. Most were still shooting prone off to an angle, sling style. He was the guy who demanded a 90-degree trigger finger, aligning the fingernail to 9 o'clock. All the things most people see today as a standard practice did not exist before Rifles Only, not in the military.

Recoil management with the way the student lined up behind the rifle, as well as loading the bipod, were born in South Texas. Others have adapted elements of our training, but if you trace the genesis, it all starts at Rifles Only. It doesn't end there: The floating of the thumb also happened at Rifles Only.

I was there that day. Jacob, in demonstrating the reasoning behind lining up correctly, moving recoil in a straight line, he introduced the

During Sniper's Hide matches, the tripod is one of the most important tools to carry. Very few real-world shots are taken from the prone position, so mastering alternate positions is a skillset the author promotes.

floating thumb. Originally, it wasn't meant as a technique, but more to show you didn't need the thumb, and its influence could be in the negative. He took his support arm and pointed it toward the target and did the same thing with his thumb. A former student later would mistakenly take this technique and introduce it as his own, but you cannot erase the fact his only background was a week at Rifles Only during this time.

We didn't teach at Rifles Only, but we held matches designed to validate the training we were engaged in. We hosted two events a year: the Sniper's Hide Cup, which is the flagship event, and the more progressive Shooter's Bash. The Bash was the testing grounds for the Cup. We would come up with new courses of fire and test them during the Bash.

Our competitions sold out in minutes. We were limited at the time to the number of shooters, so we usually capped it around 75. Today, events host twice as many people, but it all started at Rifles Only.

This is where the Precision Rifle Series was born, on the Sniper's Hide forum in direct response to the Sniper's Hide Cup at Rifles Only. We saw the PRS born in the forum and the discussions were animated during those early days. I was not a fan. I didn't see the need for a group to insert themselves between the shooter and match director. I saw it as money-making device, mainly because initially it was assumed and not coordinated with the match directors. They just thought everyone would go along with it, and, eventually, many did. We sold out events in minutes and this was just a way to insert a group into this process. If they started out offering their services for free, I would have had fewer objections, but they were charging money for an unsecured promise to give you consideration down the road.

Today, the PRS is a household name and part of my objection to it probably helped that. I skylined the series several times in my objections and that always pushes a segment of people toward it. Competitions are a good thing. I am a big fan of them and continue to shoot them to this day. While disagreements have risen over the years, I have never stepped away from competing. I was just a bit more discerning in my choices on where to compete.

Sniper's Hide has a long track record of propping up companies. We were always small-business friendly. Many products were designed on the site with the help of its membership. From the McMillan A5 stock, which is the company's best-selling design, to the Badger M5 Bottom Metal used to introduce the Accuracy International AICS magazines in a fiberglass stock.

The list is endless because we have so many years of great work under our belt. One need only look to the success of a place like GA Precision. George Gardner is a huge mover and shaker in our industry and his roots can be traced back to Sniper's Hide. We used to do limited-edition GA Precision Rifles specifically built for the membership. The Headhunter started it

all, the Harbinger introduced the Badger Bottom Metal the Valkyrie, we even had a precision semiauto AR-10 in the early years before it was cool to do so. GA Precision and Sniper's Hide were completely intertwined in the early days. Our work during those years holds up today. People continue to use the products introduced on Sniper's Hide.

The friendships, and the business relationships, are why Sniper's Hide is successful. We are a community of like-minded shooters hoping to discuss and promote the field of long-range precision rifle shooting. It's a community. It's something some people don't understand because they refuse to recognize the history of the place. We moved the needle on so many levels, it's hard to put a finger on just one part of it.

The Scout Years Explained

I want to cover the Scout years and my thinking

At Rifles Only, shooting a competition next to Jorge "No Legs," who is a top precision rifle competitor. Jorge was injured during the recent wars, but that does not stop him from competing. What is your excuse for not pushing yourself to the limits?

behind it. In 2014, I was approached by a sports network called Scout, a group of individual sites hosted under one roof that mostly focused on sports like football, baseball, etc. At the same time, I saw Facebook coming and it was offering free groups for people. By free groups, I mean anyone can create a group on his or her platform, add members without their knowledge and basically have a series of micro forums. This, in my mind, was my biggest threat.

Scout's timing was right. Just prior, a big magazine offered to buy Sniper's Hide. I won't mention its name, but it is huge in field and fishing. The offer was far too small, so I turned it down, but with the idea of selling the site still on my mind. The Scout offer, on paper, had several advantages. I could maintain ownership of my trademarks. I would remove the technical side of the house, turning over daily operation to the magazine's IT department. The biggest

benefit was a sales team to take advantage of the site's traffic for banner-ad sales. I was a one-man operation and things were too much for me to handle. With an IT department, a sales team and, most importantly, funding, I felt it was the best way to showcase shooting alongside main-stream sports.

This was key. The Precision Rifle Series people and I were talking again. I wanted to highlight our competitions alongside those other sports. If you saw shooting next to college football, how could they continue to attack our chosen sport? Little did I realize how myopic the industry was going to treat my decision.

I moved the site to the Scout servers in October, and in January prior to the Shooting, Hunting, Outdoor Trade (SHOT) Show in Las Vegas, they brought a video crew to the Sin City PRS Match the weekend prior. During this event, I instructed the video crew to create shooters'

The Sniper's Hide Cup is the longest-running tactical match of its kind. Its stages involved movement and shooting though obstacles, such as this Loophole stage.

Another angle of a Loophole shot. The author and his fellow instructors excel at stage planning and having the competitors push themselves, both physically and mentally.

Video Player Cards. These were short, hero shots that highlighted the shooter, his or her equipment, and their sponsors. Player Cards were big in high school and college sports, as they were used as selling points to potential teams. Scout did this, but it was far from roses in the early days.

I hated the software and had monster battles behind the scenes. The chief operations officer was straight out of Microsoft and considered a big deal. I fought for 13 hours straight calling his work second-rate shareware. Their promises fell flat with each new update. But I was stuck having signed a three-year contract. I demanded more, and tried to guide the ship, but I was in the minority. To make matters worse, they completely failed to sell advertising for my site. I was one of the most popular properties on the network, but I was politically incorrect. I hated every day of it, but, as is my nature, I did my best to make it work.

In the final stretch of my Scout time, they had a group event in Las Vegas. They highlighted a host of new changes and I was encouraged by everything I saw. Two months later, it all blew up as being vaporware. The CEO was accused of squandering almost $40 million dollars and

they now had two choices: sell the network or bankruptcy. Both happened. They filed for bankruptcy and were sold to CBS for pennies on the dollar.

With my contract violated, I turned Sniper's Hide back on. I never gave up control over the site. I continued to own the trademarks and simply turned the original server to an archive site. A few domain adjustments, a software upgrade and I was back in business on my own. What people failed to realize is, the site was never gone, it was just hiding dormant. The comical part with all this is the CBS reaction to

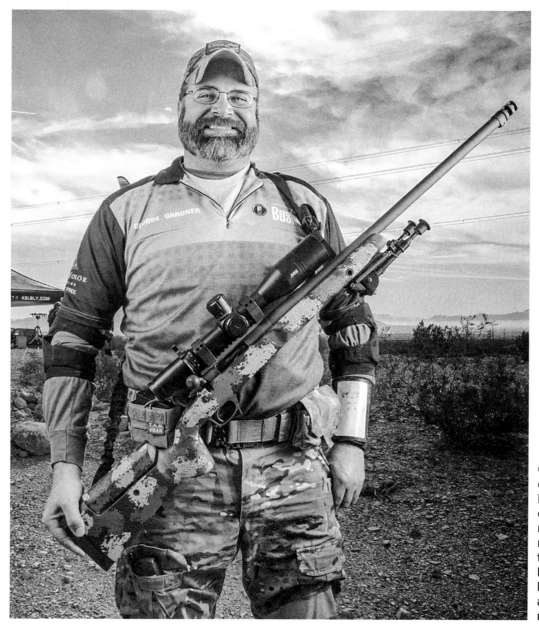

George Gardner, of GA Precision, built a lot of the early Sniper's Hide rifles. Though his most famous is the Gladius, he had others: The Headhunter, Valkyrie and Harbinger, to name a few.

The author shown mentoring a new shooter during a local competition. Passing on knowledge should be part of everyone's mindset.

my leaving.

I told the group I had reservations about being aligned with anti-gun CBS. Nobody ever called me, so I simply told the membership, go back to Sniper's Hide and I turned off the lights on Scout. It took them 20 days to realize I was gone, and when the CBS lawyers called me, it was all over but money. I was owed a bunch of money, CBS told me to go pound sand, and I demanded every piece of Sniper's Hide data be removed. About 60 days later they complied, as for me, I was out tens of thousands of dollars in the process. Scout artificially suppressed me, so I never made more than my minimums, but that is water under the bridge. Shortly after that, the original Scout team started a new site, and they tried hard to recruit me. I laughed pretty hard at their advances.

As of this writing, Sniper's Hide is stronger than ever. We are experiencing growth like never before in our history. Many people look at the golden days, with past members contributing to the discussion, but they are being nostalgic. We enjoy stronger numbers today than at any time in our 18-year history. We were growing 15 percent every day while I wrote this book. I saw it often; we are living in golden times when it comes to precision rifle shooting. We have more competition than ever, yet we grow. This is built on the strength of our members. They are loyal, they are dedicated and they are just as responsible for my success as anyone. Members make the forum. It's their efforts more than mine. In the early days, I pushed the conversations in a certain direction. Today, I write pointed articles and create videos as often as possible. The rest

is the membership. I like to think they are better educated because of the house we built. We don't suffer fools and can be quick to point out errors. Yes, this is a double-edged sword. Your reputation can go either way. But I love how the site has evolved over the years.

Sniper's Hide is a labor of love. I work on it all the time to improve the end-user experience. It's important to me that people have a good experience. I want to have a good experience because I am there every day using the site.

I don't see myself slowing down, though I am getting older and a bit less active. I enjoy writing, the videos are time-consuming, but fun to make. Videography interest me. While others are taking shooting classes, I take cinematography classes. It's my personal distraction that just happens to fit into my work: A pho-

Caylen, of Magpul fame, shooting the Robinson Stage at the Sniper's Hide Cup competition. They modeled this stage off a bronze star citation for Sgt. Robinson, USMC.

Close-up of Caylen's perfect position shooting off the tripod. Today, most tripods have improved weight ratings so this much effort is no longer needed. We balance the rifle and let the tripod do the work.

tography hobby that grew into a value-added part of the site's operation. Still images have been mostly replaced by video, but it's about growth.

My outlets for reaching new members has grown as well. Recently, we started the Everyday Sniper Podcast. This started out as a joint venture with Mike from Mile High Shooting. Today, I have grown that podcast into one of the biggest out there. If you take all the precision rifle podcasts and combine their stats, we eclipse everyone three times over. It's about the dedication to the craft. I make sure a new episode appears each week. There are no vacations. You have to be front-and-center, or find yourself searching for a new audience. That is what drives me. The same things that drove me to succeed in the military, having a no-quit attitude. I also limit my excuses by doing it myself. I have no one to blame for my failures but me, and I like it like that. People come and go all the time. I am forever. Yes, I know, that is pretty

funny, but as long as I am around, I know I can depend on me.

Success is not lost on me, and while I might not want to venture a specific path, I do understand the history and where it all came from. I appreciate those who helped me: Jacob, George, Lindy, Rob, Tony, all the early crews who stuck to each other like glue. As we age, and move off to new ventures, the names might change, but the situations are very similar. You have to adapt to the times, and I see these changes as adaptions. Still, I will never forget sitting at the bar in Greenwich while Jacob pitched me Rifles Only. That tour ended in 2011, but it will never be forgotten.

In a way, this is my dedication to all those who stood alongside me, and the site, over the years, whether it was on the Internet, training on a range, or in a competition. This is for you. Like me, or hate me, I couldn't do it without both sides. One reinforces the other. And both drive me forward.